APPROACHING AN
AUSCHWITZ SURVIVOR

| | |

Helen Spitzer shortly after liberation, summer of 1945 (from the private collection of Helen "Zippi" Tichauer)

APPROACHING AN AUSCHWITZ SURVIVOR

SURVIVOR

| | |

Holocaust Testimony
and Its Transformations

Edited by
JÜRGEN MATTHÄUS

Foreword by
MARK ROSEMAN

OXFORD
UNIVERSITY PRESS
2009

OXFORD
UNIVERSITY PRESS

Oxford University Press, Inc., publishes works that further
Oxford University's objective of excellence
in research, scholarship, and education.

Oxford   New York
Auckland   Cape Town   Dar es Salaam   Hong Kong   Karachi
Kuala Lumpur   Madrid   Melbourne   Mexico City   Nairobi
New Delhi   Shanghai   Taipei   Toronto

With offices in
Argentina   Austria   Brazil   Chile   Czech Republic   France   Greece
Guatemala   Hungary   Italy   Japan Poland   Portugal   Singapore
South Korea   Switzerland   Thailand   Turkey   Ukraine   Vietnam

Copyright © 2009 by Oxford University Press

Published by Oxford University Press, Inc.
198 Madison Avenue, New York, New York 10016

www.oup.com

Oxford is a registered trademark of Oxford University Press

The opinions presented here are those of the editor and authors, not of
the United States Holocaust Memorial Museum

Library of Congress Cataloging-in-Publication Data
Approaching an Auschwitz survivor: Holocaust testimony and its transformations / edited by
Jürgen Matthäus ; with contributions by Atina Grossmann . . . [et al.] ; foreword by Mark Roseman.
p.   cm.
Includes bibliographical references and index.
Summary: "Five Holocaust scholars reflect on the testimony of one survivor, Helen "Zippi" Tichauer
and watch her testimony—and scholarly responses to it—evolve over the years"—Provided by publisher.
ISBN 978-0-19-538915-9
1. Tichauer, Helen, 1918–   2. Holocaust, Jewish (1939–1945)—Personal narratives—History and criticism.
3. Holocaust survivors—Interviews—History and criticism.   4. Holocaust, Jewish
(1939–1945—Influence.   5. Auschwitz (Concentration camp) I. Matthäus, Jürgen, 1959–
D804.196.T535 2009
940.53'18092—dc22   2008048669

1 3 5 7 9 8 6 4 2
Printed in the United States of America
on acid-free paper

| FOREWORD |

Mark Roseman

At first sight, the subject matter of this book seems very familiar. In the United States and elsewhere, the Holocaust survivor has become an arche-typal figure, etched into popular consciousness and commemorated in films, plays, and novels. The survivor's story, the journey to the camps, the unimaginable lives within, the death marches as the camps closed, all this feels in broad outlines known to us. It is surprising, then, how original this volume manages to be, how refreshing and distinctive its tone, and what vistas of knowledge, yet to be researched, it opens up.

For, as it turns out, the postwar world has found it difficult to ask the right questions of survivors and their testimony. Recent decades have seen in the United States and elsewhere what the writer Eva Hoffman, herself a child of survivors, has worriedly described as a "memory cult" around the survivor. It is understandable, perhaps, that individuals who managed to make it through such an ordeal should be celebrated as heroic figures, though it took some decades—as well as political and cultural shifts in the postwar world—before survivors came to be considered in this light. Yet redemptive narratives of heroism and triumph seem in reality unlikely characterizations of the choices and losses that accompanied survival or of what it meant in later years to have endured and survived such experiences. Schol-ars, true enough, have been very skeptical of this kind of memory cult, but academia has often fared little better when it comes to establishing a critical but respectful relationship with the survivor.

Instead of the hagiographic narrative, scholars have been in danger of creating a different kind of "holiness," namely, by placing victims and survivors somehow outside the realm of normal human communication. This is true, for example, of much of the more or less psychologically informed work on trauma, which portrayed the survivors as emotionally crippled by their experience. And it is particularly true of the literary-critical and philosophical analyses of survivor texts and testimony, which have burgeoned since the 1980s, and which often present survivors as peculiarly unable to integrate or communicate their experience. Witnessing has appeared almost an impossible act, and at least one celebrated commentator has argued that the survivor could communicate only silence. To many survivors (and indeed to many who have heard what survivors have to say), this kind of interpretation has seemed both disempowering and as creating a kind of false sacredness around the Holocaust.

Historians have been less prone than scholars in other disciplines to the invention of such shibboleths; on the other hand, history (outside Israel) has been particularly slow as a discipline to take the Nazi victims seriously as sources of information, and has tended to focus much more heavily on the records left behind by the perpetrators. Indeed, the most famous English-speaking historian of the final solution, Raul Hilberg, has explicitly challenged the value of victim testimony. In part this reflects a traditional hesitation to use oral history, in part a belief that the victims were too disempowered and crushed to see what was happening to them.

So in bringing a group of historians together to reflect so carefully on a body of survivor testimony, this volume is already entering territory where few scholarly texts have ventured. It breaks completely new ground by being the first collection I know of (if one excludes essay volumes about famous literary figures among survivors, such as Primo Levi) to devote all its analyses to one individual survivor, in this case Helen "Zippi" Tichauer née Spitzer. By adopting such a uniquely multiperspectival approach to one human being, it highlights how many different questions can be posed to the survivor and her testimony, and how much we can learn about what she saw, about the acts and relationships that influenced her survival, about how as witnesses and custodians of memory survivors shed light on the past, about the sense they made and make of their experience, about the ways in which the postwar world has made sense of them, and finally about the ways in which they as individuals and their testimonies can be used in teaching.

At the same time, this kaleidoscopic approach has the virtue of reminding us of the survivor's individuality. This is true not just of the specific trajectory that allowed Zippi to survive more than two and a half years in Auschwitz but also of the particular way she has made sense of her experience and has chosen to live with her memory. The accuracy of her recall also reminds us to avoid what in recent years has been an all too glib assumption about the effect of time and cultural change on survivor memory. Memory, too, works in very individual ways.

If this book has a special quality, however, that quality adheres as much to its tone as to its vantage point. The "false sacredness" described earlier is a sign of how difficult it has been for the postwar world to find the right kind of relationship with survivors. How far may one pose questions to individuals who have endured so much? How far dare one judge those who found themselves in such unbearable situations? To what extent can one even comprehend a past world characterized by such extremes? Survivors themselves have often felt ill-used by the world's attentions, yet it is clear that an account concerned with truth cannot afford to take the survivor's approval as its sole criterion of authenticity. Instead, it needs to steer a path between respectful engagement and critical distance.

Before I knew much about this project, I happened to be in the Center for Advanced Holocaust Studies at the U.S. Holocaust Memorial Museum working on something else, and I saw and overheard a meeting conducted in Jürgen Matthäus's room, with him and Konrad Kwiet on speakerphone conversing with someone located elsewhere. I noticed how these senior and dignified scholars were being slightly put through the mill by whoever was on the phone, and rather enjoyed seeing them (though they are both friends!) having to behave like respectful students for once. They were, I learned, talking to Zippi Tichauer, and it was clear she was a woman with the strength and self-confidence to assert her position. It also became clear that she was nevertheless open to their inquiry. That interaction has helped to produce the, to my ear, wonderfully well-pitched tone of the essays, which acknowledge their subject's humanity, while carefully exploring difficult issues. Some questions are no doubt not posed as forcefully as they might be, some avenues only glimpsed at and not traversed. An obvious example is the brief reference to Zippi's relationship to the guards in the camp and her postwar interventions in trials, in at least one case to exonerate them. Readers should be aware, as they read, therefore, that they are not just entering into a relationship with the writers, but that they are also indirectly observers of a respectful but careful dialogue between historians and their subject. That, too, is part of the legacy of the Holocaust.

| CONTENTS |

APPROACHING AN AUSCHWITZ
SURVIVOR

| | |

| Introduction |

What Does It Mean? Holocaust Testimony
and the Story of Helen "Zippi" Tichauer

This book is the outcome of a cooperative journey by five Holocaust scholars who for several years have shared individual, independent contacts with one Holocaust survivor, Helen "Zippi" Tichauer née Spitzer.[1] It represents, as far as we the authors of this book can see, the first attempt at a multilayered analysis of a single body of survivor testimony by different scholars. We feel that reflecting from different angles on what Zippi had and has to say opens important vistas toward better understanding the specific elements of Holocaust testimony and Holocaust history. Highly intelligent, warmhearted, curious, and a keen observer, Helen has stored away a wealth of information that she gladly shares with those interested in what she remembers.

Zippi's life story remains to be fully explored, yet this book is not a biography. Helen Tichauer's vita consists of much more than the Holocaust and early postwar experiences we feature here. To highlight its many facets, the contributors to the volume approach Zippi and her testimony with different questions that complement each other. They focus on order, death, and survival in Auschwitz (Konrad Kwiet); comparative humane aspects of camp life (Nechama Tec); the transformation of Zippi's earliest Holocaust account by way of translation and editing (Jürgen Matthäus); postwar Jewish life in and beyond displaced persons (DP) camps (Atina Grossmann); and the role of survivors for classroom teaching (Wendy Lower).

Helen Tichauer can look back on a rich life that spans a happy childhood and polyglot postwar experiences with her husband, Erwin, a Berlin Jew, also a survivor of Auschwitz. At the age of ninety, she lives on her own in a two-bedroom apartment in Manhattan. More than a decade ago she lost her beloved husband. After liberation they had married in the DP camp of Feldafing and—like so many Jewish "displaced persons"—embarked on long journeys to rebuild their shattered lives. Unlike many other survivor couples, however, their happy marriage remained childless. Visually impaired, almost deaf, and virtually immobile, Zippi relies not only on special reading glasses, sophisticated hearing aids, and a walker but also—and above all—on her efficiency, excellent memory, and organizational skills, qualities that sustained her through all the stages of her life.

Today, Zippi spends most of her days in her apartment on a leather sofa. In front of the sofa stands a table that serves as dining table as well as a place to store medication and file correspondence. A diet prescribes the choice and preparation of each meal; a four-month supply of medication is always on hand. In storing and taking her medication she follows strict guidelines once she has deciphered the inscription and instructions on the labels with the help of a reading machine. The tablets are assigned to different containers she refills at regular intervals. On a small sideboard between the sofa and the table stands the telephone, her lifeline to the outside world, above all with relatives and friends who, as in many other survivor families, live scattered across the continents. She also takes much time to talk to Holocaust researchers who are seeking advice and guidance, a welcome distraction from her daily routines and many practical troubles; at the same time, this is a somewhat mixed blessing because her later experiences play little or no role in these conversations, thus forcing her back to remember a chapter in her life she herself considers closed.

On the underside of her left arm Zippi bears the number 2286, her Auschwitz prisoner number, which—with its mere four digits—reveals her early arrival at the camp in March 1942. SS-enforced depersonalization of prisoners through numbers and markings was to be of key importance for her fate in Auschwitz. After having survived backbreaking labor in the main camp, she was entrusted with the task of printing the numbers of "new arrivals" on small white strips of linen that were attached to the triangles affixed to the prisoners' jackets to categorize them. Long after her stigmatization, she learned that the blue tattoo on her arm has an important Jewish symbolic value. Added together, the digits total 18. Learned friends, acquainted with Talmud and Kabbalah, informed her of the number's religious meaning: 18 symbolizes "chai" or "life." Today, Zippi pays little attention to Jewish symbolism. She attributes her survival not only to sheer luck or good fortune but also to her resourcefulness and stamina and, above all, to her professional qualifications acquired in a world that preceded Auschwitz.

Zippi has no fear of dying. She hopes, however, to be alive for a few more years, to serve as one of the last living witnesses to the horrors of the Holocaust. Having been among the first Jewish women to arrive in Auschwitz, and still able to remember crucial aspects of daily camp life attested to by few of her fellow survivors, she considers herself uniquely suited if not obliged to bear witness. She has seen and spoken to almost all of the women prisoners who passed through the registration procedures in Auschwitz and who were "processed" by her. She claims to have known all female Kapos (prisoners with supervisory functions), although she was not one herself; the same applies to female SS guards serving in the women's camp of Birkenau. Her bearing witness did not start in her old age. After liberation, Zippi was one of the first survivors who rendered an account of her experiences gained in the epicenter of the Holocaust. From the very outset— her early interview voice-recorded by David Boder in 1946—until today, Helen has been consistent in her story as well as in the way she tells it: she responds only to specific questions that are put to her, and she describes only episodes that she herself witnessed; she does not offer her own narrative.

Zippi's life covers a wide range of human experiences in extremis; her accounts come to us in different manifestations and raise many questions about the meaning and use of survivor testimony.[2] What do we know, and how much do we understand, more than sixty years after the end of the Nazi era, about the workings of a Nazi death camp and the life of its inmates? How willing are scholars, students, and the public to listen to and learn from the fascinating yet often unwieldy and discomforting experiences of a Holocaust survivor, and how much is our perception preconditioned by standardized images of persecution and survival? What are the mechanisms, aims, and pitfalls of this kind of oral history for interviewers, interviewees, and interested users? With the passage of time, can survivor testimonies be read and understood properly without input, guidance, and corrective interventions by survivors? How can those experiences be communicated to teach and educate without undue simplification and glossing over of problematic aspects inherent in both the life stories and their current renditions?

No doubt, this book will not answer all questions posed by Zippi's story and even fewer relating to Holocaust testimony in general. Still, Zippi's case helps bring into sharper focus the crucial yet uneasy correlation between personal memory, scholarly or public appropriation, and historical representation. The person remembering and those trying to make sense of Holocaust testimony are struggling with problems that emerge from differences in experiences, interests, and expectations. In putting this book together, we as well as Zippi thought that a new approach—different scholars engaging a survivor and her testimony in different ways—would help prevent the undue stratification of her rich, complex, and multilayered memories. Because the essays assembled here can be read in conjunction as well as individually, readers will detect some overlap and repetition, modulated by each author's specific approach. We hope Zippi's voice can be heard throughout this book, especially in its documentary components; nevertheless, there is no denying that this is our, not Helen Tichauer's, text.

Under the title "Designing Survival: A Graphic Artist in Birkenau," Konrad Kwiet begins the book by looking at what appears as the most prominent feature in Zippi's body of testimony. Helping with the registration and marking of prisoners became her key role in the Auschwitz women's camp; her account of her adolescence and training shows that from early on she had a special eye for and interest in the visual and the organization of space. A deep description of her story from her arrival in Auschwitz in spring 1942 to the last days as prisoner during the war reveals continuities and caesuras in her perception of reality and her attempts to survive.

Nechama Tec shows that total domination did not produce total atomization; there is evidence that help, solidarity, and resistance in Auschwitz served to a certain extent as counterreality to the order of the camp, even though the constraints severely limiting clandestine resistance efforts pose questions that to this day neither survivor testimony nor other documentation can fully answer. Forced to become a part of the January 1945 death march, Zippi had lost all the information she had carefully compiled in Auschwitz. Fortunately for us, Zippi's keen memory and her willingness to share these memories gave us an opportunity to recapture some of the historical evidence that she had to leave behind in Auschwitz.

Jürgen Matthäus presents an analysis of Helen Tichauer's first documented account on her wartime fate, a 1946 interview with psychology professor David Boder (the appendix to the volume offers an annotated English translation). Matthäus retraces how this interview was received and used: first, in the process of translation, and later, as a result of editing the translation for book publication. We can witness here a disturbing loss of immediacy, context, and meaning in a process over which the interviewee has no control.

From the 1946 interview setting Atina Grossmann takes us to the DP camp Feldafing with its many transitory arrangements for postwar life, some perpetuating earlier developments, others consequences of the Holocaust. With Nazi persecution having come to an end, Holocaust survivors found loved ones and their own years lost forever in the maelstrom of the "Final Solution." Only fairly recently, scholars have started to research how Jewish DP camp inmates tried to retrieve what seemed retrievable and how the legacies of the war impacted on the most basic physical functions. Zippi's account of her life in Feldafing complements and at the same time contradicts other sources on DP life—an indication of the extent to which the telling and receiving of stories shared by Holocaust survivors, indeed the very notion of survival, are part of an ongoing process of coming to terms with the past.

The book concludes with a chapter by Wendy Lower, who shares her experiences in bringing the voice of an Auschwitz survivor into the classroom—in this case by facilitating telephone discussions over the course of several semesters

between Helen Tichauer and American college students. There is more to the tyr-
anny of distance than just the geographic separation between Zippi in her New
York apartment and the classes on Washington, D.C., and Maryland campuses;
the partners in the conversation seem to be also worlds apart in their expectations
on what their encounter might produce and, most obviously, their background
knowledge on Auschwitz as a historical and—so prevalent in the public mind
today—as a symbolic site. The essay reflects on how and how far this distance can
be overcome.

The conclusion presents a reevaluation of our initial questions regarding
the specificity of survivor testimony and its usefulness to help better understand
the Holocaust against the background of what we have learned from talking to
Helen Tichauer. This book is dedicated to her; we owe her more than can be
expressed in the following chapters. Friends and colleagues have accompanied this
book along its path to publication, most notably Joan Ringelheim, Alan Rosen,
Michael Berkowitz, Benton Arnovitz, and Judy Cohen. We are grateful to Nancy
Toff at Oxford University Press for her dedication to the project, and to the peer
reviewers for their criticism and encouragement. In Zippi's interest as much as in
ours, we hope we have kept errors, omissions, and redundancies to an unavoidable
minimum. Whatever the strengths or weaknesses of this book, its aim is to trigger
more in-depth analyses, be they on an individual or broader basis, of survivor testimony while their originators, those few who experienced what happened during
the Holocaust and lived to tell their story, are still with us.

ᴅDesigning Survival

| | |

A Graphic Artist in Birkenau

Konrad Kwiet

Before the Second World War, women trying to enter male-dominated professions faced severe obstacles. Helen Tichauer insists she was the first woman to finish her apprenticeship as a graphic artist in Slovakia—with distinction. Being able to use one's profession to survive in the extreme environment of a German concentration and death camp required a unique combination of special skills, favorable circumstances, and sheer luck. As a specialist for sign painting in the women's camp of Auschwitz-Birkenau, Helen was the one entrusted with labeling the uniforms of inmates and keeping records for the Nazi murderers—tasks she fulfilled with efficiency and perfection. She once told me what other survivors recall, too, namely that Auschwitz was a living hell in which order and chaos prevailed. In the camp, she quickly earned a reputation for being a reliable and gifted graphic artist, virtually irreplaceable for smoothing the registration process and thus for bringing "order into the chaos."[1] Her function secured her the patronage and protection, however precarious, of both her male and female SS masters, and of inmate functionaries, all of whom relied on her services. On one occasion, when an SS guard observed her skillful production of armbands, he asked her which profession she had learned. Zippi replied: "I am an artist, a profession which your Führer also learnt" (*Ich bin eine Kunstmalerin, ein Beruf, den auch Ihr Führer erlernt hat*). The SS man laughed at the comparison.[2]

Until today, Zippi regards her camp products as more than craftsmanship. Indeed, she sees pieces of art in her detailed, colorful diagrams showing fluctuations in the numbers of prisoners as reported to the SS-Reichssicherheitshauptamt (RSHA) in Berlin and in her 3-D miniature camp model. We know about them only from her memory; after the war, the real charts and model never surfaced among the remaining documentation on Birkenau—most likely they were burned, buried, or shredded. Yet Zippi still hopes they will be found someday. In the same way as she was searching over many years for the audio recording of her 1946 interview with David Boder,[3] she continues to believe her camp artwork will be discovered. If that ever happens, it would complement her recollections; moreover, her diagrams would be important historical records for reconstructing the day-to-day history of what is commonly regarded as the epicenter of the Holocaust.

This essay tries to reconstruct Zippi's career as the graphic artist of the Birkenau women's camp. The way her biography unfolds here is in part based on her memories, shared with me in countless conversations over a period of thirteen years, and in part the result of my efforts as a historian to understand, analyze, and contextualize. The two aspects of this reconstruction effort are compatible only to a degree; in the end, we will be left with fragments, not a whole story. Helen Tichauer's memory, it appears, defies abstraction as she insists on the primacy of the factual. Instead of buying into "big questions," she sticks with what she experienced and provides precise, unadorned answers to small questions. We are left to fill the gaps in her story with meaning—our meaning. Zippi shares with many survivors an innate distrust of historians in their limited understanding of what happened in Auschwitz. She has never shown an interest in joining any debate on Holocaust memory among scholars as she suspects them of imposing on survivor stories layers of philosophical and intellectual speculation. Whenever I asked her "Where was God in Auschwitz?," her answer was always the same, occasionally expressed in a surly tone of voice: "In Auschwitz I never bothered with God. I had to survive and—like all prisoners—obey, work, eat, and sleep."[4] If I, the historian, wanted to know where God was, she suggested I should ask "rabbis, theologians and philosophers—or, for God's sake, the Elie Wiesels and Primo Levis."[5] Her refusal to replace concrete reportage with abstract reflection extends to how she depicts her graphic (in more than one sense of the word) work in Birkenau and to what she remembers about the forms and functions of art in Auschwitz.

Formative Years

Born in Bratislava on November 10, 1918, Zippi spent her childhood and teens in the comfortable environment of a caring Jewish home.[6] Her happy memories are overshadowed by the early death of her mother. At the age of six Zippi moved into the home of her maternal grandmother, and, when her father remarried and established a new family, Zippi's paternal grandmother took on the care of Samuel,

Helen Spitzer with her father and younger brother Samuel, ca. 1923 (from the private collection of Helen "Zippi" Tichauer)

Zippi's younger brother. Both families lived under one roof, though in separate apartments. Zippi recalls the cheerful hours of her youth—playing in the surrounding streets, swimming in the Danube, wandering through the idyllic landscape surrounding Bratislava, or taking part in lively gatherings of friends and clubs, especially time spent in youth and holiday camps. Later, incarcerated in Auschwitz, she often escaped into dreams, by day and by night, in order to keep these pleasant images alive along with her will to live.

As in most prosperous middle-class families, whether Jewish or non-Jewish, the Spitzers placed enormous value on the humanistic twins *Kultur und Bildung* (culture and education). Zippi remembers evening concertos and music quartets at

Helen Spitzer near the springs at Trenčianské Teplice, ca. 1925 (from the private collection of Helen "Zippi" Tichauer)

home in which she participated. She played the piano and, with even greater enthusiasm, the mandolin. She loved to dance and sing, to listen to music, and to read. In Birkenau, Alma Rosé recruited Zippi into her women's orchestra as first mandolin player.[7] There, rehearsals took place in a special barrack; the women performed outside on the *Lagerstrasse*, the camp road, in either the early morning or late evening, when the work columns were leaving or returning to camp. On weekends and on special occasions, the orchestra played in front of a select audience, made up of German camp personnel and prominent inmates. Participation in rehearsals and performances offered Zippi, as well as all the other players, an additional piece of bread and rare moments in which it was possible to suppress the feelings of isolation and demoralization. Since Auschwitz, Zippi has never again touched a musical instrument. She rarely danced since, only if invited by Erwin, her late husband, at official festivities. She continues to listen to music. I recall several telephone conversations, interspersed with her singing of popular melodies known prior to and in Auschwitz.

Zippi's family was firmly established within the vibrant Bratislavan Jewish community numbering about 20,000 from all walks of life. She grew up in a modern Jewish environment. As a young girl she prayed in the synagogue only when obliged to say Kaddish, the mourners' prayer, on the *Jahrzeit* (anniversary) of her mother's death. However, she never abandoned her belief in the existence of God, either in Auschwitz or after liberation. This is how she explained her views to me: "I can neither see God nor understand him, let alone explain him. I only accept that he has a place in the world of nature."[8] Having survived the "living hell," Helen accepted the existence of the devil. When in 1946 she reflected on her most lasting impression of Auschwitz, she referred to the slaughter of the Hungarian Jews in summer 1944. Zippi witnessed these events and remembered them in terms similar to Dante's *Inferno*.[9] In 1972, the issue of God and hell resurfaced in New York when Zippi listened to the late Lubavitch Rebbe Schneerson; she responded with dismay to his assertion that Europe's Jews were punished by God for their many sins.[10] In the early 1990s, Schneerson changed his position, admitting that the victims died for the sanctification of God's name.[11] Until today, Zippi displays an aversion to ultra-Orthodox Jews.

In addition to her artistic talents, Zippi was gifted with a quick grasp of languages. Growing up in the multinational and multilingual environs of Bratislava, Zippi spoke German, Slovak, and Hungarian fluently as a child. At school she attended classes in French and Hebrew. German remained her preferred mother tongue—and remains so to this day. In Auschwitz she learned Polish, Russian, and Yiddish, and after the war she swiftly acquired English and Spanish. Smatterings of Indonesian complete the language palette. Her linguistic skills proved to be a decisive tool in her fight for survival. From the outset she understood and mastered the *Lager Jargon*, special German phrases of command and compliance that regulated daily camp life and the work to be carried out. Moreover, she could speak in her mother tongue to the German or Austrian camp personnel and communicate in other languages with prisoners of different nationalities, especially those occupying supervisory functions. These abilities enabled her to establish contacts, to help others, and in return to win the support of others.[12]

At home she had been well trained in domestic skills: sewing and darning along with cooking and cleaning, associated with then-prevailing gender stereotypes. At school she earned the reputation of being an outstanding student, frequently topping the class. Her formal education commenced at the Jüdische Volkschule, the best German-language primary school in Bratislava. After five years she entered the Staatliche Bürgerschule, a public high school for girls. Three years later she completed her school years in an advanced class taught in a coeducational institution and broke out of the prefabricated, socially accepted gender mold. Zippi maintains that her pioneering professional career as a woman helped her to stand her ground in the camp world of Auschwitz dominated by males. A technical college offered her the possibility of embarking on a career as commercial artist, then a man's profession. Her vocational training lasted four years, combining classroom teaching and practical training undertaken in a private firm specializing in graphic art. Zippi acquired a profound and extensive knowledge of relevant areas such as colors, tools, and a range of materials—paper, linen, wood, and metal. Given her considerable talents, she found and used the most advanced techniques in drawing, painting, and printing. Design and the fine lettering of signs and other objects became central to her craftsmanship. When, after the creation of the "independent" Slovak state, employment opportunities for Jews shrank, she worked for a range of private customers and gave a training course in graphic design for Jews trying to acquire practical skills prior to emigration. Her abundant collection of products included car plates and name plates, notices and posters, advertisements and labels, signposts and street signs, house signs and railway signs, as well as trade and machine descriptions.[13]

The number plates of cars acquired a particular significance. In Slovakia as in many other countries, commercial artists completed the production of these plates. Numbers were not printed by machines as they are today but were painted by hand on metal plates. Different sets of number series were allocated to major cities, which provided each car buyer the numbers to be placed on the plate. Working with these numbers almost daily and over a lengthy period of time after she had earned her state certificate as an accredited sign writer, Zippi developed the ability not only to recognize but also to remember the date and place of the registration of cars. Later, when printing serial numbers on the uniform of "new arrivals" in Birkenau, she could rely on the experience gained in her skilled work in Bratislava; moreover, she had no problems in memorizing the numbers. Even today Zippi is still able to verify on the basis of prisoners' numbers their place of departure and the approximate time of arrival of large transports.

Ladies First

Before the war, Zippi witnessed the end of the short-lived "golden era" of Slovak Jewry, a change marked by anti-Jewish laws imposed by the Fascist Tiso regime. Following a pattern first established in Nazi Germany in the 1930s, state authorities confiscated Jewish properties and belongings, drove Jews out of their jobs, evicted them from their homes, and confined them to so-called *Judenhäuser*, Jew houses.[14] A small portion of the "aryanized" Jewish wealth was offered to the Germans in early 1942 for each Jew to be deported to the "East." Two thousand young unmarried women were the first to be shipped to Auschwitz—in two trainloads in late March 1942—under the pretext of forced labor in the eastern parts of Slovakia.[15] Prior to their departure, crammed into assembly centers under the watchful eye of black-uniformed Hlinka guards, they encountered the first acts of brutality, humiliation, and degradation. Zippi described her experiences in a one-page report entitled "Ladies First," the only testimonial piece she ever published herself.[16] The journey into the unknown lasted two days. One of Zippi's panic-stricken companions was Katia Singer, whom Zippi attempted to calm with comforting and encouraging words. In the camp, such relationships of mutual help often fulfilled lifesaving functions.[17]

On March 28, 1942, the transport arrived in Auschwitz, more precisely at an open field at the outskirts of the town. SS guards lined up the women, who without exception were exhausted, disoriented, hungry, thirsty, and dirty, five abreast in long columns and then led them through the township. When they entered the gate of the main camp, the *Stammlager*, or Auschwitz I, they saw the large sign of welcome: *Arbeit Macht Frei* (Work Sets You Free). Zippi also sighted another, much smaller sign placed on the wall to the side of the gate, a sign not recorded, to my knowledge, in any other survivor testimony. It was white, with a single word printed in black: *Konzentrationslager*. Without understanding what it meant, Zippi knew where she was.[18]

On the previous day some 1,000 non-Jewish women had arrived, transferred from the German concentration camp Ravensbrück to assist in setting up the women's camp in Birkenau, or Auschwitz II. Like so many other survivors, Zippi has graphic memories of the various humiliating and painful rituals of the arrival procedure: the confiscation of all belongings, being forced to undress and shower, the removal of hair, including pubic hair, the distribution of camp uniforms, the tattooing, registration, and then the assignment to barracks and work details.[19] Confined to a *Block* (number 9) in the *Stammlager*, through the cracks in a barricaded window, she became the horrified witness of the execution of Polish women together with their children, carried out in the small neighboring backyard. It was the murder site in front of the "Black Wall" of Block 11, containing the offices and cells for interrogation and torture, known as the *Bunker*.[20] It did not take long before Zippi learned that newcomers were "selected" (*selektiert*), families torn apart, and men and women separated. Once the equipment for and techniques of mass extermination were in place, she sighted the gas chambers and crematoria and found out what took place in these installations.[21]

The clothing storehouse (*Bekleidungskammer*), set up in the *Stammlager*, served as the area where all prisoner uniforms, including men's caps and women's head scarves, and initially footwear, were stored and distributed. Piles of shoes were later kept in the *Schuhkammer*. Today, they are powerful symbols of Auschwitz displayed behind glass in museums, as both original objects and restored arti-facts. Shoes, as Zippi and many other survivors have maintained, were often more important than bread, in high demand among inmates and constantly stolen dur-ing sleeping hours.[22] New arrivals had their own shoes taken from them and were forced to accept replacements that often differed in shape, size, and quality. The result was invariably confusion and pain. As a rule, inmates engaged in outside labor had to march to and from their work sites barefoot, carrying their shoes, wooden clogs, or felt slippers in their hands. Only at work were they permitted to wear them. Exposure to the extremes of weather, being forced to trudge along muddy, frozen, or stony roads and to work at hazardous sites made the wear-ing of adequate footwear vital for survival. It provided some measure of comfort and protection against injury. The healing of open wounds and chilblains was a painful and time-consuming process. In most cases, long-term foot infections and maladies resulted in death, as the SS "selected" inflicted prisoners for the gas chamber.

Zippi, one of the first arrivals at Auschwitz, was lucky. Because of the very limited stockpile of women's shoes, she was granted the privilege of keep-ing one pair of her own shoes. She chose her much-loved *Bergsteigerschuhe*, sturdy mountain boots with metal fittings made by the Austrian company Goiserer (the company still exists). At regular intervals, she told me, she was approached by Kapos and other inmates who demanded to hand over her valuable boots, but she managed to protect them as long as they were indispensable to her. When later assigned to the *Häftlings-Schreibstube*, the prisoner registry office in Birkenau, she struck a deal with a friend working in the *Schuhkammer*, entrusting her with the boots, and henceforth being supplied with comfortable walking shoes. Like all Jewish women, Zippi had to relinquish her civilian clothes upon arrival for a military uniform inherited from a murdered Soviet POW. Such uniforms—tattered, full of lice, and often encrusted with blood—were also given to male inmates; only prisoners transferred from other concentration camps retained their blue-gray striped camp uniform. Once the stockpile of Russian uniforms was exhausted and the demand for camp garments increased, civilian clothes were distributed. They came from the stores of clothes confiscated upon arrival. The best pieces were sent to Germany; less valuable ones were transformed into camp uniforms.

Helen (third from left) wearing her Goiserer boots at Hashomer Hatzair camp, ca, 1931 (from the private collection of Helen "Zippi" Tichauer)

Exposed to the appalling sanitary and hygienic conditions, Zippi suc-cumbed to lice, fleas, and other vermin, resulting in typhus, spotted fever, malaria, and diarrhea, as well as skin rashes, blisters, and boils. She remembers the care she received from inmate doctors, nurses, and her circle of friends. The meager food ration consisted primarily of small, often moldy pieces of poor-quality bread, with watery soups, and tea or *Kaffee-Ersatz*, a coffee substitute. This diet led quickly to undernourishment, a permanent state of hunger, and vitamin deficiency. As best she could, Zippi followed the lifesaving rules of simple hygiene. In the first months the most basic sanitary items were not available. She was compelled to use the monstrously crammed, noisy, and stinking latrine, washing, and shower facilities established outside the living quarters. Murky water was used for cleaning mouth and teeth, or to help remove the infected scabs from her skin. She collected small stones to clean and cut her nails. Weak tea served as cleaning lotion for intimate body parts. Like other women, she searched for shreds of papers or leaves, sticks or scamps to substitute for toilet paper.[23] Similar to most female camp inmates, Zippi experienced the cessation of her menstrual cycle, a result of starvation and exhaustion. She reacted with a feeling of relief because it spared her the despair and humiliation of searching for makeshift sanitary napkins. Zippi disputes the theory that the Germans poured bromide into soup buckets and drinking contain-ers to stop the menstruation of camp inmates, a claim made by many female survi-vors and one that falls into the realm of historical legend.[24]

When in August 1942 Zippi was transferred from the *Stammlager* to the women's camp in Birkenau, her living conditions improved slightly. Assigned to the *Häftlingsschreibstube*, she slept and ate in a small room located directly behind the registry office. Spared the use of the common latrine and other washing facilities, she managed to acquire soap, towels, a toothbrush and toothpaste, toilet paper, underwear, socks, a brassiere, and sanitary napkins. After eighteen months her menstrual cycle returned, triggered by better nutrition and working conditions Working in a central camp office headed and visited by German camp personal, Zippi was required to maintain a clean and well-groomed appearance. This applied equally to the "secretaries of death" working for the SS in the *Stabsgebäude* (staff building).[25] Next to Zippi's office were the *Postkammer* and *Paketkammer*, where she helped sorting letters, postcards, and parcels. Some consignments required special care: parcels with "untraceable" addressees who had been transferred or murdered. Referred to as "death packages," their contents were recorded and sent to other camp offices. Some valuable items, however, disappeared into the flourishing black market. Zippi remembers some of the items she obtained from the "death packages" (*Totenpakete*).

Upon her arrival in late March 1942, Zippi had been subjected to hard labor in the open fields outside the confines of the *Stammlager*. Assigned to a wrecking commando, she was forced to demolish farmhouses located in the "clearing zone" in and around the small village of Birkenau (Polish: Brzezinka). Hit by a collapsing chimney, Zippi suffered a painful back injury from which she never fully recovered. This work accident put an end to Zippi's first, literally backbreaking job. In search of a new, less strenuous and dangerous assignment, she did not hesitate to approach the head prisoner of the women's camp (*Lagerälteste*), Eva Weigel, a communist prisoner from Berlin. As unbelievable as it may sound, when told of Zippi's professional qualifications, the camp senior immediately arranged her transfer, confiding to Zippi that her fiancé was also a graphic artist.[26] One day later Zippi was entrusted with a task that enabled her to resume her profession.

MARKINGS IN AUSCHWITZ

Over time, with the disappearance of old Soviet uniforms for use by Auschwitz inmates, SS camp leaders recognized the need to mark prisoners dressed in civilian clothes and engaged in outside work. They decided on red stripes that were to be painted on the back of prisoner clothing. Unlike tattoos and other insignia, these stripes have never been the subject of investigation after the war, nor have they attained a symbolic meaning. Rarely mentioned in survivors' testimonies, they do not appear, to my knowledge, in any photographic image or historical record. Zippi's work started in the *Stammlager*, both inside and outside the

Bekleidungskammer, generally prior to the departure of the work columns. After mixing the right color—vermilion—with oil, turpentine, and siccatives (drying agents), she painted the two-centimeter-wide stripes onto the backs of her fellow inmates, "from the top to bottom; from the neck to the legs."[27] At the beginning she required the help of a ruler for precision in measuring and tracing the lines. Once she became accustomed to the routine she did the quick brushstroke freehand. To meet the growing demand, she also had to train helpers who were soon capable of performing the task without the supervision of their master painter.

At the end of 1942, Zippi was relieved of this task and given more time for another job she had already commenced in another work detail (*Arbeitskommando*) where her skills and qualifications were in greater demand. This assignment involved the printing of black registration numbers on small white strips of cloth, which were placed next to the colored triangle on the uniforms of "new arrivals." The triangles (German: *Winkel*), introduced and tested in the "model" camp at Dachau in 1933, served in all Nazi concentration camps as effective devices to monitor and control the inmates by creating a hierarchy and divisions among groups of prisoners.[28] The color of the *Winkel* showed the prisoner's category according to Nazi designation: red for political prisoners; green for "criminals"; purple for Jehovah's Witnesses; black for "asocials" (often prostitutes and other social outcasts); black or brown for Sinti and Roma; blue for "emigrants." Outside the women's camp, male homosexuals were labeled with pink triangles. In addition, capital letters signaled the nationality of non-Jews. A plethora of other special insignia completed the marking system, which varied slightly from camp to camp and underwent changes in the course of time. Jews were identifiable by a two-colored, six-pointed star: a yellow *Winkel* overlaid by another colored triangle, revealing the reason for incarceration.

As distributor of colored triangles and as printer of the black serial camp numbers, Zippi found a place in an *Arbeitskommando* called Politische Abteilung: Zugänge (Political Department: New Arrivals). Comprising some fifteen members, supervised by a female Kapo, and operating under the watchful eye of the camp's Security Police and Security Service, it was headed by Josef Erber, holding the rank of SS senior sergeant (*Oberscharführer*).[29] Helen Tichauer's transition from painting red stripes to printing black numbers found its expression in a joke circulating among a few German-speaking prisoners—even reaching the Monowitz or "Buna" camp (Auschwitz III) where Erwin Tichauer, Zippi's future husband, had to work as forced laborer. The joke's crude and unreal sexual imagery only works in German: "*Zuerst geht Zippi auf den Strich, dann macht sie die Nummern*"; its meaning in English would be roughly: "First she walks the line [innuendo: of prostitution], then she does the numbers."[30]

The registration of new arrivals took place first in stone buildings disguised as *Sauna*,[31] in the first weeks in the "bath house" of the *Stammlager*, and then, from mid-August 1942 onward, in the shower and reception facilities located in the women's sections of Birkenau. Arrival time and size of the transport determined the length of the day or night shift. Women prisoners registered the women. Two male prisoners from the men's camp performed the tattooing. At first they used an impractical metal stamp, then a single needle, and finally a double-needle device. The procedure lasted about thirty seconds. Lou Sokolov, the chief Auschwitz tattooist, and his assistants marked more than 200,000 inmates, almost half the camp population tattooed. Soon more men were required to do the job.[32] Zippi labeled new arrivals with cloth strips until the final days of Auschwitz. She met and spoke to thousands of women—Jews and non-Jews alike. In the later period she occasionally marked children who had been sent together with their non-Jewish mothers and/or fathers to Auschwitz.[33] The SS immediately murdered Jewish mothers with young children, pregnant women, and newborn babies. Non-Jewish children were registered and tattooed. Female children under the age of five with their mothers entered the women's camp; boys over the age of five were confined to the men's camps.[34]

After two years, the SS had women trained to replace the men as tattooist. The process followed rules and exceptions. Jews selected for the gas upon arrival were neither tattooed nor registered. All inmates were tattooed, with the exception of Reich Germans, Ethnic Germans, and inmates classified as *Erziehungshäftlinge* (education prisoners) or *Polizei-Häftlinge* (police prisoners). The tattoo stigma, introduced in 1941, had three distinct functions: to mark and humiliate prisoners, to prevent their escape, and to expedite the identification of corpses already stripped of their uniforms, particularly following mass killings or epidemics. Non-Jews who had been tattooed were not to be murdered by poison gas, with the exception of Sinti and Roma. When these guidelines were repeatedly ignored, the SS ordered to distinguish between non-Jews and Jews, the latter to be identified by a small triangle pierced under their tattoo. At the request of German industrialists, some Jews deployed as slave laborers in war-relevant factories throughout Nazi-controlled Europe remained untattooed.[35]

After the horrific and humiliating rituals of the arrival procedures, the women were lined up in columns of a hundred and instructed to queue in front of a long table for registration. Behind the table sat several functionaries, completing the entry form for prisoners. The new arrivals had to answer a few questions— name, date and place of birth, residence, nationality, profession. The personal data collected provided the basis for compiling the *Zugangsliste*, the list of arrivals, as well as for different series of prisoner cards kept and constantly updated in comprehensive filing systems. Zippi sat at the end of the table, the documents and tools needed to complete the process of registration within easy reach. Before Zippi distributed the rectangular strips of white linen with the printed colored triangles to the woman in line, she printed the prisoner's camp serial number next to the *Winkel*, using a small, simple printing device in which she placed the appropriate numbers. She maintains that she never once made a printing error.[36] It was left to

each woman to sew the piece of linen at chest height onto the left side of the uniform. Zippi provided needle and thread and ensured that the needle was returned
to her. With the registration completed, *Blockälteste* escorted the new arrivals to
their assigned barracks.[37] When asked whether women attempted to resist, Zippi
could not recall any incident of unrest or insubordination: "Reception and registration transformed human beings into stones and numbers. The women were totally
confused and disoriented, hungry and thirsty, happy to be still alive."[38]

In summer 1944, Zippi was given a free hand to design new insignia
unknown in the long history of marking Jews and only to be detected on a handful
of photographic images.[39] Because the mass influx of Hungarian Jews had depleted
the stockpile of Jewish triangles, it was left to the graphic artist to produce a
cheaper version. Maria Mandel, the *SS-Oberaufseherin*,[40] approved of Zippi's design:
a white, six-pointed Jewish star with black borders. Using treated paper, Zippi
scored a star-shaped template, which she placed on a white strip of linen. She
then dipped a felt roller in ink and stenciled the outline. This new insignia came to
be known among the new arrivals as the "Hungarian Star."[41] Soon afterward, the
entire marking system underwent a change. The different colored triangles disappeared and were replaced by a single, uniform badge—the red *Winkel*. To further
identify the prisoner's category, narrow stripes were printed over the badge, in
the accepted colors to indicate the reason for incarceration. Recalling the rituals
of registration and depicting its atmosphere, Zippi once remarked: "I am now living in darkness. Yet when I close my eyes, I see every thing in front of me crystal
clear—all the colors and movements."[42]

"Ordinary" or "normal" prisoners had to wear insignia and serial numbers.
Funktionshäftlinge (prisoner functionaries) like Kapos were differentiated by distinctive armbands, identification bands used in all ghettos and camps. It was Zippi who
marked these armbands in precise yet elaborate Gothic script, clearly signaling the
position within the SS-controlled prisoner hierarchy from *Lagerälteste* at the top via
Rapportschreiberin and *Blockälteste* down to *Läuferin* (runner); at hospital level from doctors to nurses and orderlies, at work sites from *Oberkapo* to Kapo and *Vorarbeiterin*
(forewoman).[43] Zippi never wore an armband,[44] yet she belonged to the camp elite—
another example for the contradictions of Auschwitz. She "enjoyed" the privileges
granted to prominent prisoners and those who received preferential treatment. She
was better dressed, fed, and housed than the rank and file. She was beaten up only
once, while demolishing destroyed farmhouses upon her arrival. Zippi followed
orders and another basic rule of survival—*nicht auffallen*, not to be conspicuous.[45] She
rejected the offer to wear a wristwatch, a symbol for the privileged few among prisoners,[46] but she also managed to evade tattooing with the Jewish triangle, knowing
that it could lead to sudden death if discovered at random selections.[47]

Zippi could move freely within the confines of the women's camp.[48] As
a chain smoker she relished the short but frequent *Raucherpausen*, illegal smoking

breaks, during which Polish, Russian, and much-coveted British cigarettes were savored. Sources of tobacco for women were accessible only through the flourishing black market or barter.[49] Moreover and quite unbelievably, at regular intervals Zippi was permitted to leave the camp to collect office stationery and other materials from outside depots. She was even occasionally invited to join a small group of prominent prisoners who, under the escort of an unarmed SS guard, embarked on Sunday excursions to idyllic spots nearby. Zippi recalls summer walks to a duck pond where they were permitted to bathe.[50] Nothing better illustrates the esteem for her work and her status in the camp than these outings.

Based on his experience in the Buchenwald concentration camp, Eugen Kogon uses the term *Dankbarkeits-Zwiespalt*, loosely translated: "ambiguous gratitude," to describe an adaptation process in which privileged victims are drawn closer to the SS.[51] While Zippi had no sympathy for her cruel German masters, she felt she owed them gratitude and loyalty. The masters in turn protected her because her skills ensured that their tasks were carried out efficiently and competently. After liberation, Zippi was never called, nor did she step forward to testify in the various Auschwitz trials against SS officers and their helpers. A Polish tribunal in Cracow sentenced head *SS-Oberaufseherin* Maria Mandel, Helen's main mentor, to death in 1947.[52] Irma Grese, equally feared by "ordinary prisoners" for her brutality, was condemned to death in the British Bergen-Belsen trial.[53] In 1967, Josef Erber, Zippi's SS overseer in the registration procedures, received life imprisonment in the second Frankfurt Auschwitz trial; Zippi still insists that he was innocent.[54] Helen Tichauer testified only in one case dealing with crimes perpetrated in the concentration camp at Malchow, the final destination of her death march: she swore an affidavit in the office of the German Consul General in New York, disputing the accusation that one of the SS female guards had deliberately murdered prisoners.[55] No doubt, her personal experience and long-term observations on the coexistence between order and chaos, normality and extreme violence in Auschwitz played a role in determining her assessment on who among the SS camp officers was "decent" and who was a "criminal."

ART AND ORDER

Zippi's tasks in Auschwitz combined labeling new arrivals and camp functionaries with work in the *Häftlingsschreibstube* of the women's camp, a place unexplored in the research on Auschwitz, barely mentioned in testimonies, and overshadowed by the accounts of inmates who worked in the SS *Stabsgebäude* located outside of the electrified wires and entrance gate of Birkenau.[56] For Zippi, the *Häftlingsschreibstube* was the nerve center of the women's camp.[57] Indeed, it functioned as the central office for registration and record keeping of all operations affecting more than 120,000 female prisoners in the women's camp, its subcamps, and satellite camps.[58] Entry lists and prisoner files formed part of an all-encompassing registration and filing system—a steadily growing and constantly updated database.

Just like the arrival procedures, the roll calls remained engraved in the memories of survivors, especially the tortures of punitive lineups (*Strafappelle*) often lasting over several hours. "Regular" counts were conducted twice daily, in the early morning prior to the departure of the work details and following their return to camp. The roll call sheets delivered to the *Häftlingsschreibstube* were of vital importance, since they provided information on the exact number of inmates held in all sections of the camp; the count determined the precise allocation of food and other items supplied the following day. All data collected were transferred onto colored index cards and filed in open boxes. The filing system consisted of various catalogs. The *Namenskartei* contained in alphabetical order names and locations of all prisoners. The *Berufskartei* listed the professions, filed according to name and number. These indexes served as a resource pool for the supply of labor inside and outside the camp. The *Arbeitsdienst* (labor service) lodged requests for labor; the *Arbeitseinsatz* (labor deployment) assigned workers to camp details or to slave labor in private German companies. The *Totenkartei* recorded the name and serial number of the deceased, as well as the date and cause of death. In addition, reference books such as the *Hauptbuch* registered the serial numbers, and the *Strafbuch* chronicled sanctions imposed on women for violating the *Lagerordnung*.

The work detail in the *Häftlingsschreibstube* consisted of thirty to forty women representing all nationalities and groups categorized by the Nazis as Jews, non-Jews, and *Mischlinge*, with the main positions filled by girls and women from Slovakia, Poland, and Germany.[59] The data collected and processed in the *Häftlingsschreibstube* were sent to the *Stabsgebäude* and other camp offices, and from there to the SS central offices (Wirtschaftsverwaltungs-Hauptamt or RSHA) in Berlin.[60] Some prisoner data sheets were marked with a stamp "processed by Hollerith" (*Hollerith erfasst*) at the central labor deployment office and there converted into punch cards for mechanical procession.[61] The assertion, however, that the Nazis could never have managed Auschwitz without the IBM-produced Hollerith machines falls in the realm of historical speculation. Equally untenable is the assumption that Hollerith numbers provided the impulse for the Auschwitz tattoo.[62] Zippi maintains that she never once in all her months in the *Häftlingsschreibstube* sighted a card marked *Hollerith erfasst*.[63]

From the outset, Zippi displayed a particular talent for understanding and handling the complex and confusing filing system. Indeed, she was eager to simplify and to improve the logistics of processing prisoner data. At the same time, her skills, insights, and networks enabled her not only to secure her own survival but also to help, protect, and rescue fellow inmates—Jews and non-Jews, friends and women unknown to her. She did this by the careful manipulation of cards and lists, which permitted some prisoners to be assigned to better work details and barracks. In the beginning, she assisted Katia Singer in her capacity as *Rapportschreiberin* in speeding up the roll call system. A sheet, clearly setting out prisoners' numbers, was introduced and a *Vor-Appell* conducted by each *Blockälteste* and *Blockschreiberin*.[64] This precount, taken during the distribution of the meager evening rations, pro-vided an estimate for the main roll call staged the following morning. Both counts, Zippi argues, followed the basic principle of any accurate bookkeeping, namely, the "debit and credit" (*Soll und Haben*) principle.[65] Zippi had access to all card catalogues, including the *Totenkartei*. Sifting through and updating the entries, she quickly became accustomed to the colored crosses placed behind the names and numbers of the deceased. Red marked the *Sterbefälle*, those who had died what in Auschwitz was known as a "natural death": disease, suicide, and execution. Black stood for *Sonderbehandlung*, "special treatment," the euphemism for murder.[66]

In late 1942, in recognition of her talents and achievements, Zippi was assigned to a new workplace, located behind the *Häftlingsschreibstube*. The room, which she shared with another prisoner, was equipped with tables, shelves, and wardrobes for storing and putting to use all the materials and tools required by a graphic artist. It became known among SS officials and inmate functionaries as Zippi's *Zeichenstube*, a drawing room, into which she could retreat, generally undis-turbed. Her work centered around two special tasks set by Maria Mandel: the drawing of top-secret monthly diagrams sent to the RSHA, and a miniature three-dimensional architectural camp model that, once completed, was placed under a glass cover for display. With all the statistical data at her disposal, Zippi drew each diagram on a large sheet of graph paper.[67] Several differently colored curves traced the daily fluctuations of the camp's population and the progress of the camp's operations, documenting the number and nationalities of prisoners, labor deploy-ment, and *Sonderbehandlung*. Zippi maintains that in the final days of Auschwitz she made copies, which she placed in tubes and hid behind a wardrobe. The Rus-sian liberators, so she believes, must have discovered the diagrams and kept them locked away; she hopes that one day they will reappear.

The architecture of Auschwitz is well documented, especially the gas chambers and crematoria, most recently with the help of modern technology.[68] Zippi's camp model did not incorporate the facilities for gassing, burning, and disposing of ashes because the SS had tasked her with reconstructing the women's camp only. Her model also excluded other separate camp sections of Birkenau, such as the men's camp, or the two camps liquidated in 1944—the so-called gypsy camp, and the family camp, which housed prisoners transferred from Theresien-stadt. The model served as a kind of "visual directory" to assist SS personnel and inmate functionaries in finding their way through the camp maze as none of the blocks and offices was numbered or labeled. With the help of an assistant, Zippi worked several months on the model. All the miniature buildings had to be cut from cardboard, folded, and held together by glue. Zippi placed them on a table, two meters long and eighty centimeters wide, and used fine string to mark the line of the rectangular fencing. On top of the watchtowers tiny lightbulbs served as searchlights powered by a battery at the bottom of the table. After her "masterpiece" had met with approval, the SS quickly removed it from the *Zeichenstube* and displayed it in one of the central camp offices. It can be assumed that it was shown to prominent visitors inspecting Auschwitz-Birkenau who, to preserve the secrecy of the "Final Solution," were not permitted to witness the operations of gas chambers and crematoria.

Prior to the "evacuation" of Auschwitz, SS personnel began to erase the evidence of the heinous crimes perpetrated there. Zippi recalls two episodes that left an indelible imprint on her memory. She was asked to write the address on a parcel to be posted to the Austrian residence of a female SS supervisor.[69] Holding the heavy package in one hand and allowing her other hand to skim the surface of the wrapping paper, she became convinced that the parcel contained precious metal, perhaps an ingot of gold made from the dental fillings of Jews extracted after their murder. The other episode relates to the evacuation day. Zippi was one of the first Jewish women to arrive in, and one of the last to depart from, the Auschwitz women's camp. While passing through the gate on January 17, 1945, in the company of the *Blockälteste* of the *Häftlingsschreibstube*, she was asked to close and lock the iron gate.[70] Ten days later, Russian soldiers arrived to liberate dying patients and Polish women with their children left behind in the sick bay.

AFTER AUSCHWITZ

First on foot in the freezing winter cold, than in an open cattle truck, Helen Tichauer, like many other evacuated prisoners, experienced the horrors of the death march. The bizarre order of the camp evaporated in its transformation from stationary to mobile terror system. Thousands perished from exhaustion, were beaten to death, or were shot while attempting to rest or escape. Zippi recalls the enormous difficulty in maintaining even a minimum of hygienic care. With the departure from Auschwitz, her menstrual cycle began; she also had to deal with the problem of urinating while being goaded relentlessly to march. Prisoners offered each other physical support to keep going. The first leg of the death march ended in Ravensbrück, the second in Malchow, a subcamp of Ravensbrück, located in the north German province of Mecklenburg. On the outskirts of this forced labor camp, Zippi was liberated by Russian soldiers on May 3, 1945, together with a veritable European army of "displaced persons" comprising prisoners of war, forced laborers, and camp inmates. The return home by rail lasted almost one month; when she finally arrived in Bratislava at the end of May 1945, Zippi was greeted by many with the surprise question commonly heard in those days: "You are alive?"[71]

It did not take long before Helen resumed her journey. The hostile reception in her home city, fueled by an upsurge of antisemitic sentiments, intensified her feelings of isolation and homelessness. In September 1945 she made the decision to turn her back on the place of her birth, childhood, and deportation. Like so many Holocaust survivors, Zippi joined the army of refugees who sought refuge in the displaced persons (DP) camps set up in Central Europe. In Feldafing, she met and married Erwin Tichauer.[72] Here as elsewhere, survivors began the heartbreaking and arduous search for missing relatives and friends. Following the war, Zippi was frequently asked over many years about the whereabouts of girls and women deported to Birkenau. Men in search of their girlfriends, fiancées, or wives and insecure about embarking on new relationships approached her most often. In many cases she was able to provide an answer, relying on her memory and on the clerical work she had done. She testified in person or in sworn statements that she had seen a missing person upon her arrival in Auschwitz or on work details.

Once the Tichauers had secured emigration papers to leave war-torn Europe, they moved on: first to Chile, and in 1950 from there to Australia, a country that welcomed more Holocaust survivors than any nation of the free world, with the exception of the newly established Jewish state of Israel. More than 30,000 survivors found a new and permanent home at the edge of the diaspora.[73] The first port of call was Brisbane, where Zippi's past continued to haunt her. She was accused by a distant relative of having been a Kapo, a brutal Kapo in fact. Deeply hurt and in shock, she went to court to obtain a writ to prevent the dissemination of this lie.[74] While Zippi continued to work as a freelance graphic artist, designing business cards and posters, Erwin embarked on an academic career. He accepted an offer by the United Nations and served for a short time as a representative of the International Labor Organization (ILO) in Peru and Ecuador. He then took up a position at the newly established University of New South Wales in Sydney. The Tichauers resided on the "sugarloaf," an idyllic spot on the northern foreshores of Sydney, with expansive views over the magnificent harbor. However, Zippi and Erwin never really felt at home in postwar Australia. Another offer from the UN took them to Indonesia; this time Erwin was working for the children's organization UNICEF. In the midsixties, the Tichauers finally migrated to the United States, first to Texas and then, in 1967, to New York City, where they bought a two-bedroom apartment in Manhattan near New York University. Professor Tichauer quickly earned a reputation as an eminent, highly acclaimed scholar in the fields of occupational biomechanics and industrial ergonomics; he died in May 1996.

My conversations with Zippi—in her New York City apartment, but mostly on the phone—continue to this very day. Over the years, she became more than an Auschwitz eyewitness to me, almost a mother figure. When discussing with her the final draft of my essay, the conversations on occasion became tense and emotionally charged. Whenever I did not understand what she told me and confronted her with the findings of scholars or accounts by other survivors, her response was swift and unequivocal: "Forget what others have written and said."[75] For a historian, this statement is hard to accept; for Holocaust survivors, it must be equally disturbing to read accounts by historians in which they do not recognize their own experiences. Yet, the two views are not as incompatible as they seem. "The artist," the late Raul Hilberg writes in his autobiography about the historian portraying the Holocaust as well as any other part of the past, "usurps the actuality, substituting a text for a reality that is fast fading. The words that are thus written take the place of the past; these words, rather than the events themselves, will be remembered. Were this transformation not a necessity, one could call it presumptuous, but it is unavoidable."[76] Zippi's work as graphic artist in Auschwitz and the memory she shares about the camp attest to this necessity.

Recapturing the Past

| | |

Individuality and Cooperation in Auschwitz

Nechama Tec

My explorations into resistance under the German occupation have led to unusual sources of data. Especially revealing among these sources are the recollections of individuals whose wartime experiences were somehow linked to resistance against the occupiers. The personal histories of these women and men promote our understandings of that period in general and promise fresh insights into resistance to oppression in particular. My current presentation concentrates on the wartime history of one such individual, Helen Spitzer-Tichauer, also known as Zippi.

In one of our earlier encounters I heard her explain:

As the graphic designer of the Auschwitz-Birkenau women's camp, I was responsible for mixing the paint and for making sure that a stripe was painted at the back of each dress. All the women prisoners had to wear these garments . . . the color of the stripes was red . . . only red!

Many, many years later I watched a TV show featuring a Hungarian Jewish woman, a Holocaust survivor of Birkenau. I heard her say that her camp dress had a painted yellow stripe on the back. This woman spoke with such assurance . . . right there an inner voice ordered me to correct this misconception. . . . I tracked her down in Los Angeles. . . . Over the phone I introduced myself, described my past involvement with the paint mixing and drawing of stripes. I told her that the color was red and that only a color-blind person would describe it as yellow. . . . Furiously the woman asked: "You are telling me what to say!?" I heard myself say: How dare you?? And I hung up.[1]

Significant for this survivor's sense of history, the color of the painted stripe is but a minuscule portion of the puzzle that made her concentration camp life stretch into what to her felt like eternity, covering the years 1942 to 1945. Surely this seemingly endless history had its varied beginnings.

Zippi was born in 1918 into a traditional Jewish family in Bratislava. In this year at the end of the First World War, Czechoslovakia emerged from the ruins of the Hapsburg Empire, one of the newly independent states' component parts being Slovakia with its capital Bratislava. As far back as Zippi remembers, she felt good about being a citizen of Czechoslovakia. For many years these favorable impressions about her country were untouched by hints of the approaching personal and political disasters.

When Zippi was eight years old, her twenty-nine-year-old mother died. Facing her own pain, this girl realized that her beloved grandmother, who lived in the same building, had lost her daughter. This tragedy affected the father's health, preventing him from being fit to take care of his daughter and younger son. While herself coping with the loss of a daughter, this grandmother stepped in.

Helen's mother and grandmother with family in front of their house in Bratislava, ca. 1915 (from the private collection of Helen "Zippi" Tichauer)

She took her granddaughter into her apartment and sent the younger boy to the other grandmother's home. The family kept in close touch, cooperating fully in the many problems that inevitably called for attention.

After what Zippi's grandmother saw as an appropriate lapse of time, she encouraged her son-in-law to remarry. She practically selected this widower's second wife. With this remarriage, the boy moved in with the newlyweds. In quick succession two more sons were added to the family. The two households lived in harmonious proximity until changes beyond their control disrupted their lives.

Zippi credits her beloved grandmother's tactful, unobtrusive presence for the family's close ties. Born in 1866, this grandmother was way ahead of her times. With limited formal schooling, she managed to become an avid reader. She was endowed with a lively curiosity, which applied to whatever information came her way, about people, politics, history, and much, much more. Eager to know more about the world around her, each day she consulted the available press. She shared with Zippi not only the information she had but also her special ways of looking at and evaluating that which she absorbed. The grandmother had exposed the girl to as many valuable experiences as their environment had to offer.

The Jewish community in Bratislava participated in a wide range of Zionist groups. As a young teenager Zippi joined the leftist Shomer Hatzair, officially registered as a scout organization. The boys and girls who attended this group's meetings learned most of the practical skills a scout movement had to offer. Zippi welcomed these instructions. She recalls, "I found being a part of this group fascinating...most of my friends enjoyed the things we learned....But gradually, with time, they started to indoctrinate us, politically....I did not understand the theory, nor could I follow." She had no problem learning and absorbing the practical part of being and becoming a good scout, but the lectures about Lenin and Marx created problems for Zippi. Perhaps they were too invasive. She continued to struggle with how she felt about this indoctrinating phase of her life: "I don't know why, but I could not swallow what I heard. I don't know what it was. It was foreign to me and it was something I was not enthusiastic about. It would have been the same even if it were a religious group, not a leftist political group." It seemed not to be so much the issue of "what" as of "how."

Despite this teenager's reservations, she did not give up her membership in this leftist Zionist group. Zippi explains, "I belonged because my friends were there. We had fun being together. We had often interesting lectures. In the summer we went on all kinds of excursions. We had good times, being with the young people we knew and liked. But I never had the ambition to become a leader. I also did not want to be led....And so I never had a feeling for any of the political ideas. Still I was willing to learn, without being devoted to their ideology. Today I know about Zionism more than many others. I tried to learn all they offered. But had they asked me to give up my profession, which I was in the middle of learning about, I would not interrupt my studies, I would not go to Palestine. That was too much for me."

This young girl retained her Shomer Hatzair membership for social reasons. At the same time, she attended a school for graphic designers. She emphasized that she was the only woman accepted into the program. Zippi was eager to explain what becoming a graphic designer meant. I heard her repeat that "graphic design was a very select trade. The candidates had to meet high standards. Before they were accepted they had to pass a series of tests. It was a trade school, not a university. Those who qualified and were accepted had to learn how to design letters, how to convey messages through designs . . ., you had to know anything and everything that was involved in lettering, the technology, how to produce glasswork. You had to know how to create very elegant objects . . . very beautiful glass."

Zippi knew that the world around her was changing in predictable and unpredictable ways. Before she finished her studies, in 1938, her beloved grandmother died. Much later this granddaughter was thankful for this natural death. On the world scene, in 1938, the Munich agreement between England and Hitler marked the start of Czechoslovakia's breakup as an independent country. Zippi waited eagerly for the year 1939, when she was to take her final board examinations to receive her certificate as a graphic designer. Her examination was followed by an unexpected reward. She was asked to join a prestigious German firm graphic design firm. Zippi's performance at the final board examination probably led to this job offer. In view of the continuously shifting political climate, an acceptance into such a prestigious firm was an extraordinary achievement. Not

Helen Spitzer painting lettering on the Luxor Palace in Bratislava, 1938 (from the private collection of Helen "Zippi" Tichauer)

only was Zippi the only woman who had joined eleven male graphic designers; she was also the only Jew employed in the firm. This situation did not last. The firm was forced to terminate her employment because she was Jewish.

Slovakia became a fascist, satellite state with Bratislava as its capital. To this fascist country the spring of 1942 came with a special edict, posted all over the city of Bratislava. This document ordered unmarried Jewish women, aged up to forty, to assemble at a designated time and place in western Patronka. It also explained that the agricultural eastern part of the country was experiencing a shortage of laborers, created by the enlistment of young Slovakian men into the German army. They had volunteered to fight at the eastern front, for Slovakia's freedom from the communist menace. A part of this edict argued that transfers of young Jewish women to eastern Slovakia would solve the existing labor shortages. The document included a promise that the prospective laborers would remain in eastern Slovakia for a short time, lasting only up to three months.

The emphasis on the brief duration of the work duties diminished concerns about these transfers. And yet, this partially calming effect was undermined by warnings that severe and swift punishments will be meted out to the families of those who failed to appear at the specified time and place. The Slovakian Jews knew from experience that threats by the fascist regime were real and could have devastating consequences.

The document ended with a few practical suggestions. Each piece of luggage should be limited to fifty kilos. Those who owned valuable tools should bring them. Tools would entitle their owners to jobs in their fields of specialization. The message was: proper working tools equal more suitable jobs.

In the broader context of the German occupation and the wartime context of satellite Slovakia, this edict was unusual. It did not fit into the earlier history, which involved the mistreatment of Jewish men rather than Jewish women. Thus, in German-occupied countries including satellite Slovakia, young Jewish men were forcefully seized for debilitating labor. Some of those who were caught disappeared without a trace. A minority managed to communicate with their families. When they did, their letters contained vivid descriptions of humiliating, strenuous work. Jewish men equated falling into the clutches of Slovakian fascists with debilitating life-threatening labor. In sharp contrast, up to this 1942 edict, Jewish Slovakian women were hardly ever mentioned in relation to their employment.[2]

Because of the special persecution of Jewish men rather than Jewish women, some Slovakian Jewish men went to Palestine. Others succeeded in crossing the borders to Hungary, a place that, for quite a while, offered them protection. Still others had reached countries in Western Europe: Belgium, Holland, and France.[3]

Helen Spitzer, twenty-one at the time, was very independent. To her, the prospect of having to go to another part of the country for several months did not seem like much of a problem. Knowing that a refusal to register for this program would endanger her family convinced her that she should follow the order. Besides, her father's failing health and the imprisonment of one of her brothers only strengthened her determination to protect her family. Zippi had made the necessary preparations for her departure. On that fateful Monday in March 1942, she and her luggage went to the assembly place in western Patronka. As she moved toward the area, Zippi had few regrets. She was convinced that most other Jewish women who fit into the category of prospective laborers shared her views.

I was curious if anyone had accompanied her on that day. Zippi's brisk answer was: "I was not a baby!" She shrugged and began to describe what she had witnessed at that time and place. She saw a number of Hlinka guards, the Slovakian version of the SS, swarming all over the place. Why so many? she asked herself. She was struck by their unusual self-assurance that verged on cockiness. With a commanding gesture, they directed the women to an abandoned munitions factory. In front of this building, other Hlinka guards stood ready to act. Quickly turning to the arrivals, they relieved each woman of her luggage and pocketbook. This too happened in silence—the women had no time to react.

Deprived of their possessions, including their documents, the women were pushed into an area in which old Slovakian women searched their bodies. Whatever these women found promptly disappeared. The search itself was undignified, rough, and humiliating. They never saw any of their possessions again. Still, nothing was explained, only the gestures of the guards moved them inside this abandoned factory building. The ground they walked on was to serve as their living quarters. Only later on did it occur to Zippi to wonder how much pain and disappointment could be inflicted upon human beings without uttering a word. This absence of verbal communication added to her growing feelings of isolation.

Inside, Zippi surveyed the space and the people. None of the faces looked familiar. It was a big crowd, a silent crowd. She felt totally alone, a condition that, under the current circumstances created an inner void. Next, an attractive, striking-looking woman, twenty or so, captured Zippi's attention. The woman was resting on the ground, crying with determination and rage. Touched by this lovely but obviously suffering human being, Zippi moved toward her. Zippi asked her why she was crying. But the crying itself interfered. No answer came. Zippi was not one to give up easily. She kept repeating the question gently, over and over again. Slowly the woman began to relax. She introduced herself as Katia Singer.

As a way of explanation, she mentioned that she was "not Jewish educated." Zippi wanted to know if this meant that she came from an assimilated family. As Zippi explained, Katia repeated "not Jewish educated . . . not Jewish, she did not feel Jewish, and therefore why was she with us at all? She was arrested by Hlinka guards who were looking for a Jewish musician, the lover of the lady of the house, and they took her, Katia, by mistake. They said that if they could not find him, they would take her. She was there by accident. She was not brought up Jewish. . . . She was adopted by Jews. Her adopted mother told her that her real mother was Catholic." Later on, after they became friends, Zippi realized how much a part of Katia's existence was her preoccupation with her Jewish identity. Her need to deny it again and again was strong and persistent, but the stories about her background kept changing from time to time.

While waiting for transfers, Zippi had a soothing effect on Katia. She persuaded her that at this time and place nothing could be done. No one was around who was willing, or who even cared enough, to consider Katia's "problem." The two new friends, Zippi and Katia, were in a situation that required strength, and they benefited from their mutual support and friendship. The rest of the women in this abandoned factory seemed lost and isolated from the world. Increasingly, this uncoordinated group seemed more apathetic, totally unengaged. They stayed there from Monday until Friday evening. In the end, they were pushed into cattle cars, attached to the waiting train. Only when each wagon was filled and sealed did the train proceed on its way. This live cargo shared the suffocating air in closely shut cars. Practically no light reached their interiors. Along the way, the women realized that their Slovakian guards had disappeared and German SS men had taken over.

It was dark when they arrived at their final destination: Auschwitz. For Zippi, a learning process began with the brutal shoving into a nearby empty barrack. Inside, some of the arrivals found a sleeping space on the floor. The more fortunate among them grabbed a bunk, which they had to share with another person. All this happened very fast, leaving no time for hesitation or searches.

The first prisoners in Auschwitz were members of the Polish men elite, all of whom were considered political threats by the Germans. Some were political opponents while others were at best potential or imaginary rebels. With time, the prison populations and the camp structure changed, with Auschwitz becoming "the largest and most lethal of the German death camps. . . . it was three camps in one: a killing center, a concentration camp, and a series of slave labor camps." Eventually, there were about fifty satellite camps around the three main Auschwitz structures: Auschwitz I, Auschwitz II (Birkenau), and Auschwitz III (Monowitz).[4] Once the political opponents of the Third Reich were neutralized, a new kind of power emerged in all concentration camps, including Auschwitz. This power "shattered all previous conceptions of despotism of dictatorial brutality. This was reflected in a systematic destruction by means of violence, starvation, and labor— the businesslike annihilation of human beings. Indeed, between 1933 and 1945, the camp system changed from a means "of terror to a universe of horror."[5]

All German camps, no matter how otherwise identified, were places of extreme coercion, degradation, economic exploitation, and mass murder. Some, such as Treblinka, Sobibór, and Bełżec, were built with the sole purpose of putting

Jews to death. Occasionally, they also included other prisoners who seemed to fit the definition of the racially "inferior" or otherwise "undesirable" groups.[6] In Auschwitz, and in all other German camps, slave labor was extracted from most of the Jews and other inmates, before their murder.

It was dark when the Slovakian prisoners' sleep was interrupted by loud shouts, ordering them to hurry up. Not quite realizing what this commotion meant, the women were being roughly pushed out of the barracks. The shouts continued mixed with the word *Appell*. Zippi felt that these inmates had no clue what this word meant, nor did they figure out what their handlers had in mind as they kept pushing them out. Outside it dawned on some that they were supposed to form rows. Rapid counting began. It stopped briefly, only to resume. By now wide awake, the women had probably guessed that they were a part of a roll call. With each recount, the prisoners' positions were rearranged. Repeated counting caused much confusion. SS women (*Aufseherinnen*) and their assistants, German concentration camp inmates, were in charge.

With each recount, the SS women became more abusive, swearing at and haphazardly hitting the Slovakian prisoners. Absent from this disarray was the idea that an orderly formation of prisoners could lead to an accurate count and solve the problem. The Jewish women were exhausted. As they stood, waiting for it all to end, their attention was caught by some strange-looking creatures who were moving and gesturing toward them. They had no idea who these peculiar figures were. When the counting stopped, the Slovakians dared to approach these unrecognizable visions. Zippi recalls, "We moved in the direction of these mysterious-looking persons. Only when we began to mingle with them could we tell that they were the girls from eastern Slovakia, already transformed into inmates, heads shaved, they had old Russian uniforms on. Before, we didn't know who they were! They looked so very strange! This group came on the twenty-seventh; we came on the twenty-eighth; there was one day difference in our arrivals. These women were shaved and wore the 'official uniforms.' In some way, this told us what to expect next." But being shown and being told were different from personally experiencing something for themselves.

This was the day when Zippi and the other women, like all concentration camp inmates before and after her, were deeply shamed by the shaving of their bodies. Although men were less traumatized by these experiences than women, even they concurred that compulsory body shaving was just one of the many dehumanizing measures aimed at torturing all concentration camp prisoners. For women it was much harder. Women's sexual identification is more closely tied to their body and their hair. In concentration camps, public nudity and the shaving of body hair happened simultaneously. Women experienced these events as shattering, personal blows.[7] Deeply shaken by these practices, some women could not talk about them. Others, including Zippi, could mention them only in neutral, detached ways. In fact, I heard Zippi say, in passing and casually, "Once I was shaved and in uniform, they took us for work." The work was the central message of her statement.

In sharp contrast, in an interview conducted earlier, in 1946, she was emotional when her interviewer urged her to describe her reaction to the ordeal of being naked and having her hair shaved. My free translation of what she said in German is "We could not cope with the pain. . . . we were not conscious of it. . . . we lost the ability to feel. . . . we turned into stones."[8]

With March 1942 coming to an end, the Auschwitz *Lager* had to find space for the 2,000 Slovakian women. While the presence of Jewish Slovak women signaled an accelerated pace in the process of Jewish annihilation, it at the same time sharpened racial distinctions among the concentration camp prisoners.[9] Before 1942, a certain proportion of the concentration camp inmates were also Jewish. At that earlier stage, however, Jews were registered as political and/or "criminal" prisoners. With the arrival of the Slovakian Jewish women in 1942, racial Jewish designation was officially recognized as a valid reason for incarcerating people in concentration camps. This change automatically had increased the transfers of Jews, first from different parts of Eastern Europe and later on from various Western European countries, including Belgium, Holland, France, and others. Regardless of the country of origin, the Germans used the *Lager* as the last stage of Jewish annihilation.

Separated from Auschwitz by about two miles, the women's camp in Birkenau was still under construction. Since the middle of 1942, transports of Jewish women and later on of Jewish families continued to arrive in Auschwitz. The German authorities were determined to keep the women separate from men. To accommodate the incoming Jewish women, the Auschwitz camp for men was split into two parts, with a special wall erected as a divider. The first ten blocks were used for women; the eleventh and all the rest were reserved for men.

As early Jewish arrivals, the Slovakian women in Auschwitz automatically had access to "better" jobs than later transports of Jewish women. Zippi assumed that only a small minority of the Slovakian prisoners became foremen (Kapos). Some of the Kapos distinguished themselves by behaving cruelly toward their fellow prisoners. One such notorious example was Cili, a sixteen-year-old Slovakian woman who was in charge of barrack number 25, a waiting place for Jewish women who were selected for gassing. Cili's arrogance and sadistic violence must have helped create the opinion that Jewish Slovakian functionaries were abusive. Research about the Kapos' behavior and their ethnic origin is lacking. Examples of Kapos from different countries show extreme cruelty and extreme goodness. Through their concentration camps the Germans had created environments that aimed at humiliating and debasing prisoners before their murder. Inevitably, such environments led to expressions of both extreme evil and extreme kindness.

Familiarity with the German language gave some advantages to the Jewish Slovakian women over those who were unfamiliar with German. Slovakian women were also suitable for jobs requiring German writing skills. Predictably, office work was competitive. Office employment offered protections, such as shelter from the capriciousness of the weather. The clothes the prisoners received could not protect them from cold. Wooden shoes without stockings, coupled with mud-filled, unpaved roads, made marching to and from work a hazardous undertaking, especially during the fall and winter. An office job often offered more adequate clothing and better opportunities for washing.

The initial and early decision to build a woman's camp in Birkenau was followed by a transfer of 1,000 German women prisoners from Ravensbrück, a women's camp established in 1939. Depending on the time, the Ravensbrück prisoners had come from a variety of European countries. However, the 1,000 Ravensbrück women who were selected for transfer to Auschwitz were all German. Some of these prisoners were identified as political opponents of the Third Reich. For some, internment had begun before Ravensbrück came into existence. Others were semipolitical prisoners, like the Jehovah's Witness women, who became Ravensbrück inmates because they refused to swear allegiance to Hitler. Others among these German prisoners were hardened criminals, thieves, prostitutes, and the chronically unemployed or so-called shiftless elements. Finally, too, some of these women were guilty of violating racial laws. This usually involved "Aryan" women who were accused of being sexually involved with "non-Aryans," usually Jews. In short, whomever the German authorities decided to see as actual or potential threats to the Third Reich could be among these former Ravensbrück prisoners.

Curious and eager to learn, Zippi tried to assess the situation around her. With the initial official, devastating introduction to the camp behind her, she learned that not only were the women's barracks not ready, but the entire system was poorly run and in need of order. The chaos that dominated the morning roll call spread into all other aspects of their lives. Even the distribution of food suffered from haphazard arrangements.

Touching on that early period in Auschwitz, Zippi notes, "We got a piece of bread or something. We had something to drink, from the kitchen. We always had to go to the kitchen to get a big, big pot. It was always the same food. It was a very disorganized place when we got there. There were four people for one loaf of bread. No knives to cut the bread. They wanted to be more efficient, so they took one loaf of bread and told five girls, 'This is for you.' Of course, the girls would be fighting each other."

Aware of the disorderly and chaotic circumstances in the camp, Zippi was searching for guidance on how to live, how to deal with the surrounding horrors. An action-oriented person, she recalls her experiences:

When I realized that there were German women from Ravensbrück, I tried to contact them. These were inmates who had been in camps for years. Some of them were from the day of the Reichstag fire [February 28, 1933], Communists, all kinds. . . . There were also some professional criminals and women who had Jewish lovers. I wanted to learn more and know what a concentration camp was. We were brought there and were told nothing.

Many of these women wanted to connect to us also as well. Some of them were fine individuals who readily shared with us their experiences. They also wanted to know about the world; we were of interest to them. In those days, all the high prisoner officials were Germans. You had the SS, at the top. Each SS had an inmate functionary, who helped him or her. Those German inmates who worked for the SS would come back to the camp after work. I knew some of them. I would introduce myself to others. . . . Sometimes, it was a political prisoner, sometimes a Jehovah Witness, et cetera. You had a cross section of the whole German population in the camp.

Throughout 1942, with the accelerated pace of Jewish annihilation, many more Jewish transports came to Auschwitz. A greater influx of prisoners required new ways for processing their growing numbers. Arrival of Jewish transports into Auschwitz coincided with the loss of all their personal belongings. Whatever they carried with them when they boarded the trains had to be left behind. These stolen properties landed in an Auschwitz barrack area known as Canada. Here, under the supervision of special guards, the inmates emptied each piece of luggage, bundles, and packages. All contents landed on the ground. Here they waited to be sorted according to the German specifications.

Prior to the accelerated arrivals of Jewish women in 1942, German and other non-Jewish inmates worked at sorting the belongings of the incoming prisoners. These laborers were identified by their striped uniforms, which later were also worn by some German functionaries. When in 1942 more Jewish transports continued to arrive, the newcomers had to wear uniforms left by the deceased Soviet POWs. With few exceptions, practically all Soviet POWs were murdered in Auschwitz in most cruel and inhumane ways.[10] The continuous flow of Jewish women into Auschwitz depleted the supply of these POW uniforms.

The SS felt that prisoners could not be dispatched for outside jobs without clearly marked identifications. Needing to find substitutes for the Soviet uniforms, the SS authorities eventually decided the Jewish women inmates should wear the poor-quality dresses, the ones deemed unsuitable for German consumption. They also felt that these discarded dresses had to be clearly and uniformly marked. The solution was to paint a red line across the middle of each dress, in the back. Because the Germans insisted on separating women from men, they wanted a woman for this job. Zippi, as the only known graphic designer in Auschwitz, was a perfect choice. Her work as a graphic designer within the women's camp developed gradually. At first it involved the mixing of the paint, making sure that it would end up as a specific shade of red. Next, she took each of the worn-out dresses and painted on the back a line in the middle, from the top of the dress to the bottom.

As the arrival of Jewish women prisoners increased, the demand for these specially painted dresses grew. During the second part of 1942 and beyond, the transports of Jewish women were followed by transports of Jewish families. Some of these new arrivals came from Slovakia and other eastern and western parts of Europe. Because mothers were identified more strongly with young children than fathers, their fate was more closely tied to their children. For the Germans, young Jewish children had no economic value. In addition, Jewish children were considered undesirable because they promised a Jewish future, which automatically transformed them into a threat to the purity of the Aryan race. Concerned about the orderly and efficient murder of Jewish children, the Germans insisted on keeping mothers and their young children together; hence, of the concentration camp arrivals, mothers with small children were first to reach the gas chambers. In fact, the vast majority of Jewish mothers were gassed with their small children.[11]

The small minority of Jewish women who were admitted into the camp, an estimated 10 percent, was supplied with additional kinds of identification. Besides the dresses with the red stripe in the back, a specific number, printed on a badge, also distinguished each woman. Zippi, who was involved with making these badges, describes the process: "I had the white badges with the numbers; they had to be sewn on the uniforms. I had to print the numbers. Each prisoner had to sew the badge on herself. I supplied them with the needles and thread. They had to return the thread and the needles. Only then were they taken to the barracks. I engaged some people to do the stripes, since I was so busy, but I had to mix the color. I created some jobs for some people."

The numbers sewn on the dress corresponded to the numbers tattooed on the women's arms. The kinds of jobs Zippi could offer to inmates were more desirable than outside work, which was both heavy and life-threatening. I wanted to know if all those who had benefited from these offers were Slovakian prisoners. She admitted that most of those she had placed in jobs were Slovakian. But, she added, that this was so only because Slovakian women were more likely to be around her. After all, many of them came together, and many of them lived in the same barracks. Zippi insisted that, in principle, she tried to help regardless of who the people were. Seeing this as an important point, she mused: "I can only speak for myself. For me, it made no difference who the people were. I had one ambition: to help. I used my position to help. Political prisoners would help each other if they belonged to the same political party. But this was not my way. For me, what was important was to survive and to aid anyone I was in contact with ... whoever approached me, I tried to help."

In August 1942, the Slovakian Jewish women who arrived together were transferred to a barrack in Birkenau. This sharing of a common barrack created a semblance of continuity in a disjointed, humiliating environment. It allowed for most friendships, old and recently made, to continue.

In the slavelike environment of the concentration camp, many inmates established collective support systems and coping strategies. Most of these cooperative efforts originated in the barracks. The more detrimental and life-threatening the circumstances are, the greater is the need for mutual cooperation and help.[12]

Zippi felt that prisoners could not isolate themselves from each other. The surrounding circumstances, in themselves, forced them to share. In fact, on the most fundamental level, all inmates had to share their beds, with two prisoners assigned to each bed. Potentially, there was the possibility of stealing, but those who shared the same bed were in a better position to guard each other's belongings, especially food. Mutual help, sharing, and cooperative relationships collectively gave comfort to these prisoners. Besides, these mutually gratifying associations made the prisoners feel human. Zippi considered herself lucky that the young woman who shared her bed was very decent and caring. She remembers warmly the benefits of their mutual help and how important it was for each of them. Zippi's recollections reiterate and explain these mutually derived gratifications:

> There was always somebody with whom you had to share. There was nobody who could survive without sharing, at least, with one person. It was also economically worthwhile. We would exchange bread against margarine. We were sleeping together. This girl was very religious.... Together, we had two pieces of bread and two pieces of margarine. In order to fill up better, we would exchange the margarine for bread. We shared our meals, our rations. In Slovakia, she had lived some distance from where I lived. I had known her brother, but not her. This brother would come to us for a Shabbat meal, which helped him economically. He was a poor boy. She was a very fine person, glad to know me because she knew that in the past we had helped her brother. She lives now in Israel. She is very religious. She came from a very good family. She was always decent and good. Just as the nationality made no difference to me, it made no difference to me that she came from a very poor family. Such differences didn't matter to me....
>
> She never ate sausage because it was not kosher. I ate her sausage and gave her something else. If we had sardines, I would give them to her. She wouldn't eat bread, so she got potatoes. I would give away my bread sometimes so she would get potatoes. Sometimes, we would

get additional food, more bread or something. Once in a while, we also received vouchers for food. Jews that did certain kinds of work could use the vouchers in the canteen in the camp. They could get mineral water, mustard; men could buy cigarettes; women were not allowed to smoke. Occasionally, I would buy mustard. We would have potatoes on Sundays, and I would make a salad, with the mustard.

But Zippi did not limit her friendships and cooperative efforts to the young woman with whom she shared a bunk. She was friendly with most of the women who lived in her block. Zippi's friendship with Katia Singer continued in the camp and beyond. In Auschwitz-Birkenau, Zippi was hit by the revelation of how capable and good-natured Katia was. The day after their arrival in Auschwitz was a real eye-opener for most of the Slovakian Jewish women. The chaotic counting and recounting seemed endless and exhausting. It was clear that the SS women and their Ravensbrück German prisoner assistants were in charge. Being in charge also meant being responsible. However, they were not clear on what they were in charge of or responsible for.

The SS women and their Ravensbrück assistants were expected to collect clear-cut information about the number of prisoners, their jobs, their health, their food intake, their recreations, and whatever changes and fluctuations were taking place in every part of their lives and surroundings. All information had to be readily available in easily accessible ways, preferably in clearly written reports. Some of these reports had to reach the headquarters in Berlin, at specified times.

The SS women and their German assistants were overwhelmed by the demands of their work. It was hard for them to understand the extent of information they had to absorb and how to share it with those who could dismiss them for any mistakes and any inconsistency. In short, many of these SS women had a hard time grasping what their duties were.

The Jewish Slovakian Katia Singer had special organizational gifts and became a God-sent presence for the distraught SS women and their German assistants. Some of Katia's prisoner friends were also amazed by her ability to move from the chaotic to the orderly, clearly grasping and reporting the information that the authorities required. Those around her saw Katia's handling of the roll call as miraculous. A roll call under the direction of the SS women could take several hours. With Katia, it would last less than fifteen minutes.[13]

In a short time, Katia was appointed to the high position of *Rapportschreiberin*. She was in control of all the women prisoners. If anything went wrong, she had to attend to it. All the women's barracks were under her jurisdiction. Twice each day, Katia was in contact with functionaries from every block. They had to report to her and tell her exactly how many people had died, who had been transferred to where. The figures had to be correct. Katia, who was respected for her work, guided others in how and what they had to do.

All concentration camp prisoners dreaded the idea of becoming hospital patients. They were well informed about the deplorable conditions of the place. They knew that when they were hospitalized, instead of being cured, they would move closer to death. Indeed, for many, the road from the hospital led straight to gassing and the crematoria. This knowledge convinced them that they had to keep their illnesses secret. Concretely, it meant that no matter how sick they were, they forced themselves to keep working. For Zippi, this method served her well twice. Her health improved spontaneously without any outside intervention.

The third time, however, the system failed her. In the latter part of September 1942, Zippi had struggled with typhus. She continued her duties, hoping to hide her condition. Then the *Blockälteste*, the German prisoner in charge of her block, discovered the truth. Zippi recalls: "One morning, this *Blockälteste* informed me that I was shaking in my sleep. . . . I must be very sick, and people around me are afraid that they will contract my illness. She had to move me to the hospital. That was it."

In these days, the women's hospital consisted of several barracks, which were a part of the medical compound. Zippi was admitted into block number 27, a dirty, overcrowded room. Water was scarce. Instead of beds, the patients were assigned to filthy mattresses, spread on equally filthy floors. There was no medication. The patients waited. They hardly knew for what. Soon, what they had feared the most was about to happen. Zippi recalls: "On October 1, 1942, Birkenau had a big selection. I was a hospital patient, lying on the floor, feverish, feeling very, very sick. . . . An order came for all women patients to assemble in front of the hospital." There, they had to sit and wait for the trucks to collect them. Depleted of energy, they obeyed.

While the women waited, trucks filled with other women passed close to them, moving in the direction of the crematoria. Sitting passively, Zippi caught bits of the SS men's conversations. What she heard confirmed her initial fears. Somehow she had pieced together information that block number 25, which served as a collection place for women who waited to be gassed, was emptying out. Then she heard the SS men hinting that they would have to fulfill their quota for the day. To Zippi this meant that her group was next in line. In a haze, she absorbed the reality of her approaching end. Then, seemingly out of nowhere, Zippi saw the German prisoner Hanni Jäger, the woman who was Paul Müller's secretary, the commander of the women's Birkenau camp. Zippi called out to this secretary with all the strength she could muster, begging for help. The woman's expression of horror and the nod of her head showed that she knew what was at stake.

Indeed, later on, Zippi found out that this secretary rushed to her powerful boss, the SS man Müller, begging him to save Zippi's life. This German woman was a Birkenau inmate because she had violated the racial law by having an affair with a Jewish man. Told about Zippi's predicament, Müller dispatched Stiwitz, one of his SS officers, with instructions to release Zippi. When Stiwitz approached Zippi, she assured him that she was not sick at all but was fit for work.

But Stiwitz had to follow orders. First, he subjected Zippi to a strenuous physical test involving rigorous climbing of stairs and jumping over hard-to-cross ditches. Somehow Zippi passed these taxing exercises.

Next, this SS man took her to the hospital compound to check if she had a fever. The nurses and doctors on duty cooperated fully in solving the patient's predicament. They declared her free of fever and in good health. In no time what seemed like a miracle happened. Zippi was free to go. As she was about to move toward a newly found life, through the window she saw how the hospital patients who had waited with her were being loaded onto the standing trucks and taken off to be gassed. In her block alone there were about 1,000 women. Zippi was the sole survivor.

Weighing about seventy pounds, barely able to move, in a daze, half deaf, Zippi forced herself to attend to her duties, to act "normal." The idea that out of this vast multitude of martyrs, she alone was spared continued to weigh upon her. What she felt, she could not put into words. Very gradually, out of her emotionally blurry self, two sentiments resurfaced. One was a feeling of gratitude to those who, pushed by the desire to save her, stood up for her. At the top of that list were the SS man's secretary and the hospital employees. Towering over Zippi's feelings of gratitude was a determination to remember those who were murdered for no reason at all.

By May 1943, Zippi and an ethnically mixed group of inmates were transferred to block number 4 in the women B compound of Birkenau. In this group of women prisoners, about 60 percent were Jewish, the rest were Polish, Ukrainians, Yugoslavs—a partial mosaic of the occupied European countries. The accommodations in this block were improved, with sheets on each mattress and spaces set aside for storing the prisoners' personal belongings. Still, the beds were arranged in trilevel, with two women assigned to each bed.

The Polish political prisoner Anna Palarczyk was appointed the *Blockälteste* of block number 4. She argues that most prison functionaries faced the problem of balancing the SS orders with the needs of their fellow prisoners. Anna explains: "We had to fulfill the SS orders, at the same time, we were preoccupied with helping our women prisoners. . . . We had to act in ways which seemed to satisfy the SS demands, but we were mainly concerned with the welfare of our fellow prisoners. In our hearts, the idea of how to serve our prisoners took precedence over what the SS wanted. . . . To find the 'right' mix was very hard."[14]

Anna acknowledges that not all inmates who wielded power felt this way. Some of the inmate functionaries were cruel toward their fellow prisoners. She offers two examples. One was the beautiful Stanislawa Starostka, sentenced to death after the war. The other was Cili, the previously mentioned vicious Kapo of block number

25, who was severely punished after the war.[15] The Polish *Blockälteste* Anna admired Zippi's special ability to pretend that she was satisfying the orders of the SS, while in reality she concentrated on helping the prisoners. Anna thinks that Zippi was successful in reducing the suffering inflicted upon some of these prisoners.[16]

When dwelling upon her official duties, Zippi liked to emphasize that only the women's camp in Birkenau had an official graphic designer. To her, this meant that women were just as capable as men and that, at times, they could achieve even more than men. Perhaps this satisfied Zippi's sense of justice.

Inevitably, the role of graphic designer of Birkenau offered some privileges. Zippi had the freedom to move around in most parts of the camp, provided that an SS guard accompanied her. She liked to emphasize that she lived and worked "in the prisoners' office [*Häftlings-Schreibstube*] and was known as *Zippi aus der Schreibstube*."

The May 1943 move to block number 4 in Birkenau provided a separate design office for Zippi, *eine Zeichenstube*. Prominently displayed in this office was a model of Birkenau, a creation of this talented graphic designer. SS men and SS women admired this model and would bring camp visitors to see it.

Questions about Zippi's official duties led to some interesting revelations. She mentions: "I established the filing system in Birkenau. We had different categories that applied to our lives... everything was arranged in a great variety of ways, by profession, by origin of country, by barracks, there was a special catalog system of the hospital compound, who died, who was sick, et cetera.... We would also solve some official problems."

What kind of problems? "For instance, if a factory wanted 100 women for a certain job, with specific anatomical features, or special skills, such as narrow fingers, they would ask for it."

Did they know the size of the prisoners' fingers? "Not really.... We only knew that if you were fifteen to sixteen years old, you probably had smaller hands. Actually, most people were skinny at that time anyway."

Did you ever have the opportunity to put someone on a list or take someone off a particular list? "Yes, I could do these things, and I did them." She then qualified her answer by pointing out that such changes happened very rarely and required much caution.

Zippi continued, mentioning that she "had to produce monthly reports of all movement in the camp, outside the camp, transfers to various camps, what happened in the hospital compound, in the different punishment blocks and much, much more."

Almost an endless range of questions could be raised about the nature of these movements. Some of these seemed innocent: "How many people changed their locations?... Where from and where to did they move? Which work details changed in what ways, et cetera.? I knew who had moved where, when, and for what reasons. The evidence I received I had to arrange in clear, precise, and accessible, graphic summaries, and diagrams." Behind these designs there was much powerful indirect information about behaviors of high-level officials involving potentially compromising political secrets.

Zippi's more accessible and clearly arranged graphs and diagrams had to reach the Berlin headquarters at specified times. She elaborates:

> Before I delivered these summaries, I made a rough copy for myself. Nobody knew that I had my own rough copy of what I was about to deliver to the authorities. I would do my work during much of the day, and often into the night. Sometimes only around six in the morning, I was done with my official work, including my rough copy. I would send back all the original materials I received earlier, together with my summaries in the form of clear graphic curves and diagrams. This way they were not likely to suspect me that I kept any of the evidence they delivered to me. Because of my input into these reports, I was well informed about what was happening in many concentration camps around us. Because of my own secret copy, I could and did share information with others who made good use of this evidence. All I had to do was to consult my own draft to check the data. But no one knew that such a draft existed. I had to be "clean"!

Up until the present, when questions about her membership in the underground come up, she denies that she ever belonged to any resistance group. Concerned with facts, she insists that whatever connections she had to various underground groups were never formalized. For her, not formalized meant nonexistent.

Moreover, one could never be too cautious. The Germans were very vigilant. Spies and collaborators were swarming all over Auschwitz and Birkenau, all of them hungry for evidence about illegal activities. Fear and distrust were rampant.

Along with the many dangers and suspicions was a need for human contact. In the evening, before the official curfew, the prisoners would eagerly connect with each other. Zippi had many visitors during this permitted stretch of time. There was a doorwoman (*Nachtwache*) at the barrack where Zippi had an office. She would admit Zippi's callers and direct them to her place. Directly or indirectly, most of these individuals were connected to a variety of underground groups. Zippi remembers warmly these varied contacts, which reflect a tapestry of various groups. Still, woven into Zippi's descriptions of these visitors was a recurring assertion: "I never said that I worked for the underground. I never knew anything, and I never asked."

Nevertheless, descriptions of some of those she had direct and indirect contact with are instructive. Among these individuals, for example was

"Vera Foltynova, a member of the Czech underground in Auschwitz,...
[who] would smuggle plans to Terezin [Theresienstadt]. She needed
help; she would never approach me directly. Still, she got the information
she needed.... A French woman, Marie Claude, was in the underground;
she visited me. She was the main witness after the war in the Pilecki case,
a prominent leader of the Polish underground. Josef Mikusz was Pilecki's
representative in Birkenau. Mikusz would visit me several times a week.
When he wanted to meet his mistress, I made my office available....

Michal was a runner. When Michal would come to my office, most
Polish women would come to listen to the news. He would report to
these Polish prisoners the information he had. The Poles watched out
for my welfare because I allowed them to use my office.

The chief electrician, Heniek Porebski, lived in Birkenau, the only
man to live there. He was connected to the underground.

Among my visitors was also a French Jew, a Bundist,[17] Moniek
Eisenstadt, when he needed facts he came to me... he specialized in
information about French women—he knew he could come to me. But
all this was verbal; nothing could be written down. I had access to certain information, and if they needed it, they would come and I would
give it to them; but there was no evidence for this. None.

While herself never directly involved in the visitors' underground activities,
Zippi did provide the setting for significant illegal exchanges. She had acted as
a catalyst, an enabler for the underground. At the same time, she had never committed any potentially compromising information to writing. She made a point of
avoiding direct exposure to illegal evidence. Curious by nature, Zippi showed no
curiosity about specific underground plans for future operations. She kept her distance from life-threatening entanglements. But keeping a distance never interfered
with her feelings of compassion for the most oppressed and humiliated segments of
the concentration camp inmates.

Zippi's sensitivity to the plight of prisoners focused on the Polish Jews.
Indeed, Zippi had prefaced her contacts with Roza Robota, a prominent, mysterious figure of the camp's Jewish underground, by emphasizing how disadvantaged
the Polish Jewish inmates were.

She recognized that the earlier arrival of the Slovakian Jews coupled with
their knowledge of the German language and culture gave them some advantages.
In contrast, the Polish Jews who reached Auschwitz and Birkenau in the second
part of 1942 and beyond were starved, exhausted both physically and emotionally. The vast majority of the Polish Jews, an estimated 90 percent, were gassed
on arrival. Included in this majority were the sick, the old, children, and mothers
accompanied by young children. Moreover, the small minority of Polish Jews who
were admitted into the camp were the most deprived inmates.

Instead of German, these Polish Jews spoke Yiddish, which had no appeal to the representatives of the "master race." The few functionary positions that might have been filled by Jewish prisoners were already taken by the more qualified Slovakian Jews. Aware of the deplorable plight of these Polish Jewish latecomers, Zippi was positively predisposed toward them. In a way, she was emotionally ready for Roza Robota's evening visit in 1943. When Roza came, she introduced herself as a fellow member of the Zionist group Shomer Hatzair. She explained that she remembered meeting Zippi at one of the group's gatherings in Poland. Zippi recalls their first encounter:

> We spoke a little. Then she said that she would visit me again, and was gone. I thought that the whole business was an excuse, but it didn't matter to me. A few days later, she brought me an apron. Our uniform was a blouse and a skirt; only some of us had aprons. It was a little thing, but I appreciated it. Two weeks later she came again, with another apron. . . . I told her that I didn't need it, that one was enough. She disregarded my comment and asked me to give her my old one and she would give me a new one . . . this she did every two weeks. These were beautifully made aprons. . . .
>
> On my part, I encouraged her to ask me for favors. She did. Sometimes she wanted me to find a better job for someone in need. I did. . . . Occasionally, Robota would bring me bandages and I would give those to whoever could use them well. She also brought me women's panties, a great luxury. . . . I distributed those to very grateful women. Roza found them in her place of employment, the *Bekleidungskammer.*

This storeroom was a place in which Jewish women received their camp garments before they were officially registered as camp inmates. Roza's workplace was close to crematorium number 4, but Zippi paid no attention to this fact. Yet she noted that Roza's visits occurred only in the evening. It was customary, and probably safer, to move around during the permitted evening time.

Zippi briefly mentioned the October 7, 1944, uprising by the Jewish Sonderkommando group.[18] This tragic revolt was closely tied to Roza Robota. Zippi was reluctant to dwell on this, saying, "I only heard that Roza Robota was hanged. . . . I didn't go to see the hanging; I didn't want to go; I could get out of it, so I did. Hardly any of the Jewish women who had helped smuggle the gunpowder for the revolt knew about Robota's role in this uprising. . . . Only very few of the Jewish women knew about each other's participation, but hardly anyone knew about Roza'a role. . . . Four women were hanged, including Roza Robota. . . . I didn't know, and I didn't want to know anything about it."[19]

This graphic designer had to shield herself from any further exposure to Robota's story. But Robota's underground role, which led to her murder, created history, much of which remains a mystery to this day. The aprons that Zippi received from Robota were probably a significant and undiscovered part of this mystery. Supposedly, a former Birkenau inmate, who had worked as a seamstress in the sewing section and moved to Australia after the war, had made these aprons for Roza. In retrospect, it seems that Roza Robota made contact with people by supplying them with these fine aprons. Zippi muses:

> I never spoke about this to anybody before. Some of the aprons had pockets sewn inside. She must have used these pockets for carry-ing something in the aprons. I don't know what she did with them. I never noticed in my aprons any special pockets. I would put a heavy table on top of an apron... next day it would look as if it had been ironed.... Then, I began to think: why was she so anxious to have my old apron? I saw that at the edges of the aprons were those little layers.... Maybe she stored her merchandise in the aprons until she delivered it; no one would have bothered her if she carried an apron. I might have carried the powder on me. After two weeks, she would come and take my apron. It just could be that way. I was probably like a live bomb! It could be that when she brought the apron, she had the powder in it. It just could be that way. But it doesn't make sense; why would she bring it to me? The woman who wrote the article wrote about certain pockets, but all I remember is the special fold at the edges.

Were these folds an unusual feature of the aprons? I heard Zippi say: "That's all I know, really.... This was the genius of that woman, that I did not suspect her."

When I approached Zippi, I had hoped that our contacts would broaden my understandings about the Holocaust in general and about resistance in particu-lar. These hopes were fulfilled in a variety of ways.

The mere presence of a Jewish graphic designer in the Auschwitz-Birkenau compound was an oddity, hence a learning experience. Perhaps more surprising was the fact that a Jewish slave laborer like Zippi had access to sensitive and politically explosive information. In itself, this access suggested some cracks in the powerful German bureaucracy. It also showed German reliance on Jewish experts. Moreover, I was surprised that the Auschwitz-Birkenau authorities never learned about Zippi's sharing of information with various resistance groups.

As I continued to follow this graphic designer's history, I learned how tenuous the line was between Zippi's submission to the SS demands and her con-tinuous offers of help to various resistance groups and individuals. These illegal contacts almost automatically have raised the issue of whether or not she belonged to a resistance group. The answer depends largely on the definition of resistance, a concept for which both extremely broad and extremely narrow definitions are useless. In the end, the value of a concept depends on how much it explains and how much it clarifies. Usually, the literature about a particular subject tends to direct us to more balanced definitions. As a rule, resistance to German oppression has concentrated on collective opposition, usually organized by like-minded, cooperative individuals.

Another frequently appearing feature of resistance has to do with self-identification of special resistance groups and/or individuals. World War II literature about resistance includes variations on the ability and/or desire of groups and individuals to reveal their social or ethnic identities. Under the German occupation, in particular, some people could not disclose their ethnic backgrounds. Being a part of a hated minority in a hostile environment involved many serious dangers that could lead to murder.

Consistently, until the present, Zippi has been insisting that she was not a resister. And yet we know from her history that she had close and meaningful connections to different individuals who belonged to a variety of resistance groups. I accept her self-definition as a nonresister. Still, Zippi's denials point to some interesting associations between membership in a group and direct involvement with activities that are a part of that group.

Zippi's case broadened my views on the relationship between resistance membership and participation in illegal activities. Zippi acted as a catalyst, an enabler for various anti-German operations, without becoming a member of those groups. Undoubtedly, her keen intelligence coupled with inherent imperfections in the German bureaucracy shielded her from paying a price for her illegal connections. Zippi's case is instructive, showing that her indirect contacts with resisters would occasionally move her beyond awareness. As a rule, she preferred not to probe, not to know. There was danger in knowledge, and Zippi tried to distance herself from it. She was willing to share the information she had only on condition that others were likely to benefit from it. Up until the present, in a setting unconstrained by dangers, Zippi continues to share what she remembers with those she thinks would benefit from her recollections. I am glad to be among those with whom she continues to share her extensive, seemingly endless knowledge about life in extremis.

3

Displacing Memory

| | |

The Transformations of an Early Interview

Jürgen Matthäus

On September 23, 1946, Helen Tichauer gave an interview to American psychologist David Boder as part of a project aimed at recording the wartime memories of so-called displaced persons (DPs) in Europe. Brief as the encounter was, Zippi would not forget it. Instead, the memory of this interview has become a firm part of her life story; to this day she refers to it when asked if she could tell what happened to her during the war: one should read or listen to, she would say, this early interview because "everything is in there."[1] Many authors have written about Holocaust testimonies, their meanings, and contexts based on broader patterns in the transformation of survivor and public memory.[2] In this essay I address a different, more basic, but less frequently asked question: What makes one and the same testimony—Tichauer's 1946 interview—take on different meanings in the processes of its being recorded, translated, and communicated?

I am not claiming here any monopoly in having gotten her story right, nor do I suggest that only the first telling of and the first listening to a survivor's account should form the basis for analyzing that person's life story, although the special value of early Holocaust testimonies is as generally evident as it is visible in Zippi's case.[3] Still, problems inherent in processed versions of a historical source need to be addressed because they influence our understanding of the Holocaust. The forms and effects of the transformations presented in this essay pose the question of how we as scholars can live up to our claim of attempting to properly understand survivor testimony when we treat it not as a source that needs to be critically scrutinized as well as preserved in its originality but as a quarry for the mining of suitable data or as raw material for the construction of new narratives on the past.

I focus here on the effects of different interventions in the course of Helen Tichauer's 1946 testimony recording and later use. In order to follow the steps in the transformatory process described here, the reader needs to know which texts this essay refers to. I start with the voice recording of her 1946 interview with David Boder (subsequently: Tichauer Interview);[4] next, we will look at Boder's 1950s English translation of the recording published by Boder himself (Tichauer Topical Autobiography),[5] and conclude with an interview version published in Donald Niewyk's more recent *Fresh Wounds: Early Narratives of Holocaust Survival* (Tichauer Fresh Wounds). By tracing the origins and later permutations of Helen's interview, we can see some of the mechanisms and effects of communicating Holocaust testimony. In the process reconstructed here, the recorded interview becomes the object of two related, yet contradicting developments: amplification through increased accessibility and textual reformatting, and displacement to the point where shared memory—that is to say, a person's communicated recollection of historical events—virtually disappears behind externally produced layers of signification.

Recording Voices, Documenting Trauma: The Boder Interview Project

Before we get to Helen Tichauer's interview, let us look briefly at the pioneering 1946 recording project and its originator. Born Aron Mendel Michelson in 1886 in Liepaja (Latvia, then part of Russia), David Boder received his higher education in Vilna (Lithuania), St. Petersburg, and Leipzig (Germany) before he came to Mexico in 1919, where he changed his name and worked as a psychologist at the Mexican National University as well as in state prisons. In 1926, Boder emigrated to the United States and settled down in Chicago to teach at the Lewis Institute, which in 1940 merged with the Armour Institute to become the Illinois Institute of Technology (IIT). His professional preoccupation with the psychology of language and the utilization of modern technology must have influenced his initiating and directing a project that was to become the first scientific attempt at recording in audio format the stories told by survivors of Nazi terror. His Jewish background, a sense of the unprecedented crimes committed during the war by Germans all over occupied Europe, and his urge to reach a broader audience for his psychological findings also played a role but are more difficult to pin down as causal factors. Clearly, his interest was triggered by what he called, toward the end of the Second World War, "the enormous discrepancy between the abundance of visual material collected on subjects of the war and the meagerness of first-hand auditory material available on the same subject."[6]

The war in Europe was still raging when, on April 30, 1945, Boder out-lined his research interest and methodological concept. "For psychological as well as historical reasons," he argued, "it appears of utmost importance that the impres-sions still alive in the memories of displaced persons of their sufferings in concen-tration camps and during their subsequent wanderings, be recorded directly not only in their own language but in their own voices." Throughout his project, Boder was to insist on the crucial unity between personal memory, choice of language, and reconstructing the past. In his mind, these persons were "entitled to their own Ernie Pyle";[7] in the absence of such a communicator of collective experiences, "the exact recording of their tale in their own voices" seemed to him "the nearest and most feasible alternative."[8] It took more than a year before Boder was able to implement his ideas. After an arduous bureaucratic struggle for support, in summer 1946 he managed to commit his employer, the IIT, and the Psychology Museum in Chicago (which he had helped founding) to his project. He arrived in Paris on July 29, 1946, and immediately established contact with relief agencies, most nota-bly the American Jewish Joint Distribution Committee, which helped him with identifying suitable interviewees. For his work in Germany, Boder could rely on the support of the United Nations Relief and Rehabilitations Administration (UNRRA). There was no scarcity of interview candidates: at the end of the war, about 7 million displaced persons lived in camps on German territory occupied by the Western Allies, among them roughly 50,000 Jewish survivors.

The term "displaced person" (DP) comprised all those who, as objects of German wartime policy, had been expelled or deported or had escaped from their homes. Intermingled among survivors of the German universe of camps, forced laborers and POWs were those who had collaborated with the occupier, some even as assistants to the German murder of Jews and other "undesirables" in East-ern Europe. Jewish DPs represented a fair share of the small percentage of victims who had escaped the Holocaust alive. Between spring 1945 and summer 1946, during the time David Boder was busy preparing his project, the composition of the DP camps in the western, and particularly the American, zone of occupation in Germany changed significantly. They became the transit stations for tens of thousands of Jews from Poland and other Eastern European countries desperate to escape postwar persecution and to live elsewhere, especially in British-controlled Palestine. In late 1946, the number of Jewish DPs in western Germany had grown to about 185,000 persons. For many, it took years to settle in the country of their choice. The last Jewish DP camp in Germany closed in early 1957—as it turned out, that year also marked the forced end of David Boder's project when his fund-ing ran out.[9]

Not all DPs were willing or able to tell their story, yet anyone willing to listen could hear talk about the past. Collecting the spoken word in its original form distinguished Boder's project from others. During his tour through European

Erwin Tichauer in uniform with his new wife Helen in
Feldafing, January 1946 (from the private collection of
Helen "Zippi" Tichauer)

DP camps in the summer of 1946, he interviewed roughly 130 persons and preserved their stories (and also songs) on about 190 forty- to fifty-minute spools
of carbon wire, thus amassing more than 120 hours of audio documentation—
an unrivaled collection in terms of proximity to the events, diversity, and scope.
Boder collected most of the interviews (seventy-three) during five weeks in France;
in Germany he recorded thirty-seven interviews, but only three in the Feldafing
DP camp, including those with Helen Tichauer and her husband, Erwin.[10] Until
1957, supported by grants from the U.S. Public Health Service, Boder and a small
team of assistants produced full-length English translations for a little more than
half of the recorded interviews. These seventy translated interviews were incorporated in his sixteen-volume publication *Topical Autobiographies of Displaced People*
that, together with indices and additional material, filled more than 3,000 typed

pages. Mimeograph copies of the series went to specialized libraries; in 1954 Boder published a journal article in which he presented some of his findings on survivor trauma to his fellow psychologists. Five years earlier, he had aimed at a broader audience with a book titled *I Did Not Interview the Dead*. It featured translations of eight of his 1946 DP interviews; for reasons we do not know, Zippi's was not among them.[11]

From the beginning, Boder was aware that his interview project could provide only limited insights into the experience of Holocaust survivors. Immediately after the war, Annette Wieviorka observes, "the survivors did not emerge as a coherent group in any part of society."[12] In the DP camps, they fragmented along lines of nationality, gender, and age; as a sad reminder of the Nazi past, former prisoner status, time of arrival in the Nazi camp, and place of imprisonment also mattered. The experiences of enduring and relentless persecution, the loss of loved ones, the destruction of what before the war had been home, and the confrontation with the scope of genocide created deep wounds. "A victim of a catastrophe," Boder wrote later, "may not always be its best historian, but his reports, like items of folklore, give a definite portrayal of moods, and may render valuable *leads* for historical, anthropological, and psychological follow-ups."[13]

What was Boder aiming at when he conducted the DP interviews? We can get the best clues from his *Topical Autobiographies* selection published in the 1950s. Among the seventy persons whose interviews he chose to include in this series of translated testimonies, Jewish survivors formed the majority; yet the members of the sample differed widely in age (from fifteen to seventy-five), social background, and political outlook. In deciding whom to talk to, Boder was not out to get as many stories as possible: "I prefer to listen to less people who tell me much than to many people who tell me little," he told one interviewee.[14] The length of the accounts ranged from twenty minutes to four hours; as a rule, use of notes by the interviewee or the presence of others was not permitted. Whenever Boder had the impression that a narration was "rehearsed," he would tell his readers.[15] Aware of the subjectivity of survivor testimony and looking for traces of trauma, he detected signs of tension between historical events and their individual recollection: interviewees frequently mixed up dates and numbers, failed to recall names, or conflated personal experience, hearsay, and postwar information. On the other side of the microphone, Boder sometimes misunderstood due to lack of factual knowledge, language difficulties, or distraction from the outside—phenomena Boder noted on occasion when later translating a testimony.[16]

The conditions for recording interviews with DPs in Europe in 1946 were anything but favorable. Frequently, power lines and recording equipment presented challenges; sessions were disturbed, recording wires had to be changed, or the interview ended abruptly for reasons not clear from the record. Once his wire recorders had been set up, Boder let the interviewees talk (and asked them questions) in the language of their choice. Most of the interviews took place in German or Yiddish; in some instances, narrator and interviewer alternated between two or more languages.[17] In what Boder described as a "semi-non-directive" interview technique,[18] he started by asking for the person's name, date and place of birth, his or her fate since the beginning of the war, and the "high points of experience." Compared with more recent oral history interview standards, Boder's approach seems quite interventionist: he frequently interrupted the flow of the narration and also deliberately "redirected" the interview; on occasion, he expressed surprise or even skepticism in reaction to what his interview partner had said.[19] Hard-pressed for time, Boder tried to speed up or cut short the last interviews in one camp before his departure to another—at the end of Helen Tichauer's interview in Feldafing, he stated that he had to stop because his car was waiting to take him to his next destination.

Contingencies and logistics mattered not only when recording the interview material but also during its subsequent processing. As the carbon wires used for the original recordings became too brittle, Boder copied them onto two sets of steel wire. The National Institute of Mental Health that financed the duplication received one set of spool copies after 1950, but—not being interested in "this type of basic data"—sent them on to the Library of Congress.[20] The other set was kept by Boder and used for the translation and transcribing of the interviews for his sixteen-volume *Topical Autobiographies*. Not all material gathered in Europe in 1946 could be later traced; among the losses was the testimony by Erwin Tichauer, Helen's husband, whose interview originally consisted of two spools, of which only a short, almost inaudible fragment remains. Boder again used wire recorders for translating from the original language into English.[21]

In 1957, after the publication of his *Topical Autobiographies*, when he had to terminate the project, Boder regarded his work as far from completed. One remaining key task was to translate those interviews not contained in the *Topical Autobiographies* series into English. More important and true to his initial approach, he saw the need to transcribe all the interviews "in their original language as recorded."[22] As it turned out, neither of his visions was to come true in his lifetime. Boder's project predated by about two decades what Annette Wieviorka calls "the era of witness" prompted by the Eichmann trial in Jerusalem. Not only had Boder been too early; his approach, with its emphasis on individual survivor accounts, seemed too anecdotal, and audio recordings too unwieldy a form of documentation. His *Topical Autobiographies* gathered dust in many U.S. libraries as mainstream historians widely ignored them until the 1980s, when they started to perceive survivor testimonies as important Holocaust sources.

Today, for any nonpsychologist interested in Boder's project, his scientific aims and findings seem less relevant than the material on which they were based. The interviews convey an amazing variety of testimonial evidence in an overwhelming directness that stems from the medium in which they are recorded and from their chronological proximity to the events. During some sessions, Boder is gripped by what Lawrence Langer calls "the complex immediacy of a voice reaching us simultaneously from the secure present and the devastating past."[23] This immediacy carries over into the translated interviews included in the *Topical Autobiographies* selection; yet it is most intense if one listens to the material in the form in which it was collected by David Boder in 1946: as voice recordings of survivors, conducted in the language of their choice. Based on this material, Boder's preferred "study of the 'single case'"[24] has the greatest potential for Holocaust studies—a field that interviewer and interviewees, but also historians, in 1946 could not imagine would exist and thrive more than fifty years later.

Most of the DP interviewees seem to have quickly forgotten about their encounter with David Boder, which is hardly surprising given the impromptu nature of the recording and the interviewees' striving for postwar normalcy. Helen Tichauer did not. In late 1950, she approached Boder to ask for his advice on how to get her husband's autobiographical account on Auschwitz published; because Boder could not help, the brief contact broke down, not to be restarted.[25] Half a century after the interview, Helen Tichauer wanted to listen to what she had said in 1946; after the death of her husband in May 1996, she began to search for Boder's recordings. Through her telephone conversations she solicited help from friends and scholars—Joan Ringelheim, her most long-term confidante, and also from Konrad Kwiet and me. In 1998, as a result of coordinated efforts by staff at the USHMM and the Library of Congress, Zippi finally managed to receive a copy of her audio testimony.

If previous experiences told David Boder how to conduct his interview project, and if Helen Tichauer had talked about her wartime experiences before summer 1946, neither he nor she mentioned a narrative frame of reference relevant to her recorded story. At the time of the interview in September 1946, several such referential models existed: Jewish groups inside and outside DP camps, in Poland and in other countries, had long started to collect survivor testimonies for their shtetl, city, or community of origin; newspapers and radio stations reported on Nazi atrocities and on the fate of victims in conjunction with the International Military Tribunal in Nuremberg, where proceedings opened in November 1945; and since their liberation survivors inside and outside DP camps had shared parts of their harrowing experiences with family members, friends, and relief workers.[26] Even earlier, sociologists in the United States had published on the impact of catastrophe in Germany after 1933 as experienced by men and women who later emigrated.[27] In this sense, Boder was not navigating uncharted terrain; yet, as Helen Tichauer stresses, the talk of the DP camp was not the past, but the present with its immediate needs and the future with its challenges and promises.[28] The project's proximity to the events—chronologically, geographically, and (for those who gave their interview in German) also linguistically—offered the chance for individual memories to transcend whatever formalized discourse already existed and to let the personal narrative develop as freely as possible.

Zippi's testimony, conducted some fifty days into Boder's recording trip, shared several features with his other DP interviews. Boder published his English translation in the late 1950s as part of the *Topical Autobiographies* series; more recently, it became electronically accessible via the IIT's "Voices of the Holocaust" Web site that features Boder's translations and some voice recordings.[29] Yet until now, as for most of the *Topical Autobiographies*-volumes and the other more than sixty 1946 recordings not translated by Boder, neither Helen's actual audio interview nor a transcript in the original language has been available online.[30] Tichauer's experiences and choice of language also put her in good company with others who were Jewish, spoke in German, and gave extensive testimony (hers lasted three spools, each at more than forty minutes). Clearly, her background met the key criteria Boder had defined when planning his project, namely, to record "the rank-and-file experience" as authentically as possible.[31] How did Boder interact with Tichauer in the course of the interview, and how did her recorded account change later in the process of translating it for his *Topical Autobiographies*?

From Spoken German to Written English: Testimony and Translation

The obvious question for anyone listening today to Helen Tichauer's 1946 testimony is: Why is it in German? Her choice of this language (and that of more than thirty-five of Boder's interviewees) appears astounding for a number of reasons.[32] Since the Nazi era and especially in the context of Holocaust discourse, German carries with itself a heavy load that caused its descent from internationally acclaimed parlance of culture and humanism to being regarded as the language of Nazi terror and genocidal inhumanity. For many, including a linguistically trained scholar like David Boder, however, German sounded similar to Yiddish, the language of destroyed Eastern European Jewry. For remembering the dead, Elie Wiesel claims, "there is no language like Yiddish"[33]—a dictum that highlights the historical distance between German and Yiddish despite their linguistic relatedness. Yet how do we deal with those survivors who—like Zippi—were brought up in the language of the perpetrators and use it to communicate their experiences? We can best perceive the trouble with German if we compare its current assessment to what appears to be its counterimage: not Yiddish, but English.

In terms of proximity to the events of the Holocaust, English is widely seen as detached, yet at the same time closest to current Holocaust perception. English has become the lingua franca of Holocaust discourse, a development resulting from the leading role of English-language media products of all kinds, from scholarly books to fictional literature and movies, and greatly increased by the emergence of the field of Holocaust studies especially in English-speaking countries. The omnipresence of English has consequences for our understanding of survivor experiences. As Alan Rosen points out, one camp of scholars sees historical reality jeopardized whenever English prevails, whereas others claim English facilitates the reconstruction of this reality by serving as a buffer against trauma, as the language of choice to create a "balance . . . between medium and message."[34] These interpretations are not necessarily mutually exclusive: according to James Young, many survivors regard English "as a neutral, uncorrupted and ironically amnesiac language" well suited to telling their story.[35]

However one assesses the value of English-language Holocaust discourse, it is clear that German has characteristics diametrically different from those ascribed to English. Adapting Young's assessment, in the context of the Holocaust in general and of giving testimony in particular, German appears as *the* enemy language, completely corrupted and traumatically hypermnesic. Yet there are good reasons why Helen Tichauer and other Boder interviewees chose to speak German. For all of them, German was either their mother tongue or the only language in which they could converse with Boder without the mediation of an interpreter. In addition, we have to consider the role of language during and after the Nazi era: during the war, command of German meant reduced risk of annihilation and thus increased chances for survival, especially in a camp setting where access to lifesaving privileges required a degree of direct, long-term, if extremely lopsided interactions with those in positions of power. To communicate one's experiences after the war, German, with its Nazi-invented euphemisms and camp jargon, seemed well suited. Not surprisingly, then, those survivors who had experienced terror mostly in camps run directly by Germans (as opposed to ghettos with Jewish councils as intermediates) and who were asked to tell their story, as David Boder put it, "directly not only in their own language but in their own voices," preferred this language over others.[36]

Alan Rosen writes about Primo Levi's postwar use of German that for Levi "vocabulary and pronunciation serve as organic artifacts of what happened in the camps," thus becoming an important part of his "strategy of commemoration."[37] For other survivors who had adapted to the "*Lager* jargon," this might have been the case too; unlike Levi, however, Tichauer had learned German before she arrived in Auschwitz and thus associated very different events, feelings, and impressions with this language she had grown up with in Bratislava. She was born in a city where her social environment consisted predominantly of people of non-Slovak background, with German an established mother tongue for many Jewish families, including the Tichauers.[38] Helen's grandmother read the esteemed *Kronenzeitung*, a

German-language newspaper from nearby Vienna, the metropolis of the Austro-Hungarian Empire that maintained its cultural dominance in the region even after its demise at the end of the First World War. Like many Jewish children in Bratislava, Helen went to a German school and received her formal education in German. While Slovak was part of the school curriculum and also picked up by Helen in the streets, there can be no doubt that German had a greater influence on her—even today she refers to German as her *Muttersprache*.[39]

Yet, in the 1946 interview setting, proximity to the events came at a cost for the survivor: the risk of rekindling one's own traumatic experience. Similar in function to Yiddish, protective linguistic buffers could be erected by deliberately adopting a garbled version of German that created distance and expressed distaste.[40] As we will see in the case of Helen Tichauer, there was another, perhaps more intriguing way of containing trauma, namely, by using a polished, at the same time individualistic, "high German" intermingled with camp slang and geared toward descriptive precision—as opposed to emotive expression. This language use reflected not only her experiences and narrational preferences during the interview but also her perception of reality in the camp. We will deal with this perception and its linguistic implications later; what is noteworthy at this point is Zippi's lack of linguistic distancing and her high comfort level with speaking in German that ties in with this language's capacity to closely approximate historic reality.

People being separated by a common language is not an usual phenomenon in a conversation setting; disparate levels of linguistic proficiency also played a role during Boder's 1946 interviews. It remains unclear how well versed David Boder was in the German language; in his grant proposal for the interview project, he listed German next to Russian at the top, and he corresponded with his mother in German. No doubt, German was part of the diverse Eastern European linguistic landscape in which Boder was socialized. Yet by the time he worked on his *Topical Autobiographies*, his German skills had declined to the point that he decided to rely on a translator, Bernard Wolf, for texts in Yiddish, Polish, and German.[41] If forgetting a language is "a process that is in part governed by attitude and will,"[42] one could speculate whether Boder and Tichauer did not approach the interview in Feldafing from opposite ends. Irrespective of Boder's German skills, they were vastly different from Tichauer's. After almost three years in Auschwitz, she had blended elements of the *Lager-Deutsch* into her German vocabulary. As a result, her German narrative served quite naturally as medium and as message. We will investigate this closer in the following paragraphs.

Asked today, Zippi insists there was no preparation for or introduction to the interview prior to the start of the recording. She remembers being interviewed because her name had been mentioned to Boder by fellow Auschwitz survivors among the members of the Feldafing DP camp administration, most likely by her husband, Erwin, who headed the camp police.[43] It is clear from Boder's

English-language introduction to the spool, however, that they had talked before, if only immediately prior to the recording session, about her background, the nick-name "Zippi" she was known by in Auschwitz as well as in Feldafing, and about her husband, whom Boder had interviewed earlier in Feldafing. From one of Helen Tichauer's first remarks it appears as if Boder had asked her to focus on those parts of her story that she regarded as particularly "interesting." While thus not com-pletely unprepared, she had little idea what Boder wanted to achieve with her interview.

In view of the impromptu setting, Tichauer's narrative flows remarkably evenly; in fact, one can discern a coherent structure that resembles literary forms of storytelling. Because a narrative, as Antoine Prost observes, "cannot be sepa-rated from the explanatory links it establishes between the events that constitute that narrative,"[44] its structure needs to be included in our analysis. The Tichauer Interview unfolds in what can be called three "acts" or "chapters"—delineated by Boder changing the recording spools, accompanied by his framing each spool with a brief prologue and a postscript that provides basic orientation on place, date, and interviewee—with climactic elements concentrated toward the end of the first and the third "act." As in a classical story line, but unlike many other oral testimonies,[45] chronology and context form key structural elements; in terms of content, the scope of the narrative ranges from a historical "foreword" by her on the political situation in Slovakia via personal experiences in Auschwitz to her plans for the future. Digressions from the chronology or reflections on her own experiences—either induced by Boder or volunteered by Tichauer—provide explanation and exemplification; for the most part, she has no problem coming back to her core story.

Within these parameters and mindful of the problematic subjectiv-ity involved in "streamlining" a complex source, I have structured the roughly 120-minute Tichauer Interview into thirteen broad topical themes introduced mostly by Boder via leading questions or—in the absence of direction from the interviewer—by Tichauer herself. For these broad themes I have used the follow-ing headings:

1. Transport to Auschwitz
2. Arrival
3. First day
4. Work and death
5. Typhus, September 1942
6. Selection, February 1943
7. Numbering and marking prisoners
8. Evacuation
9. Ravensbrück

10. Day of liberation
11. Return to Bratislava
12. Episodes from Auschwitz
13. DP camp Feldafing and future plans

Each of these themes can be subdivided into further subtopics with direct, indirect, or tangential relevance to the testimony's core.[46] Instead of going into the details here and without retelling the narrative in an abbreviated form—an undertaking that would convey more my reading of her story than this story itself and thus run counter to the aim of this text—let us explore how testimony and language correlate in what I believe to be crucial passages of the interview. For this purpose, Boder's interventions in German during the Tichauer Interview and his later comments in the Tichauer Topical Autobiography (be they more formalistic editorial queries, explicit content statements, or interpretative remarks) will be integrated here as they shed light on the interaction between the two interview participants at the time of its recording and on later stages of representation and interpretation.[47] Needless to say, any fault I might find with Boder's interventions is subject to the same scrutiny applied here and does not diminish his momentous achievement in facilitating and preserving this early set of Holocaust testimonies.

After Boder's prologue in English, the German interview starts with an error by him in properly recording the interviewee's name—an understandable yet significant mistake because it distorts a key component of personal identity and because it gets perpetuated in Boder's translation, as well as in more recent texts based on his *Topical Autobiographies*. Instead of using the form with which Zippi identifies herself ("Helene Tichauer, *geborene Spitzer*"), Boder translates "Helena Tischauer, nee Spitzer." At the opening of the interview, Boder introduces another, emotionally charged marker when he sees her tattoo number—2286—and asks her where it is from, which at once establishes the Auschwitz focus of the interview. In response to an open-ended question by Boder on how she came to Auschwitz and what happened later, Zippi starts her testimony by placing her story within the broader context of anti-Jewish policy in Slovakia. She describes the background to the deportation of 60,000 Jews from Slovakia as part of a political bargain between the Slovak government and Germany, and provides specifics of those responsible on the Slovak and the German side.

Helen's implicit aim here, as throughout her testimony, is to be as precise as possible in the naming of dates, procedures, and the persons involved. Boder supports her in that effort by asking to focus on events that directly affected her. Beyond trying to communicate the correct names, events, dates, and so on, Zippi seems eager to use the most appropriate German expressions and grammatical constructions. The limits in doing so are defined by her ability to verbalize the events she recollects and by the tension between correct German terminology, on the one hand, and camp jargon, on the other. Clearly, she wanted her testimony to be properly told, first but not necessarily foremost to David Boder, who recorded her words and would thus ensure their preservation. The communication and interaction between Tichauer and Boder is key to the understanding of her testimony. Already in this opening sequence of the interview it becomes clear that their backgrounds, interests, and preferences are different though not completely incompatible.

Her striving for precision in expressing what happened should not be confused with aiming at stylistic perfection. Less than five minutes into the interview, in the first explicit editorial comment he makes in his Tichauer Topical Autobiography, Boder notes on her use of the German term *Maßregeln* (reprimanding, disciplining) that "she seems to be cautious about her High German grammar," missing the proper meaning of the German term by translating it as "measures." In the context of this interview passage, Boder also gets the facts wrong: when Zippi uses the acronym and proper name of the SS-Reich Security Main Office—RSHA (Reichssicherheitshauptamt), Heydrich's central security police and SD office in Berlin that planned the Europe-wide deportations of Jews and other "enemies of the Reich"—Boder fails to understand and notes that "the meaning of these letters are [*sic*] not clear."[48] Similar misunderstandings and incorrect translations of what Helen said can be traced throughout Boder's Tichauer Topical Autobiography: dates and names came out wrong,[49] words were not identified or were left out,[50] the meaning of German terms became garbled,[51] and sentences took on a new meaning, partly opposite from what Tichauer had said.[52] Probably the most distorting misreading occurs toward the end of the interview when Boder implies that Zippi was "the draftswoman for Dr. Mengele."[53]

In any interview process and particularly in the challenging setting of DP camps in immediate postwar Germany, mistakes like these are unavoidable. In no way do they invalidate Boder's claim to get it right, in terms of both recording and later translating the testimony in his Los Angeles office. Boder himself was aware of the "great complexity involved in the task"—from the proper reading of badly audible interview passages to the assessment of emotional expressions— and did what he could to overcome its inherent problems. Instead, the differences between the spoken word (the Tichauer Interview) and its annotated translation (the Tichauer Topical Autobiography) attest to specific limits of understanding and representing. These limits result from the way Tichauer tells her story, as well as from the lack of contextual knowledge, insufficient firsthand experience, preconceived expectations, and limited linguistic proficiency on the part of the interviewer. Their effect is profound: in the process of translating and transcribing, Boder misses information and misinterprets the precision aimed at by the interviewee as lack of clarity or stylistic posturing.

Helen's attempt to be precise in her choice of words dovetailed with what she wanted to convey. Unlike Primo Levi, Jean Améry, and other former Auschwitz prisoners whose autobiographical works have—predominantly through English translations of their texts—greatly influenced postwar discourse about Holocaust survival, Tichauer tends not to reflect on her thoughts and emotions in the camp; in fact, she avoided communicating them to Boder or anyone else she later spoke to. Yet, listening to her account and the way she conveys it allows more than just glimpses at her disposition, in terms of her perception of events in Auschwitz and their representation during her interview. We can witness here in a somewhat unusual form what Annette Wieviorka calls the restoration of "the dignity of the thinking person,"[54] a dignity that Nazi Germany, through its propaganda and persecution policies, had denied its victims.

At the same time, by concentrating her reflection on recollecting what she had witnessed as exactly as possible—from the language used to the events depicted and the persons involved—Helen verbalizes one of the defining features of life in Auschwitz: the absence of transcendence. For her, thinking in Auschwitz meant primarily memorizing camp experiences, something other prisoners preoccupied with work, food, and sleep had no opportunity to do.[55] Many years after the war, Jean Améry described the following incident in Auschwitz: dragging himself back from work with his fellow prisoners, the sight of a flag waving in front of a half-finished building evoked in him the memory of a poem.

> "The walls stand speechless and cold, the flags clank in the wind," I muttered to myself in mechanical association. Then I repeated the stanza somewhat louder, listened to the words sound, tried to track the rhythm, and expected that the emotional and mental response that for years this Hölderlin poem had awakened in me would emerge. But nothing happened. The poem no longer transcended reality. There it was and all that remained was objective statement: such and such, and the Kapo roars "left," and the soup was watery, and the flags are clanking in the wind.[56]

Let us now look closer at some of Helen Tichauer's "objective statements" that took the place of transcendence in her 1946 interview.

THE LANGUAGE OF ORDER: MESSAGES AND MEANINGS

The predominant feature of Zippi's narrative as recorded in the Tichauer Interview is her longing to establish order in the chaos, to provide orientation in a setting devoid of a uniform set of logic and morality. Describing the procedure of registering, marking, and tattooing prisoners plays a key role here for conveying her own perception of reality within which rules and order existed. Direct expressions of her preoccupation with order surface roughly twenty minutes into the interview, when she describes her waking up after her first night in Auschwitz and encountering "something completely unknown," namely, "the word *Appell*." This attempt at counting the newly arrived female prisoners failed, "naturally," as she explains, "because there was a terrible chaos" (*Denn es war ein furchtbares Chaos*) due to the fact that the prisoners were completely disoriented and the SS guards initially lacked procedural practice. Later, with the help of able prisoners, that would change. In the camp, elements of order, even if solely imposed by the Germans, were not merely important for providing referential structure; they also had direct relevance for the survival of prisoners. Instead of many hours, an *Appell* "if performed skillfully" (*wenn er geschickt gemacht war*)[57] could be over in ten minutes so that prisoners could get back into the barracks without further jeopardizing their physical condition.[58]

Similarly, she presents her lifesaving release on October 1, 1942, from the Auschwitz sick bay while other prisoners were gassed as a case of applied *Lager* logic: knowing that "one should not/has no right to/be sick," she pretends to an SS officer that she was without fever and gets sent to a fellow prisoner who checks her temperature.[59] This woman "knew exactly what it was all about" and assured Zippi that, even if she had high fever, she would say nothing, thus preventing her from being gassed together with the rest of the sick prisoners.[60] The moral frame of reference that Tichauer describes in the action of the prisoner nurse clashes headon with the genocidal order imposed by the SS and masked by German-language euphemisms—most notably *Sonderbehandlung*. Articulating what could be called the irresolvable tension between her survival-oriented perception of order and the SS system of organized mass extermination, Tichauer remarks toward the end of her interview that "one never knew what one is facing. Never" (*Sodass man nie wusste, woran man ist. Nie*). As translated in his Tichauer Topical Autobiography, Boder gives this sentence a more existential ring by changing it into present tense;[61] during the interview, he uses her statement to close the Auschwitz-related part of her testimony and to conclude by asking her about life in Feldafing and her future plans.

Boder seems to have been aware of having reached the outer limits of what was analytically fathomable within the parameters of his project. Yet here as elsewhere in the interview, Boder's interest in emotional expressions of trauma created a disparity between the interviewee's intent and the interviewer's interpretation. In the passage that deals with selections, roughly in the middle of the interview, Tichauer tries to describe the reality behind the term *Sonderbehandlung* and the treatment of new arrivals in Auschwitz "who came with RSHA transports, that is *verlockte* Juden." In the Tichauer Topical Autobiography passage quoted here, Boder not only retains the German word used by Zippi—the adjective *verlockt*—but also comments in a footnote on what he regards as its dual meaning and the "great difficulty" it poses for the translator. In addition to the dictionary definition of the word as "enticed, allured, trapped," Boder comes up with a second meaning: "covered with locks, with long, curly hair, possibly due to neglected appearance, or due to religious traditions of the Khasidic sect." In his Tichauer Topical Autobiography, Boder provides no clue to where he got these two definitions; regarding the second one, he clearly confuses the word with the homonym *gelockt*. How this error occurred is alluded to in his further comment on Zippi's use of this word: "In general it seems that the recollections are deeply affecting her mood. She loses control, in places at least over the process of verbalization, causing substantial contradictions and instances of confusion in the narrative."[62]

Indeed, one can find signs of confusion in this passage of the Tichauer Interview: queried, Helen corrects her earlier statement to the effect that these Jews deported on orders by the Berlin RSHA were *not* gassed. However, Boder's comments in his Tichauer Topical Autobiography seem triggered less by contradictions in her story than by his misunderstanding of the word *verlockt*, which he does not ask her to explain during the interview. His unusually long comment in his translation indicates that he is fascinated with the correlation he imagines to exist between this word and "the Khasidic sect"—interestingly, he does not use the term "Jewish" in his footnote. We can witness here either an overinterpretation of signals he is getting from Tichauer or a projection of his own expectations onto her narrative. The latter seems more likely because the Tichauer Interview recording shows no sign of a mood change on the part of the interviewee: the tone, pronunciation, and speech patterns Tichauer adopts throughout this passage do not differ notably from most other parts of her testimony. In addition, when Tichauer uses the term *verlockt* again toward the end of her interview, Boder correctly translates it as "enticed" and adds no further comment on its implications.[63] To this day, Helen Tichauer remains shocked about this misinterpretation, which, together with other mistakes in the Tichauer Topical Autobiography, confirmed her impression that Boder had been too ignorant and was too rushed to make proper sense of her testimony.[64]

Whatever its root cause might have been, Boder's interpretation points to the difficulty of reading the mind-set behind a testimony that seemed devoid of expressions of the very thing Boder was mostly interested in: trauma. One could speculate whether Zippi's unrelenting insistence, in her recollecting effort and most likely in her survival attempts in Auschwitz too, on providing factual information while avoiding analysis protected her against trauma or merely covered it up.[65] It is important to recognize that by taking pains to preserve the original voice recordings, Boder himself facilitated if not encouraged interpretations conflicting with his own, especially in identifying and assessing signs of emotion. Zippi's choice of language and style including terminology and intonation as documented in the

Tichauer Interview provides important clues, even if the identification of emotional markers remains highly subjective.

While Boder focuses on what he perceives as manifestations of trauma, the flow of Helen's narrative includes a broad variety of emotional expressions. In the Arrival and *Appell* passages of the interview she explains what happened to her in the course of disembarkation, the removal of hair, and the registration—elements of experience most closely related to sexual humiliation and thus most likely to imply trauma.[66] After Tichauer had described in detail the mechanics of the tattooing process in Auschwitz, Boder asked whether that hurt much—a question that caused her to pause; her voice had audibly changed when she answers: "Hurt? We did not feel pain any more." In his Tichauer Topical Autobiography comment, Boder notes her "very emotional" appearance and presents an accurate rendering of her revealing description how arriving in Auschwitz transformed her and her fellow prisoners "into stone." Shortly thereafter, when Boder asks whether the women prisoners were beaten by the SS guards during the chaos of the first roll call, she grasps for words and finally says that they—the newly arrived prisoners—were "actually unconscious" (*eigentlich bewusstlos*) or, as Boder aptly puts it in his Tichauer Topical Autobiography, "in a daze." He urges her to talk about it, but she insists she cannot do that and repeats—with Boder noting in his translation: "Animated and in a high pitched voice"—her sense of having been "unconscious."[67]

Two equally emotional interview segments surface in the Evacuation section. In describing the end of the gassings in Auschwitz after the blowing up of the crematoria in the fall of 1944, Zippi mentions without clear correlation to the concrete historical context "little children from my own family," which prompts Boder to comment in his translation that her "narrative becomes ambiguous." He was right, yet ambiguity works both ways: when she goes on by describing the evacuation from Auschwitz and the shooting of, according to her estimate, 40,000 prisoners en route, Boder asks how many prisoners had left Auschwitz altogether, and he finds her answering—"in an almost casual manner"—"over one hundred thousand." This prompts Boder to ask "with astonishment" whether all these had left at the same time. The upsurge of sentiment, in this case by the interviewer, dies down again, only to resurface toward the end of the Tichauer Interview: in the Episodes from Auschwitz section Zippi talks about the liquidation of the Gypsy camp and, according to Boder's comment in his translation, "chokes with tears." When one listens to the recording, this outburst—unlike most of Boder's other comments on the interviewee's emotion in his Tichauer Topical Autobiography—is indiscernible as her narrative continues evenly throughout this dramatic description of events.[68]

Is it justified, one might ask, to question Boder's comments, in this instance on her choking with tears, based on what one hears or does not hear in the Tichauer Interview? Granted, he made this comment ten years later when

listening to the 1946 recordings and translating them for the Tichauer Topical
Autobiography in his series; yet he might have remembered what he had seen
during the interview—he was there and thus should know. But the same applies
to the interviewee, who to this day insists she did not weep or show visible
signs of emotion during the interview.[69] It is hard to fathom how much Boder's
looking for evidence of recognizable trauma patterns and the interview setting
he created influenced Tichauer's testimony, including her emotional response. At
the same time, Boder's interest might not have been solely scientific, including—
as Alan Rosen convincingly suggests—a religious agenda.[70] That Boder was not
a purely facilitating agent and recording observer cannot be doubted; it becomes
clear from his interventions, but also from Tichauer's reserved response to some
of his questions, especially those that probed her perceptions at the time of
being in Auschwitz. Despite the dichotomy in the interests of interviewer and
interviewee, they were not completely at odds, as her matter-of-factual style
conveyed as many emotive messages as another person's outspoken references
to feelings. David Boder's translation for his Tichauer Topical Autobiography
brought Helen's testimony closer to an English-speaking audience; at the same
time, it created a distance from the authentic source and, beyond the realm of
Boder's influence, a basis for further deviations from the original testimony.

From "Verbatim Translation" to "Idiomatic English": The Unmaking of a Testimony

Until the tape recordings of the 1946 Boder interviews became available to
researchers in the late 1990s, the closest one could get to the original source were
Boder's publications, primarily his sixteen-volume *Topical Autobiographies*, containing seventy autobiographical accounts, and, for a smaller selection of testimonies,
his book *I Did Not Interview the Dead*. Somewhat ironically in view of what Boder
had in mind when recording the testimonies in 1946 in the languages preferred
by his interviewees, English-language scholars had and still have an advantage
in terms of access to these publications; not surprisingly, then, they began to be
heavily used after the Holocaust had evolved, especially in the United States, into
a distinct field of academic study.[71] The IIT's Web site "Voices of the Holocaust"
for the first time offered online access to the original recordings of some of Boder's
interviews. This presents a valuable service to many who cannot find their way
to the archived recordings; yet even on the IIT Web site, the majority of the testimonies collected in 1946 are available only as electronic copies of Boder's *Topical
Autobiographies* translations.[72] Zippi's audio testimony is not among those few featured online; in addition, the English translation of her interview offered on the

Web site perpetuates Boder's mistakes in his Tichauer Topical Autobiography and adds some new ones.[73]

New technologies that combine different media undoubtedly have decisive advantages over print publications in terms of outreach, as well as for properly presenting original visual and audio sources. Still, articles and books reach different audiences and achieve different goals, as the steady wave of newly published titles on the Holocaust proves. The quarry in the form of David Boder's legacy gets increasingly mined on both tracks, printed and virtual. *Fresh Wounds: Early Narratives of Holocaust Survival*, edited by Donald L. Niewyk and published in 1998, uses thirty-six testimonies from the Boder collection. In addition to several interviews Boder had already incorporated in his *I Did Not Interview the Dead*, Niewyk includes many more from the *Topical Autobiographies* series in his own anthology. His book also features Helen Tichauer's interview (Niewyk refers to her as "Helena T.") and thus increases the visibility of her story; at the same time, *Fresh Wounds* presents a new, troubling stage in the process of transforming Zippi's testimony.[74]

In introducing the subject of his book to its readers, Niewyk explains the uniqueness of Boder's project in terms of its timing and textual qualities. The "crucial importance of survivors' testimonies" lies, in Niewyk's words, in bringing us "as close as we are likely to get to the multifaceted essence of the experience." He assures us in his editorial introduction that, even if "close attention to survivors' accounts buys texture and historicity at the expense of coherence," we need to take this risk in the interest of understanding the fate of the victims. Nothing seems better suited for this purpose than oral testimonies, with their "spontaneity and raw directness," especially those created soon after the Holocaust. From among the heterogeneous mix of DPs interviewed by Boder, Niewyk's preference is for those Jewish Holocaust survivors who did not "freeze up" or "were unable to tell coherent stories." In terms of editorial technique, Niewyk wants "to let the survivors tell their stories as clearly and intelligibly as possible, always in their own words, but with much redundant material excised, and, in a few cases, the narratives reordered for chronological coherence." He admits his compilation is not for everyone. "Those for whom every hesitation, repetition, and convolution may be heavy with meaning," he suggests," ought to consult the original recordings or transcriptions."[75]

As we have seen, throughout his project Boder produced (with the exception of a few interviews conducted in English) no transcriptions that resemble what his interviewees had said "in their own words"; instead, for some he compiled English-language translations published in his *Topical Autobiographies* series that, as meticulously as they try to convey the original style and meaning, remain a far cry from the recorded audio interviews. Niewyk's acknowledgments indicate that he was aware of the original voice recordings and their availability. Yet for him, Boder's translations are the *original* source: he assures his readers that "every effort has been made to honor Boder's fidelity to the distinct character of the original text while rendering it in more precise and idiomatic English."[76] No doubt, Boder's translation of Tichauer's interview and, by inference, of other survivor testimonies would indeed benefit from greater linguistic precision, but in order to reconstruct or preserve the words of the interviewee, one needs to compare Boder's *translation* with the original *recording*. The editor of *Fresh Wounds* did not do this; instead, as we will see by analyzing his version of Zippi's testimony, he produced an entirely new text.

I noted earlier the strong correlation between message and format in Tichauer's testimony: for her interview with Boder in Feldafing, she chose to speak German, preferred certain German words and phrases over others, and precision over emotion in expressing what she wanted to convey. In addition, her narrative with its component story elements developed in chapterlike stages that Boder was careful to replicate in his translation. That being the case for her as much as any other interview in the Boder collection, one wonders at the start of Niewyk's book how he intends to reconcile his commitment to the "distinct character of the original text" with his preference for "more precise and idiomatic English." His editorial preference is clearly for the latter: the interviews, Niewyk warns, "required such extensive editing that employing ellipses in every case would clutter the text"; style was "regularized" in terms of punctuation, capitalization, and spellings of proper names; furthermore, the reader is asked to note "that retranslation into more idiomatic English is so extensive in this version that no effort has been made to identify the passages that deviate from Boder's early transcripts [sic]."[77]

Commenting on *Fresh Wounds*, Alan Rosen rightly notes that "it is regrettable that Niewyk has chosen to filter out what doesn't conform to standard English."[78] Given the linguistic and editorial steps involved in the process of producing Boder's Tichauer Topical Autobiography, standardizing an unfiltered text is just one of the problems we can identify here. In addition, what standard can and should be used to "retranslate" survivor testimony into "more idiomatic English"? In a review on a controversial yet well-written book on the Treblinka death camp, Auschwitz survivor Jean Améry notes an "incompatibility between literature and an unlikely truth" (*Inkompatibilität von Literatur und einer unwahrscheinlichen Wahrheit*) and voices his preference for a nonartistic, even helpless or clumsy style over literary elegance.[79] What literary style to choose might be a matter of taste; still, in view of the events depicted, one cannot and should not expect testimony by Holocaust survivors to come to us in well-worded, neatly structured prose.

Niewyk's choice to include three dozen survivor testimonies in a 400-page book forces him to cut their size. Moreover, his preference for "more precise and idiomatic English" leads him to replace the free, at times turbulent and meandering flow of the testimonies' narrative with a clearly defined yet narrow channel of fabricated syntax. In the case of Helen's interview, this streamlining involves massive interventions: omitting large parts of the Tichauer Topical Autobiography, inverting sentence and narrative structure, and changing terminology even where Boder had retained the German.[80] Overall, the result is a text that resembles very little of the content and fewer of the implications of Zippi's spoken words. If one puts the original voice recording, Boder's translation, and Niewyk's rendition next to one another, it becomes obvious that, in terms of being true to its source, Tichauer Fresh Wounds is miles away from Boder's translated text, and on a different planet than the interview recording.[81] Going further in our comparison by exploring specific passages in these texts might appear as overkill that borders on the forensic; still, it is only by exemplification that we can assess what streamlining and reformatting did to the voice of one survivor Niewyk's book claims to amplify.

True to his aim of producing idiomatic English, Niewyk selects segments from Boder's translation that are literary in style, fast in pace, and dense in content. Given the absence of ellipses, the passages linked together in Tichauer Fresh Wounds form a seamless unity. Contextual elements retained or newly inserted to convey the semblance of interview immediacy (questions by Boder) or to annotate content (a short introduction on "T.'s" life story and a rudimentary footnote apparatus devoid of information on its sources or on further reading) also help to create the illusion as if Tichauer Fresh Wounds were close to its source. Interestingly in light of Niewyk's claim "to honor Boder's fidelity to the distinct character of the original text," he retains none of Boder's editorial comments while adding more factual mistakes to what Boder got wrong. It is mysterious how some of these errors came about: that Zippi's reference to the city of "Loslau" (German for Wodisław Śląski) turned into "Wroclaw" in Boder's translation and into "Breslau" (German for Wroclaw) in Niewyk's text might appear conclusive, but why Helen's final place of confinement before liberation, subcamp Malchow ("Meistro" in Boder's translation), would turn into "Mirow" in *Fresh Wounds* remains the editor's secret.[82]

The key problem with Tichauer Fresh Wounds is not factual errors (no book is without them) but the disregard for what should have been its primary source—Zippi's interview recording—combined with the way it treats its real source, Boder's translation: as a smorgasbord of textual tidbits from which to pick and choose, leaving only a skeleton of the interview's structure, not to mention its original style, wording, and meaning. A few examples may suffice. One of the narrative segments Helen addresses toward the end—identified earlier in this essay as Tichauer Interview chapter 12, Episodes from Auschwitz—is taken out of its context and moved up in the Tichauer Fresh Wounds story line, presumably to increase its effect and to establish clear-cut chronology. Where Boder has Zippi choking with tears, Niewyk writes—without having listened to the tape on which her reactions, as we have seen, are hardly audible—"she wept."[83] What emerges in the end is a new text that, compared with Boder's translation, conveys select information devoid of context or subtext and imposes a faster pace as well as a totally different, more dramatic style. Readers of the *Fresh Wounds* piece on "Helena T." can decide for themselves whether it works more or less effectively than Boder's Tichauer Topical Autobiography, not to mention the original Tichauer Interview; there can be no doubt, however, that Niewyk's text is further away from the original source than any of its other renderings.

Tichauer Fresh Wounds brings into sharper relief the problematic relationship between memory, historiography, and current perceptions. Within Holocaust studies—a field often criticized for its being rooted in current interests—the danger of misrepresenting the past is particularly potent for the amorphous, constantly changing genres of testimony and memoir literature.[84] Survivor testimony is as crucial and irreplaceable as it is loaded with problems: some unique to this source type, others standard features of historical documentation. Addressing these problems can take different forms: from scrutinizing how a testimony comes to us and assessing its originality and facticity to choosing how to represent, analyze, and interpret it. In cases where the historian's unavoidable subjectivity in approaching a topic and the need to generalize dovetails with simplification or adaptation to what the public might expect—for example, new, more moving, and more dramatic material—the complexities of historical reality disappear behind a streamlined or otherwise distorted version of the past. Representations by those receiving and using testimony raise the issue of authenticity with at least the same urgency as alleged or real discrepancies in the stories of survivors.[85]

Irrespective of whether Holocaust testimonies attain iconographic importance or receive—like Helen Tichauer's 1946 interview—only limited attention, their public perception is in most cases based not on the original source but on edited, often translated renditions, texts that claim to be true to the spirit if not the letter of the source. New technologies and sound editorial standards offer good prospects to put this claim to the test by increasing the accessibility of Holocaust documentation previously buried in archives. No doubt, the events and experiences of the Holocaust can only be communicated to a degree; a certain, often amorphous threshold will prevent us from fully understanding what happened. Testimonies like Zippi's might not spell out what we would like or expect them to reveal. Yet, they are the sole basis for reconstructing with any prospect of success not only what actually happened but also how what happened is remembered and communicated by survivors and subsequently by historians. Instead of survivor memory or language failing in the face of Auschwitz, in the case presented here the failure seems to be on the part of its recipients, especially those who communicate testimonies in a selective or decontextualized manner. Historiography is the effort to approximate what happened in the past. We cannot get closer to this past by moving away from original sources that verbalize it.

TABLE 1. Themes and Sub-Themes in Helen Tichauer's 1946 Interview and Its Later Versions

I. Tichauer Interview (German-language voice recording in USHMMA, RG-50.472), 1946	II. Tichauer Topical Autobiography (English translation in Boder, *Topical Autobiographies*), 1957	III. Tichauer Fresh Wounds (English edition in Niewyk, *Fresh Wounds*), 1998
A. Spool 149 (44:55 min.):		
Spool introduction	p. 2044	[editor's introduction to "Helena T."]
1. Transport to Auschwitz:	pp. 2045–2050	Extracts pp. 355–356
- History		
- Family, background		
- Rationalization		
2. Arrival:	pp. 2050–2056	Extracts pp. 356–358
- Disembarkation		
- First impressions		
- Initiation		
3. First day:	pp. 2056–2059	Extracts pp. 358–359
- Chaos and order		
- Prisoner categories (i)		
- Camp organization		
4. Work and death:	pp. 2060–2066	Extracts pp. 359–360
- Gassings		
- Numbers (i): prisoner numbering and marking		
B. Spool 150 (37 min.):		
Spool introduction	p. 2067	-
5. Typhus Sept. 1942:	pp. 2067–2074	Extracts pp. 360–361
- Sick bay		
- Selection (i)		
- Zippi's survival		
6. Selection Feb. 1943:	pp. 2074–2078	Extracts pp. 361–362 [break in narrative sequence; see below 12.]
- Camp bookkeeping (i)		
- Selection (ii)		
- Prisoner categories (ii)		
7. Numbering and marking prisoners:	pp. 2078–2083	Extracts pp. 364–365
- Camp bookkeeping (ii)		
- Numbers (ii): file card catalogue		
- Auschwitz model		
8. Evacuation:	pp. 2083–2087	Extracts p. 366
- Blowing up of crematorium		
- Fate of her family		
- March, guards		
- Cattle cars, food		
9. Ravensbrück:	pp. 2088–2089	Extracts p. 366
- Experiments on prisoners		
- Chaos		

(Continued)

TABLE 1. *(Continued)*

I. Tichauer Interview (German-language voice recording in USHMMA, RG-50.472), 1946	II. Tichauer Topical Autobiography (English translation in Boder, *Topical Autobiographies*), 1957	III. Tichauer Fresh Wounds (English edition in Niewyk, FRESH WOUNDS), 1998
C. Spool 151 (37 min.):		
Spool introduction	p. 2090	-
10. Day of liberation:	pp. 2090–2094	Extracts pp. 366–368
- Camp Malchow		
- Goldberg, escape		
- Hiding with others		
- Russian approach		
11. Return to Bratislava:	pp. 2094–2098	Extracts p. 368
- Ex-prisoners and POWs		
- Fate of her brother, family		
12. Episodes from Auschwitz:	pp. 2098–2107	Extracts pp. 362–363 [out
- Fire, chimneys		of audio testimony sequence]
- Gypsies, Hungarian Jews		
- Theresienstadt		
- Deception		
13. DP-camp Feldafing and future plans:	pp. 2107–2111	Extracts p. 369
- Lt. Smith		
- Wish to leave		
- Contact with Germans		
- Zippi's and her husband's emigration plans		
Overall length: 118.55 min (3 spools)	pp. 2044–2111 (68 pp.)	pp. 354–369 (16 pp.)

4

Living On

| | |

Remembering Feldafing

Atina Grossmann

People have no memory, people don't believe me what I remember.
—Zippi Tichauer, 2007

Memory and History, Historian and Witness

As we rewrite the history of the post-1945 years in the aftermath of 1989, we are only now rediscovering what was amply obvious to contemporaries: that occupied Germany in the immediate postwar period was the unlikely, unloved, and reluctant host to some 250,000 of its former victims, housed both in and outside of refugee camps mainly in the American zone and in the American sector of Berlin. A significant number of the millions of people uprooted by war and persecution who remained on western Allied territory as "unrepatriable" displaced persons (DPs) were Jewish survivors of Nazi genocide and involuntary migration—precisely the people both the Allies and the Germans had least expected to have to deal with in the aftermath of National Socialism's exterminatory war.[1]

Since the mid-1990s there has finally been a proliferation of publications, conferences, films, and exhibitions on Jewish DPs gathered in occupied Germany, pushed in large part by the efforts of the baby boom "second generation" born in DP camps or communities. Yet, despite the truly overwhelming amount of source material, historical, sociological, visual, and literary, and a substantial and ever-growing secondary literature, we are just beginning to think about the social, rather than the political, history of the approximately 250,000 Jewish DPs.[2] Ongoing conversations with Zippi (as she has always named herself when my telephone rings with her familiar voice) Tichauer and other former DPs have only sharpened my sense of how much we still do not know and do not understand about the experience of "living on," of continuing and reclaiming life after catastrophe.

In my own recent book, I explored this process—often represented as "life reborn"—and aimed to reflect on how everyday interactions ("close encounters," I called them) between Jewish survivors and their German surroundings, and among Jews, Germans, and Allies in occupied Germany from 1945 to 1949 were shaped by, and led to, experiences of gender and sexuality. I was fascinated by the paradoxical fact that the Jewish baby boom of 1946–1947, the most concrete assertion of "living on" after a Final Solution designed to exterminate all of European Jewry, was the occasion for pragmatic and yet intimate encounters among defeated Germans and surviving Jews. I was intrigued more generally by the varied quotidian contacts—between Jewish mothers and German nannies, between Jewish men and German women, between Jewish employers and German employees, between German residents and the DPs who marched through their towns brandishing both baby carriages and banners demanding free emigration to Palestine—and the many other interactions between Jewish DPs and the Germans among whom they lived. These surprisingly close encounters seemed to me to raise fraught questions about both coexistence and revenge. Or, to put it another way, I was—and still am—interested in how, during the liminal immediate postwar years when Jewish survivors were such a significant if temporary presence in occupied defeated Germany, the simultaneously intimate and public spaces of the body, the family, and Zionism all produced a discourse of "normalization" as well as "futurity" under the "abnormal" conditions of postwar refugee life.

"People do not know me at all, they think I'm just a survivor. Just an old lady," Zippi recently told me. But her memories of life in Feldafing—the DP camp in Bavaria that featured so prominently in my research—continually challenged me to think further about how those experiences and the nature of Jewish DP life in general have been narrated and silenced in survivor memories, and how we as historians selectively both use and disavow those memories. As one of numerous historians who have benefited from her knowledge, unflinching honesty, and astonishingly detailed recall, I have found myself continually negotiating the links and gaps between Zippi's stories of Jewish life in the foothills of the Bavarian Alps, where she and her husband, Erwin Tichauer, worked and lived, and the archival evidence that first led me to the questions about Jewish life and "close encounters" between surviving Jews and defeated Germans that I kept asking her.

I met Zippi at a relatively late stage of my research. At a scholars' workshop on gender and the Holocaust convened at the United States Holocaust Memorial Museum in summer 2004, Joan Ringelheim, a true pioneer on those issues and then the director of the Oral History Department at the museum, insisted that there was someone I absolutely must contact: an Auschwitz survivor with a remarkable, almost photographic memory, who gave rigorously precise answers to informed questions, thereby confounding much of what we thought we had learned about the limits of eyewitness accounts.[3] Zippi had been interviewed at length about her experiences in Auschwitz, but, Joan urged, she could tell me much I did not know about the DP camp that had already provided some of my most compelling material. Decades earlier, I had heard fragmented stories about Feldafing from the former DP parents of my college boyfriend. I had visited the town, searching for signs of the Elisabeth Hospital in which he had been born in the restored luxury of the Hotel Kaiserin Elisabeth on the picturesque shores of the Starnberger Lake some twenty miles outside of Munich. I had interviewed the German woman who as a young town clerk had registered the many births and marriages of the Jewish DPs. I read memoirs and scoured voluminous archival sources. The records of the two main aid organizations, the United Nations Relief and Rehabilitation Administration (UNRRA) and the American Jewish Joint Distribution Committee (JDC, "Joint"), as well as the semiautonomous Central Committee of Liberated Jews of Bavaria, and—most revealingly—the files of the Feldafing camp administration, with its many departments (from religion to health and sanitation), all documented daily life in this first all-Jewish DP camp in the American zone.

Zippi's stories, however, transmitted over a period of several years, at first during visits to her New York apartment, darkened against the sun that hurt her almost blind eyes and overflowing with the books and papers of her private Holocaust archive, and then in numerous long telephone conversations (somehow we often called each other just when I was on my way to the airport for yet another conference), always both reinforced and subverted what I was uncovering in other sources. Further complicating the relationship between history and testimony, or, as I suspect Zippi would prefer, between history as understood by the historian and history as transmitted by the eyewitness, is the circumstance that even my best efforts to convey Zippi's (sometimes utterly against the grain) challenges to my research findings are of course my renditions of what she told me—frequently (especially more recently) not during anything resembling formal interviews (or oral histories) but on the phone, with me frantically scribbling notes on whatever piece of paper happened to be available.

The Road to Feldafing

Zippi's journey to Feldafing DP camp was typical of many of the survivors who found their way to the American zone of occupied Germany. Pushed westward from Auschwitz as the Red Army moved into the Reich, she survived the end of

the war in the women's camp at Ravensbrück and its notorious satellite camp in
Malchow. During the final "evacuation," or death march from Malchow, she and a
friend managed to flee. Zippi's painterly skills helped to eliminate the damning red
stripe she had previously imprinted on the outfits of so many concentration camp
prisoners (*KZniks*), and they mixed in with the masses—freed forced laborers,
camp inmates, and POWs, even SS on the run—streaming along the roads of war's
end. It was *"ein grosses Chaos"* that now, unlike in Auschwitz where she perceived
order as potentially lifesaving, served Zippi well.[4] The Red Army rumbled by;
the exhausted, brutalized troops who brought terror for many (not only) German
women signaled liberation and kindness for Zippi and her comrades. The soldiers
threw food at the starved, and when, like many Jewish survivors, Zippi decided
that her first act as a free person would be to try and return to the home in Slovakia
from which she had been deported, she and two Polish girls were offered a ride by
a friendly Soviet captain. He promised that all army vehicles would stop for them;
they had orders to transport the liberated home. And in Zippi's telling, she seems
to have had good luck, unlike other women survivors who report sexual threats
and attacks by the very same Soviets who fed and helped them. She acknowledges that as the Red Army approached, the prisoners had debated whether to
try and flee toward the Americans, but Zippi reasoned that it did not matter who
rescued them—"We want to be liberated. And it is a pity to give away our last
strength.... We knew that the day of liberation through the Allied forces, no
matter by what nation, will be our day, yes?"

"On the road," she informed David Boder in September 1946, "we met a
great variety of people, and all were nice and ... helped us wherever they could."
Was the journey really so safe, or did Zippi simply think that after Auschwitz
and the death marches, such more "minor" (my quotation marks) dangers posed by
the Red Army liberators were not worth mentioning to an interviewer either in
1946 or more recently?[5] These are among the many questions that I never managed
to ask, in part perhaps because I thought she would deem them simultaneously
trivial and disconcerting.

When Zippi finally arrived in what had once been home at the end of May,
she discovered "the vast graveyard" that awaited most survivors. Her father, step-
mother, and two younger brothers had been deported to Lublin and presumably
murdered. But, amazingly and less typically, Zippi, who had spent the previous
years, as she explained to Boder, in "living hell," recuperated some of her former
possessions, saved by a former teacher, including a coat from before the war, an
item that she cherished throughout her DP years. She also found one brother who
had managed to join the partisans. But the brother had recently married, and Zippi
says that she wanted to leave him unburdened to start his new life.[6]

At this juncture the story became confusing, in part because, ironically,
Zippi, who so values precision and order in her accounts of the Auschwitz years,

is deliberately vague about her immediate postwar itinerary. At some point she joined a group of the *Bricha* (Hebrew for "flight") 1—taking survivors through Vienna to Munich in the American zone and on to Feldafing; she seems to have gone back and forth across the borders more than once.[7] But, she warns me, the story of those journeys is off-limits; all the many postwar years have not freed her of the fear that her technically illegal border crossing *after* liberation could have consequences, might jeopardize her restitution. Zippi has survivor reflexes; still worrying about bureaucratic traps, she knows how to be evasive and is vigilant about what she will and will not reveal.

In any case, along with several thousand other survivors, Zippi landed in the DP camp in Feldafing, a former Nazi academy (*Napola*)—or, as she tells Boder, a Hitler Youth school (he refers to it as a "20 acre or so reservation, if we could call it that")—in a bucolic town "in beautiful rolling country" on the shores of the Starnberger Lake. Feldafing's core inhabitants were Jews rescued from the bomb-strafed cattle cars that were trying to carry KZ inmates away from General George S. Patton's ever-advancing Third Army. On April 29, 1945, Lieutenant Irving J. Smith, an American Jewish officer, entered the nearby town of Tutzing and found more death march survivors, over 1,000 "starving, almost raving maniacs, half paralyzed with hunger and fear."[8] The Americans, joined by an UNRRA team, quickly took over the former Nazi academy, drafted dozens of German doctors and nurses, turned a former hotel into a hospital, requisitioned the services of the *Napola* cook and some of the town's elegant villas, and began to organize daily life. Under Smith's command, the initial Jewish DP camp population, composed of survivors of death and forced labor camps and death marches liberated in Bavaria, rapidly grew to about 4,000, as more Jews arrived from Poland, most of them so-called infiltrees who were fleeing renewed antisemitism after having been repatriated from a harsh but lifesaving exile in the Soviet Union.

Lieutenant Smith has a rather mixed reputation in many sources that note his reluctance to identify himself to his bedraggled and traumatized brethren as a Jew, but Zippi had nothing but praise when Boder interviewed her in 1946.[9] Zippi, who always appreciates people who work efficiently and rationally, credits the overwhelmed officer with saving lives because of the "intelligent manner" in which he introduced a graduated feeding program beginning with gruel that the survivors could manage to digest. There were very few fatalities; at Feldafing at least, the survivors did not die in the immediate aftermath of liberation—unlike the many thousands who did not survive the early efforts to save them. Of Smith, Zippi said "in cooperation with my present husband and others as well, he worked day and night for the good of the people here" (*Zum Wohle der Menschen*); "after weeks they recuperated...Feldafing had the smallest death [rate] among other camps which were then installed."[10] Soon UNRRA, which operated under the authority of the U.S. Military Government, officially took over the camp. By September 1946, when Zippi talked to David Boder, she knew that of 60,000 Jews deported from Slovakia, she was one of the 450 "girls" (and 150 men) who had survived.

Reclaiming Life: The DP Marriage and Baby Boom

In 1946, occupied Germany, far from being *judenrein*, counted a Jewish birthrate estimated to be "higher than that of any other country or any other population" in the world.[11] Only a year after liberation, in perhaps the most important manifestation of this drive for "normality" after trauma and in such "abnormal" postwar conditions, and at the same time as Germans were bemoaning their losses, Jewish DPs were marrying and producing babies in record numbers. In a "steady rush of weddings,"[12] DPs married, sometimes within days, neighbors in the next barrack or distant kin or acquaintances from what had once been home. Many of the newlyweds barely knew one another; there were "so many marriages, sometimes really strange marriages that never would have happened before the war."[13]

Both disapproving and admiring, occupation and relief officials discerned an "overpowering desire to end the loneliness," or at least to be "half as lonely." Finally freed from constant fear and deprivation, survivors' "young bodies and souls yearned to live," and nonplussed observers were moved and impressed by survivors' "amazing recuperative powers" and apparently irrepressible "zest for life."[14] Over and over again, relief workers and interviewers heard the same message from women: "All I wanted right away was a baby. This was the only hope for me."[15] Zippi tells me about the first baby she remembers being born in Feldafing, of a Greek father and a Hungarian mother, two people who shared no language but an urgent need to escape the loneliness of survival. Zippi, it turns out, was responsible for distributing rations for expectant mothers in the Feldafing DP, and as her rendition of the improbable coupling already indicates, she provides a backstory to my "baby boom" after catastrophe narrative that is even darker, certainly more complicated, than the one my sources impose. Her memories provide a cautionary counterimage to the ubiquitous photos and films, both contemporary and in more recent publications, that circumscribe the DP years under the rubric of Jewish "Life Reborn," albeit in highly gendered ways: weddings and women with baby carriages, cradling newborns, holding toddlers by the hand, and caring for children in DP camp kindergartens.[16]

Zippi remembers that it was blushing young men—with "red faces which I will never forget"—who arrived to collect food for their newly pregnant brides. The young women themselves, who were so often proudly posed with their infants, were too embarrassed by their unfamiliar state—and presumably the sexuality it implied—even to appear. And the awkward young fathers Zippi evokes also bear little resemblance to the young men, strong, well-muscled, in short T-shirts, who appear in photos and films as athletes on the soccer fields, or strutting in the marching formations of the DP camp police, which her husband Erwin headed in Feldafing. Inevitably, as Zippi sees so clearly, these images that underline the attempted return to (gendered) human "normality," obfuscate as well as make visible; they efface the pain and the scars also carried by tough bodies and smiling young parents.

As Zippi's memories indicate, romantic and sexual longing mixed with a tormented sense of inexperience, of having missed out on some crucial youthful socialization and pleasures. The quick marriages—"Hitler married us," some DPs wryly noted—promised some sense of comfort and stability to people who possessed neither, but they were often also cause for more anxiety and insecurity. Young people were tough way beyond their years but also painfully aware of their own sexual and social losses. Women especially had buried within them complicated uncommunicable stories, about prostitution and rape, about instrumental sex, or even about genuine love affairs—and all the "gray zone" situations in which sex functioned as a crucial currency of survival. Yet, bearing a "healthy, normal child"[17] defined a certain return to normality for most Jewish DPs, whether they had survived under Nazi occupation or under harsh conditions in the Soviet Union, even if it often seemed to offer only a kind of make-believe normality, a "parallel life" to the memories of the preceding trauma.

The archives of the Joint, UNRRA, the health departments of the Central Committee and the local DP camps delineate a comprehensive and effective medical system, virtually the obligation to health. These were precious babies, and they were carefully monitored. DP leaders, camp administrators, and relief workers were committed to the notion that survivors required resocialization into proper standards of hygiene and morality, and they mobilized all the principles of modern social and preventive medicine, from immunization and cleanliness campaigns to home visits by nurses and hygiene lectures in clinics and schools to assure not only the survival but the good health of the next generation. Yiddish posters and pamphlets urged mothers to visit the camps' sick bay regularly and to be conscientious about pre- and postnatal care. Precisely because gendered roles and sexed bodies had been so catastrophically unsettled by the Nazi Final Solution that aimed to produce desexed *Musselmen* and prioritized the annihilation of mothers, children, and the "unfit," life was reborn and identity remade through the reconstruction of gendered roles and sexed healthy bodies.[18]

Like all helping professionals dealing with a client population, JDC and UNRRA nurses complained about noncompliance with their well-meant advice in matters such as breastfeeding and nutrition. Zippi's memories suggest, however,

Helen and Erwin Tichauer at Lake Starnberg, June 1946 (from the private collection of Helen "Zippi" Tichauer)

that women's reliance on nonmedical resources and counsel may have been the result not only of their recalcitrance but also of the fact that expert medical care was not as easily available as the pamphlets and official reports claimed. She insists, for example, that there was no real clinic inside the Feldafing camp, and no specialized gynecological station; the busy maternity ward in nearby Elisabeth Hospital was supervised by a dedicated DP physician with no obstetrical training. Zippi is concerned not with files and charts—which she can no longer, in any case, read— but with the agency of individuals. On the most basic level, as she observes, "the treatment was food." It was prescribed for pregnant women as if it were medicine, individually calibrated, by Dr. Henri Heitan, the JDC's (and, according to Zippi, also UNRRA's) medical director in Feldafing, a man who emerges both from the archives and from Zippi's testimony as an extraordinarily dedicated and talented physician. Whether because of more complex expert intervention or simply the regular supply of good rations, especially fresh milk, and careful attention, both Zippi and the files agree that infant and maternal mortality rates were extraordinarily low (especially in comparison with the parallel German figures).[19] A bit mischievously, she adds that as the person responsible for distributing the ample rations ordered by Dr. Heitan ("*Ich habe das Zeug verteilt*"), she feels personally responsible for some of those overly chubby DP babies we admire in photographs and newsreels.

In another conversation, she notes—a bit to my surprise, since she is so committed to orderly procedure—that when the young husbands picked up these supplemental rations, they could also acquire equally valuable goods, such as coffee and chocolate, which could be bartered on the gray and black markets that fueled all economic exchange for Jews and Germans alike after the war. It was also Dr. Heitan who decided to use a confiscated castlelike former hotel and Wehrmacht hospital in the Bavarian Alps as a sanatorium and vacation retreat. According to Zippi, all the Feldafing newlyweds were offered an overnight stay in this fairy-tale setting. Every new couple was entitled to a brief honeymoon in Schloss Elmau. Is that really true? I have been to Schloss Elmau for conferences, awed by its magical setting, and intensely aware of its layered history; but now I wonder, did Zippi and Erwin also go there after they married? I cannot remember if she told me, and there is no reference in my notes. The list of questions for Zippi only grows with the writing of this piece.

CLOSE ENCOUNTERS: MULTIPLE MEMORIES

Zippi and I spar over the central contention of my book. She is adamant that the Jewish DPs had "nothing to do with local townspeople. There were high-ranking Nazis there." Indeed, most DPs would report, "My world was divided into two, inside the camp, and outside, outside were the enemies, the people of Amalek," referring to the biblical king who had tried to exterminate the Jews. But I argued strongly that even as they claimed—and to some extent still do, in their recollections—to live in entirely separate antagonistic worlds, on the same terrain, divided by memory and experience, Germans and Jews continually encountered each other, albeit always regulated and observed by the occupiers and the relief organizations: in political contests over memories, definitions, and calibrations of victimization, over entitlement to victim status, and the material as well as moral consequences of that designation, that is to say, compensation and restitution. They also continually interacted—in uneasy, sometimes cordial, only very occasionally violent, overwhelmingly pragmatic ways—as they negotiated the nitty-gritty of everyday life, from the black market to medical and child care, feeding people, taking care of children and the sick, establishing businesses, administering the camps, in sports, entertainment, even sexual relationships, and in a small stigmatized but visible minority of cases, marriage.

I insist: archival, literary, and memoir evidence makes abundantly clear—talking back to and, perhaps more accurately, past much articulated Jewish (and German) memory—the "enemies" were part of everyday life, inside the camps protected and administered by U.S. Military Government and UNRRA, as well as outside. For both Jews and Germans, and in what I think of as a strange dance of distance and intimacy, trust and suspicion, the immediate larger past, while its shadow was always hovering, was frequently silenced and marginalized in favor of an explicitly temporary—and this is key—but mutually advantageous interaction. In the book, I used the term "productive forgetting," but another perhaps better description would be strategic forgetting. I am struck by the irony that today, both in memory and in historiography, that forgetting which made possible these close encounters, both hateful and cooperative, has itself been forgotten, deemed insignificant and discomforting, by both Jews and Germans. If we read sources carefully—sometimes even against the grain of received memory— we can, however, tease out a sense of those relationships, as commonplace as they were complicated, simultaneously loaded with symbolic meaning and part of everyday life. And I try to do that also with the data—and I do believe that she conceives of her carefully tended store of memories as data for the historian— that Zippi offers me. This is especially important when what she tells me seems to contradict what I have found in the archives—until, that is, I ask more questions, listen more carefully, and realize that perhaps the stories are not contradictory but complementary, limning the same place and situation with different perspectives.

The DPs' many babies and even the truncated family life of stateless refugees led—improbably—to connections with the Germans among whom Jewish DPs lived. Jews gave birth in German hospitals where they were attended by German physicians, midwives, and nurses. At the height of the baby boom, Elisabeth Hospital in Feldafing had 1,200 beds, twenty-eight German doctors, and seventy-one German nurses; with time, more DP staff was added.[20] Jewish marriages and births were registered in German town halls.[21] Local German women, hired, paid for, and regulated by camp welfare authorities, cared for the babies, did the DPs' laundry, and cleaned the Jewish homes and barracks. German doctors wrote the medical affidavits (*Atteste*) certifying that Jewish women needed help with babies and housework. Germans entered DP camps daily not only as baby nurses but as cleaning women and men, tradesmen, and skilled workers such as plumbers and mechanics, teachers and doctors.

Zippi challenges what I consider one of my most significant research finds: the DP camp files that document the regular employment of German women as baby nurses and nannies for Jewish women. No, Zippi insists, she does not remember any German women taking care of babies. Here her memory slams straight up against the history I want to write. The Feldafing camp records are filled with lists of German personnel working inside the DP camps. Indeed, despite—or perhaps in part because of—their conviction that the people outside the camp were "the enemies, the people of Amalek," Jewish survivors were often of the opinion that this German labor was a kind of restitution: "We have worked so much for the Germans, it is about time the Germans now worked for us."[22] In order to assure not only the survival but the good health of the treasured next generation, DPs had no compunctions about requests for German baby nurses or medical specialists, to help exhausted, lonely, sick, and very young, inexperienced parents. I tell Zippi about the lists of German workers (her resistance helped persuade me to publish such a list from YIVO's Feldafing files in my book), name some names, offer to show her the documents. But she has trouble reading, we would have to project my copies on a special screen, and so I leave the stories—those in the archives, those in the interviews and memoirs of other DPs, and those preserved in Zippi's memories—side by side; as part of an excruciatingly complicated story about "living on" that needs to be told in as layered (multilingual even) a fashion as possible.

What I define as "close encounters" Zippi sees as necessary, distanced, and mostly distasteful interactions. The fresh milk she distributes to the young mothers and babies is brought in every morning from German farms, but she does not see—or want to see—the farmers. She liked, as she stressed several times, to swim in the beautiful Starnberger Lake; she appreciated the landscape but not the people who inhabited it. And while Ita Muskal, the Romanian DP who gave birth to my college boyfriend in Feldafing, fondly remembers Hans, the former Napola cook with a "good heart" who supplied her with margarine, peanut butter, and dried and canned goods such as the ever useful Quaker Oats, peas, sardines, and tuna fish, which the Germans prized and the DPs disdained, enabling her brief career as a "businesslady" small-time black marketer in Feldafing, Zippi is certain that there never would have been a German cook in the DP camp. The religious Jews would not have allowed it, she tells me. I sense also that Zippi would not have wanted to trust a German cook with preparing her food, certainly not one who had previously worked for the Nazis. Is this a case of different kitchens, of different chronological moments, of different memories? These are differences that cannot be resolved by the historian—and in this case I have not uncovered the "facts" in any archive. Again, the stories have to coexist. For Ita, Hans represented, despite his history, the possibility of at least temporary coexistence; for Zippi, such a person could not have existed.

Even though, as the wife of the DP camp police chief, she resided outside the DP camp in a nearby German town, she insisted that she lived in an Allied enclave and had no interactions with local Germans. In 1946, however, when she was living in Tutzing, she phrased this somewhat differently. When Boder asked her, "Tell me, do you have any contacts with the Germans around here?" she replied, "Actually, no, because the Germans of Upper Bavaria have no desire/ interest/to establish a contact with us. They have no intention whatsoever to feel in some way guilty." It is not so much that the Jews hate the Germans, but that the incorrigible Germans have not changed. "In fact," she notes, "we experience no hatred whatsoever. But we feel that we are actually still hated. Still hated!" Somewhat implausibly, she thinks that because Bavaria was a center of the Nazi Party, it was even more nazified than the rest of Germany.[23] Ironically, the Bavarians themselves insist on their innocence precisely because they are Bavarians and claim, as did Minister President Wilhelm Hoegner in an extraordinary speech to the Congress of Liberated Jews in January 1946, that they too had been victimized by the "Prussians."[24] And in an interesting turn in the course of one of our conversations, she avers both that she "never wanted to have contact with the population," but also that "we would not mind to have contact with them but they don't want to have contact."

When I press her, Zippi acknowledges that Germans did provide doctors and nurses as well as cleaning personnel; Feldafing had a German pharmacist. But again her perspective is quite different than mine. While I was so struck by— and struggled to understand—the pragmatic and at least superficially harmonious relations among German nannies and Jewish mothers, Zippi remembers the story of a woman suffering from appendicitis who was so terrified at the prospect of being operated on by a German surgeon that she had to be forced into the lifesaving procedure literally at gunpoint. And the German doctors she remembers by name were carefully vetted; they had to prove, she says, that they had been anti-Nazis. Most vivid is Dr. Rudolf Rein, whom Erwin had found on the *Strassenbau*; a highly trained surgeon who had refused to join the Party, he had been caught by Allied denazification measures, disqualified as a physician, and relegated to road construction "like any other German." Erwin, recognizing something different in him, pulled him off the road, and the doctor became, as Zippi put it, a respected "collaborator" with the Jews. Together with a well-known plastic surgeon, Dr. Kriebel, who did the reconstructive surgery necessary to put Zippi's skull and other bones, broken from years in Nazi camps, back together again, Dr. Rein treated Zippi's broken leg around the turn of the year 1946/47.

The more Zippi and I debate such encounters and especially those between German nannies and the Jewish mothers, the more carefully I have to listen. I have friends born to Jewish survivors in postwar Germany who still remember their German nannies with a certain amount of affection. Not a few have remained in touch over decades and generations. Zippi has no such sentiments; she is clear on her opinion of this pervasive practice, simultaneously so intimate and so pragmatic, that defined the relationship between Jewish mothers and the Germans who often delivered and cared for their babies. It was, she says, a "big big mistake." "They depended on the German women. A Jewish young woman to get her instructions and knowledge from an ex-enemy," was, she firmly believes, "a scandal." But, tellingly, Zippi blames neither the young, inexperienced parents desperate for advice on caring for their *Meschiaskinder* (miracle children of the Messiah, as they were sometimes called) nor the DP camp officials who administered these positions.

Rather, she blames outsiders, both Jewish and not, the UNRRA and Joint social workers, for allowing the young Jewish women to remain "helpless." Zippi had no use at all for this "lousy group of social workers," mostly unmarried women, "spinsters," as Zippi derisively calls them. Like their bewildered and traumatized charges, they also knew nothing about motherhood, and therefore it was left to German women, more practiced in raising children, to care for the Jewish babies. Moreover, Zippi reveals, the young female aid officials were jealous of her, the DP who snatched a desirable and important man; they tried to save Erwin by telling him not to marry a displaced person.

Poorly trained, themselves subordinate to military control and exigencies and facing novel challenges, these young women, attached to UNRRA and the Joint, were confronted with a completely unprecedented situation, dealing with people whose experiences, languages, and culture they did not understand. UNRRA's necessarily inexperienced teams had to learn quickly how "to remain sufficiently vulnerable to other people's sufferings whilst remaining tough enough not to break oneself."[25] Zippi is contemptuous of their unprofessionalism, their lack of comprehension about what they were coping with. But she also remains angry and frustrated that they did not provide more help, could not provide adequate child care, could not control youngsters socialized in the ghettos and camps who desperately needed guidance and understanding. These young aid workers "could not help." Therefore, "They [the DPs] had to help yourself." In practice that often meant seeking help from the "ex-enemy"—those German nannies I had been so surprised to find in the archives.

Neighbors and Enemies, Violence and Policing

Zippi's and my different (and yet, as I keep discovering, complementary) takes on "close encounters" extend also to the question of violence between Jews and Germans. In my book, I maintained—against conventional wisdom, most historiography, and much received memory—that Jews and Germans did not live in entirely separate worlds and, moreover, that their encounters were also often mutually useful and relatively harmonious. I observed that there was surprisingly little direct violence between Jews and Germans. I stressed this point precisely because it is so rarely made, but carefully noted also that the degree of mutual suspicion and resentment that on occasion flared into violence must not be underestimated. Zippi does not fundamentally disagree, but as Erwin's wife, she has a very different perspective on the question of violence and revenge, filtered through Erwin's job as DP and UNRRA police chief in charge of the entire region. Many Nazis were still hiding in the woods, Zippi says, especially in the early months after the camp's establishment. One DP policeman was killed in the line of duty, she vividly recalls, and shows me photographs of his funeral.

The police force was mostly organized out of men who had some military experience, former soldiers in the Polish or Greek army, whom Erwin considered disciplined (and implicitly, I think, far removed from the taint of Jewish police who had served in the ghettos of Nazi Europe). But the threat of outside attacks was contained fairly quickly, and the main task became internal policing. Here, too, Zippi's position as the wife of the man charged by the DP self-administration and UNRRA with maintaining law and order affords her a particular lens. At the same time that the DP police protected Jews from Germans, there was, Zippi tells me, regular exchange among German, American, and DP officials. German police arrested Jews and handed them over to DP police. Erwin, who had, Zippi proudly informed me, set up "the first professional Jewish [police] station," was also close to the head of American Military Police. If he needed their assistance or if he wanted to retrieve Jews detained by the MPs, it took "only one phone call and Erwin picked them up." Mostly, however, the DP police were responsible for order within the camps. They dealt with stolen vehicles, speeding, illegal ritual slaughtering, and, she is quick to include, family fights and domestic violence. Speaking of some minor crimes, she knows whom to blame; the main offenders came from Łódź, which, she tells me, was famous for its professional thieves. DP police, however, were careful to observe certain limits; they tried to control the ever problematic unsanctioned cattle slaughtering and egregious black-market offenses, for example, trafficking in fake penicillin with water-filled ampoules, but not the ordinary gray-market dealings that exchanged cigarettes for fresh vegetables or a pretty fabric. Honor Court tribunals (*Ehrengerichte*) were reserved for more serious violations like selling DP identity cards to Germans, probably Nazis trying to conceal their identity, Zippi remarks.

ZIPPI AS "TOP MANAGEMENT": THE "WITNESS AS WITNESS"

Erwin's role as police chief also provided the occasion for one of Zippi's most provocative takes on DP life in Feldafing. She is still angry at the social workers who did not "really have anything to do with the survivors," who could not understand them and had not shared their experiences. But in her own way, Zippi, who without irony described her position in the camp as part of "top management," also inhabited a world separated from her fellow DPs. First of all, her background was different. She was a German-speaking Slovakian Jew, whereas most of the DPs were Yiddish-speaking and from Poland or Lithuania. She was older than most of the survivors, already twenty-seven when she was liberated, and therefore an exception among camp survivors, who were almost uniformly in their late teens and early twenties.

Tellingly, even though much of my work and so many of my questions to Zippi focused on issues of reproduction, sexuality, and daily life, I never dared to ask her about why she, unlike the great majority of young married women in the DP camps, did not get pregnant, why she and Erwin joined the marriage boom but not the baby boom. Zippi always insisted, "Ask me anything," but I did not ask, and when I circled the question, the answers were sufficiently evasive that I did not probe further. Had the many physical torments she suffered in Auschwitz—which required so much treatment already during her time in Feldafing—left Zippi unable or at least unwilling to risk bearing a child? Did she not want to be like other women survivors, who prompted contemporary psychoanalytically oriented psychiatrists and social workers to diagnose a desperate "hypersexuality" and to explain the baby boom as a "manic defense" against catastrophic experience and overwhelming loss?[26]

More generally, and to a sometimes shocking degree, Zippi is unsparing in her stories about the DPs whom she and Erwin were part of—and yet also separated from. They lived outside the camp, in the nearby town of Tutzing, in a house requisitioned by the U.S. Military Government for American and UNRRA personnel. They ate in the American mess hall, their meals prepared by Puffi, the "very good" and correspondingly fat survivor who cooked for the entire team. They drove to Feldafing in Erwin's *Dienstwagen*, a jeep with a chauffeur, which Erwin preferred to drive himself. He was paid in real American dollars and could do their shopping in Munich at the PX. Erwin was practically an American; he had fought with the U.S. forces after his liberation from Auschwitz (this too is a story that I never quite unraveled), and he was part of the American team, many of whom in fact were themselves Jewish and spoke Yiddish. As an afterthought, almost too obvious to mention, Zippi notes that the housekeeping (although not, as we have seen, the cooking) was done by a German family, who were expected "to do all the necessary work." The owner of the building was the widow of a former mill owner who "screamed and cried" that the villa had been confiscated, but really she received "good payment" in dollars for which, under the circumstances, she should have been grateful. So here, too, just as I always suggested, the Germans were present but in clearly subordinate positions. I am fascinated by these encounters and by the power shifts they represented; Zippi has no interest in discussing such daily interactions, which for her did not signify any kind of meaningful relationship. I sense that she finds my curiosity irritating, misplaced.

Erwin was the police chief, she was his wife, and she also controlled an essential part of food distribution. "I was top management"—Zippi uses the phrase often, and I can imagine her, physically debilitated but recently married and full of life, throwing herself into that role, always intent, as she had been already—under drastically different circumstances—on improving conditions for those whose fate she shared. She insists that she was not "the big shot's wife" and is nonplussed when I asked whether she even identified as a DP. What a silly question, she retorts in the German we often used in our conversations. Of course she *"war auch ein DP,"* she did not work for UNRRA or the Joint. She was only a camp employee (*"Nur eine Angestellte von der Lager-Verwaltung"*).

Zippi takes the social workers to task for pushing young Jewish mothers to hire German helpers, but in other contexts, Zippi's critical take on the social workers extends also to her fellow DPs. Her most jarring counter to the now standard narrative of initial mistreatment of survivors by uncomprehending American troops comes with her decidedly contrarian memory of General George S. Patton's now notorious inspection of Feldafing in September 1945. It is with this story that Zippi's highly particular position as both insider and outsider (on all levels), as survivor witness and critical observer of survivors—the witness as witness— becomes stunningly evident.[27] When Patton, after touring the camp, concluded in an infamous outburst that "Others ('Harrison and his ilk') believe that the DP is a human being, which he is not, and this applies particularly to the Jews, who are lower than animals," he may have been dismissed by an Eisenhower, already embarrassed by the Harrison Report, which sharply criticized U.S. handling of Jewish survivors, as unsuitable to be the first American military governor for Bavaria, but he was certainly not alone in his disgust. As Zippi sadly but also matter-of-factly recalled, "The toilets were clean, but in the halls, there they made their business." Survivors "didn't know what a toilet was, they knew what was a latrine." Zippi, the widow of the Feldafing DP Police chief who accompanied Patton and Eisenhower during their highly publicized visit, is convinced that Patton's reaction was influenced by his disgust at viewing DP quarters where new arrivals were relieving themselves in the hallways. The German men who came in daily to hose down the barracks had unfortunately not yet arrived when the inspection tour passed by.[28] Indeed, DPs' expectations of menial services provided by Germans extended to the most lowly jobs, including, in another complicated reworking of conditions endured under the Nazis, literally cleaning up Jews' excrement.

I included in my book a photograph showing a handsome Erwin Tichauer helping to escort Eisenhower through Feldafing. Zippi fills in the emotions behind the photograph, as I try to imagine the scene; Erwin was intensely proud of his role. The American generals attended services—it "happened" to be Yom Kippur—and she recalls Eisenhower speaking from the *Bimah* (elevated platform with desk from which the Torah is read) of a makeshift synagogue. In fact, Zippi reports—in another one of her narratives that goes utterly against the conventional grain—that Erwin rather liked Patton, the tough commander who has been vilified for his antisemitic sentiments and statements about survivors. The two men had some kind of personal rapport; did Zippi really tell me that they went horseback riding together? Ever relentlessly realistic, Zippi does not shy away from defending Patton's comment on the survivors' condition. The "lower than animals" remark was, she says, "appropriate" and not antisemitic, in fact, "one hundred percent right."

Here it would seem that Zippi shared the nonsurvivor viewpoint, agreeing with American occupiers, international relief workers, Germans, Zionists, and Jewish observers alike who perceived the DPs as "human debris," an "unattractive lot," as I. F. Stone, the American Jewish leftist journalist covering the underground *Bricha* route to Palestine, noted about his first impression.[29] Either apathetic or bounding with hostile aggression, they seemed oblivious to the most elementary rules of hygiene and the proper use of latrines, "obsessed" with food, and uninhibited in regard to the opposite sex. New arrivals horrified officials by smearing excreta on the walls of toilets and vandalizing DP camp facilities, or simply with the filth generated by roaming chickens and clogged toilets (or toilets used for laundering), with German plumbers called upon to clean up the mess. Yet Zippi's response *is* different; it comes from inside an experience that even the most sympathetic aid workers cannot fathom. From her point of view, phrased in the most matter-of-fact terms, Patton had come unannounced to inspect living quarters, and there had been no time to prepare the quarters for public presentation. It was no surprise that people and youngsters who knew only ghetto and KZ life and then suddenly found themselves in a well-polished, modern Hitler Youth academy would urinate or defecate right on the marble floors.

CLOSE ENCOUNTERS: SEX AND ROMANCE

At the same time, Zippi is also direct and matter-of-fact about topics that are still treated gingerly in much of the literature on Jewish-German encounters in the postwar period, namely, the romantic and sexual encounters, and in a stigmatized minority of cases, marriages, generally between Jewish men and German women. By 1950, more than 1,000 such marriages had been registered. Surely there were many more relationships, both fleeting and more permanent. They were driven in part by the surplus of men resulting from the skewed sex ratio (approximately 60 percent male/40 percent female) among Jewish survivors, and the easy access afforded by German women's employment as nurses or domestic servants. The tensions aroused by these connections are evident in DP literature, the records of bitter debates within the camps, and even prosecutions by DP tribunals, leading to, in particularly nasty cases, banishment from the camps.[30]

Determined to construct a fuller story about fraternization and sexual relations between Germans and Jewish DPs, I, for example—not wanting to offend—euphemistically asked Zippi to tell me what she remembered about Jewish men "going out" with German women. She looked at me indignantly and burst out, "Jewish men did not *go out* with German women, they *slept* with them!" Opportunities presented themselves easily, she recalled. German women came to clean the DP quarters, and in the daytime there were plenty of available beds; "it was very easy to go to bed." As one male DP explained in retrospect, "It is hard to believe—and even harder to understand—how that happened . . . many German women were attractive and knew how to handle their love affairs." He meant perhaps that, toughened and scarred by war, they not only were savvy about sex and birth control but also knew not to make too many unrealistic demands on men highly unlikely to remain with them.[31] Moreover, as Zippi points out, Jewish DP men were surprisingly desirable fraternizers; they had a "rich" store of goodies like cigarettes and chocolates to offer, were generally present for a longer period of time than occupation soldiers, and did not require any knowledge of English. Unlike the GIs, they often knew German, and in any case, Yiddish was close enough.

For young male survivors who "didn't know anything about women" except anguished memories of their murdered mothers and sisters, German women, themselves often refugees, lonely, and eager to "have some fun," provided an easy and relatively carefree introduction to sex, unburdened by the obligations and associations attached to Jewish women. As another male survivor ruefully recalled, even though German women had "gained a reputation for easy virtue and are held in contempt by the group," they were "as a whole . . . more physically attractive than the refugee women, if only for the reason that they did not live under such bestial conditions." He acknowledged that while most such relationships were motivated by "a mixture of revenge and the desire to taste the forbidden fruit," there were also "singular cases" of "deep reciprocal feelings" in which "the answer would simply have to be that a man and woman met and fell in love."[32] And there was perhaps some added satisfaction in the knowledge that they were engaging in a bit of "*Rassenschande*," that "Hitler would not have agreed with it, he had other things in mind for me."[33]

Zippi saw these encounters more darkly; they could, she knows, be "cruel." For Jewish men, she insisted, "a German woman was dirt," easy to exploit and easy also to leave behind with an illegitimate child. She is still haunted by one painful episode in which a Jewish DP, whose wife had been unable to bear a child, simply appropriated his half-German offspring. With his wife's blessing and over the mother's objections—she was a "beauty," Zippi notes—he passed it off as his own, and they took the boy with them to the United States. Asked whether this might be an exceptional story, she snorted, "If there was one, there were more." Most of these half-Jewish illegitimate children, however, remained with their mothers. Unlike the "mixed-breed" offspring of African American GIs and German women, in a postwar situation where single mothers were entirely common, with a "Jewish baby, nobody knew" (and the facts are correspondingly impossible to verify). Zippi disapproved strongly of such liaisons, but she also understood the consequences for the German women who got involved with Jewish men and were then—almost always—deserted as their partners married fellow DPs and left Germany behind. The women were scorned by their own families and communities, and neglected and abandoned by their Jewish bed partners. But in Feldafing, she clarifies, such sexual encounters were not punished, and "nobody tried to spy" on what people did in bed; the DP police and the Honor Courts had more important matters to attend to.[34]

THE LIFE AFTER: WHERE TO GO

Again and again, Zippi defied my carefully researched and hard-won conclusions about DP life and the conditions of "living on" among the *She'erit Hapletah*, the saved remnant, as the survivors named themselves. She became neither a mother nor a Zionist. In fact, as a German-speaking Jew from Slovakia, she differentiated herself even in 1946 from the majority of Polish Yiddish-speaking fellow DPs who had fled their former homes and had no desire to return to the vast (and sometimes dangerous) graveyard that postwar Poland had become. Zippi acknowledges—and with this she is more in tune with French or perhaps Hungarian survivors than the Polish and Lithuanian Jews who dominated DP life—that if she had not "found this man," Erwin, "my husband, who is actually from Berlin and is a German Jew, but considers himself now actually stateless," she "should have liked to live in Czechoslovakia, would have liked to live there very much, because I felt there always very well. I used to be always very happy there," and "felt a bond with Czechoslovakia."[35] And she knew already in 1946, "In Germany he [Erwin] will never again feel comfortable. In this country in which he has lost everything."[36]

Here, too, Zippi does not fit the dominant picture; she remains the sharp-eyed critical observer who understands but does not necessarily share the more pervasive experience or vision. The Jewish collective of the *She'erith Hapletah* was, I had come to understand, invented, out of but not in the crucible of the Holocaust, in the transitional protected and highly ideologized life of the DP camps. Jews publicly identified as survivors of Nazi extermination plans even if, as was the case for many of them, they had escaped because they had landed, either by choice or by force, in the Soviet Union. They committed to Zionism and Jewish identity even if they were not religious and did not go to Palestine/Israel or left again after having gone, because as Joint education director Koppel Pinson discerned, "The Zionists were the only ones that had a program that seemed to make sense after this catastrophe."[37] But Zippi, it seems, was not convinced. She knew very well that, as she informed Boder, "the people, in spite of maintenance, in spite of lodging, in spite of everything, are already very impatient, because everyone has only one single aim in view, to leave the country," the cursed German soil (*verfluchte deutsche Erde*, as the DPs said), "which once was hell" for them. But when Boder asked about her going to Palestine, she answers carefully: it is mainly the youth who want to live in a Jewish national homeland. She is unimpressed by the demonstrations demanding free entry to Palestine so often featured in contemporary films and photographs—invariably with mothers and baby carriages at the front. Of course the people demonstrated; after all, "They had nothing else to do."[38] To the question of where the DPs really wanted to go, Zippi has a clear answer: "Go? They have one aim. Out of Europe." Then there are those who have relatives in America who dream of going to live as "free workers" in the United States. In the event, Zippi would, in a sense, follow a typical DP trajectory; in 1947 she too went to a place where there were some relatives, joining Erwin in what turned out to be a temporary sojourn in Chile.

Again and again, my conversations with Zippi forced me to question my own arguments, and finally to argue that there can be no homogenized unified story of the DP experience even as we historians are obligated to present a narrative that is coherent if confusing and complex. Moreover, I was repeatedly struck by all the multiple ways Zippi's memories talked back to, talked past, and finally connected with—although not necessarily in a straightforward manner— what I found in the archives, secondary literature, memoirs (both published and unpublished), and other oral histories. As with many DPs, many of Zippi's memories of camp life have to do with the lively but often severely fractious political life that developed among the DPs, picking up on prewar divisions but in an entirely different context. Zippi is still outraged (and her enduring sense of outrage, is, I cannot help but think, part of her survival strategy) at some colleagues—Bundists (Jewish socialists), she says—who tried to manipulate camp finances and cheat her out of her wages. She is surely not alone among DPs who referred to some of their fellow displaced as "the biggest crooks on earth." Indeed, one of the most painful legacies of the Shoah and its aftermath for Zippi—and, one suspects, for many other survivors who may not be as blunt as Zippi—is the sense that "what Jews do to Jews is the most awful thing." Directly after the catastrophe, as is evident in early testimonies, survivors were much more open about the inevitable conflicts among themselves, the divisions the Nazis had imposed and exploited. Here, too, Zippi usefully complicates any clear lines, reminding me of cases she experienced where "thanks to a good Kapo, they are alive." Now, many of those stories have been marginalized; as Zippi snorts with her inimitable simultaneously amused and outraged style, "Everybody is playing Alzheimer's."

Yet, in regard to the other point that became so unexpectedly central to my research—and which still seems to me to pose monumental issues about how we define "survivor" and think about survival—namely, the fact that the majority of East European Jewish survivors escaped the Final Solution because they had fled or been deported to the Soviet Union, Zippi resists my questions. For her, Feldafing was a world of camp and ghetto survivors. In one of our conversations when I again tried to ask her about the influx of East European "infiltrees" starting in fall 1945 when she too was in Feldafing, she has nothing more to report than that those from the Soviet Union "somehow suddenly appeared" (*sind irgendwie erschienen*)—and, besides, they were all "Trotskyites," another major issue that I leave aside. Yet in the end, the fundamental point remains: none of her outrage—her bitterness, her frustration, her sense of opportunities lost—mitigates Zippi's essential solidarity with the Jewish displaced of whom she was part. On the contrary, it fuels her determination to give honest, clear information.

Living On: Extending Definitions of Displacement

In important ways that I feel we historians of the Holocaust and its aftermath should have explored more fully, Zippi and Erwin's insider/outsider, helper/participant role extended into their postwar life when they joined the ranks of the "helping professionals," those aid agency workers whom Zippi so disdained when she knew them in Feldafing. Indeed, when asked, Zippi can talk with great verve about their "life after." Erwin's UNRRA experience led to his being recruited by the International Labor Organization (ILO), which sent him on missions to Bolivia and Peru in the 1950s. When the couple moved to Australia from Chile, they were dispatched to Indonesia, and Zippi continued in her role as Erwin's partner in humanitarian work. In an echo of previous challenges, she used the graphic design skills that had served her (and her ability to remember) so well in her wartime and postwar life to devise, for example, cans that could preserve milk for babies whose mothers were not healthy enough to breast-feed. Their life went on—in enormously creative and productive ways. They moved to the United States, first to Austin, Texas, and then to New York, where Erwin was a professor of bioengineering at New York University, garnering the Manhattan apartment in the East Thirties from whence Zippi manages her archive of papers, photographs, and memories. Auschwitz was, Zippi says at some point when we have once again come to that central and inescapable topic, "one miniature part of my life." Erwin had been her first questioner. He knew how to ask the specific questions to which she would be able to respond.

Her unsparing honesty makes Zippi a judgmental witness, unafraid to breach taboos but also keenly aware that her testimony prevents her from serving as the kind of "professional" witness that she disdains. She is proud that in all the "sixty years after the liberation" she has never accepted even "one cup of coffee" in exchange for her "service" as a survivor witness. Zippi is also exquisitely aware that, on a broader scale, her memories now have much more currency than they did in September 1946 when David Boder was the first outside interviewer to ask about her experiences during the war and its immediate aftermath. Zippi is clear, however, that she does "not think Holocaust should be a business." She never went out to tell her story. "But," she says, "I answered when people asked."

Zippi does not have much faith in us, the historians laboring to tell her story and the story of the Final Solution and its aftermath. "When the survivors are gone, light a match," she warns because no one can really understand or interpret what happened. She suspects that we understand "nothing." The experts know so little; they talk about Auschwitz without even looking at a map. And yet at the same time she too labors so hard—despite her virtual blindness, despite her many physical ailments—to educate us, to try and help historians develop a reliable and comprehensible story, precisely because, ironically, the survivors who can understand will also never be able to tell a coherent story: "People didn't know what was going on." They were "sleeping, working, eating," trying to survive.

So in the end, Zippi who knows the limits of narrative and memory and can say with credibility, "I never heard a real story," does entrust us with the duty to report on what had happened. "I'm a good simplifier," she says, noting her appeal to those who would try to understand her experiences. But she also sets high standards, always admonishing the historian to be vigilant about facts, telling us precisely what she is certain she knows and what she does not, and insisting we always check and countercheck. She holds strong opinions, but she does not treat her story as a sacred inviolable memory; it is a source that can and should be verified. And always she demands, "You should have questions." Nobody knows, she complains, because nobody really asks, even today, even in the wake of the "memory boom." Because, Zippi says, "People don't know what to ask." She recognizes the "anxiety of historical transmission" that grips historians as the survivor/witnesses grow older and older and die away, but she will not be rushed into generalities. She insists rather on the careful, precise, and entirely circumscribed evidence that she can provide. She will not permit "pious condescension" by interviewers.[39] It is Zippi's particular gift to historians that despite this, despite our inevitable stupidity—and I use the word advisedly—she still answers our questions—sometimes impatiently, sometimes with exasperation, but always with the greatest of care and commitment.

CHAPTER 5

Distant Encounter

| | |

An Auschwitz Survivor in the College Classroom

Wendy Lower

The first report cards are starting to appear on Holocaust education across the United States. One of the common criticisms of the state of the field is that the phrase "lessons of the Holocaust" remains ill defined and its attendant clichés timeworn and unfulfilled. Take, for example, the typical scenario of a university student who is asked on the first day of class why he or she enrolled in a course on the Holocaust. Many if not most will respond almost reflexively with familiar imperatives such as "never again!" or idealistic but encouraging calls for tolerance, or for an end to hate and neo-Nazi movements. Of course there is much to be learned from the history of the Holocaust, but what classroom approaches have developed over the years? University professor Deborah Lipstadt acknowledged that she teaches "the particulars" and "let[s] the students apply them to their own universe," adding that "they never fail to do so."[1] Focusing on the particulars, on localities and individuals, illuminates the vexing combination of clarity and ambiguity, the very paradoxes and concrete, harsh realities, human problems, and moral dilemmas that constitute the history of Holocaust. As historians engaged in the teaching of the subject matter will agree, learning comes about through a critical analysis of the narrative and its various sources. In recent decades, increasing value has been placed on witnessing and the use of survivors or taped testimony as the most emotionally moving and "authentic" of primary sources.

What is the objective of this exercise of bringing Holocaust survivors into the classroom? At the very least, it is hoped, eyewitnesses force students to confront the fact that this horrible event took place, to appreciate how Jews became its main victims, and to be on guard that it can happen anywhere again.

Multi-pronged educational efforts led by teachers, survivors and their families, human rights activists among others backed by private and public institutions (such as museums, memorial foundations and schools) see in the tragedy of Holocaust history an opportunity to promote certain ethical and civic values and to orient the moral compass of citizens living in a democracy. Aims espoused include the development of more empathetic, tolerant individuals who understand the cruel ramifications of unchecked racism and antisemitism.[2] It is difficult, indeed almost impossible, to measure whether Holocaust education will over time achieve these lofty goals. And regrettably, the very endeavor can digress into an exchange of emotions that few educators let alone students are equipped to understand or integrate into the subject matter. Holocaust education has been prone to this form of "affective" teaching or "experiential learning." When Christopher Browning first offered his short course on the Holocaust in 1975, he was concerned about the emotional aspects of the subject but soon realized that "my course on the Holocaust was a legitimate academic subject, not just an occasion to feel deeply moved by an encounter with unfathomable evil and suffering."[3] Browning's university course was a "rare event" in the mid-1970s. But he was not alone.[4]

Holocaust Survivors as Eyewitnesses and Teachers

When did Holocaust survivors start speaking in educational settings, specifically in classrooms? Of course, one cannot rule out that survivors in the United States spoke to students prior to the 1970s, but it seems that this phenomenon arose with the spread of Holocaust education that accompanied what Thomas Fallace calls the pedagogical "affective revolution."[5] These early initiatives took off in the late 1980s and 1990s with the growing public awareness and interest in the Holocaust, spawned by a number of events such as the popularization of the Anne Frank diary, the NBC television series *Holocaust* (1978), the opening of the U.S. Holocaust Memorial Museum (1993), and the success of the film *Schindler's List* (1993), all of which has been recounted by scholars Peter Novick and Jeffrey Shandler, among others.[6]

In addition to their cumulative effect, these developments were representative of a generational shift. Enough time had passed; there was enough distance from the events, and a growing understanding that the Holocaust was something different, not just another atrocity during wartime. Survivors, many of whom had already spoken out, written their memoirs, established networks, and published memorial books (*Yizkher Bikher*) about their former European communities, found a growing audience ready to listen to their harrowing stories of suffering and survival. Many aging survivors who had already braved video interviews for Yale's Oral History Project, the Fortunoff Archive (and other local initiatives), or privately on tape recorders also mustered the courage to tell their stories to strangers who now seemed to be appreciative listeners, specifically to students. This was often driven by an admirable sense of moral obligation and historical justice "to bear witness," to remember victims, and to work toward genocide prevention for future generations.

Actually, my own first encounter with a Holocaust survivor serves as an example—anecdotal, but in many ways typical for the time. In the small town in northern New Jersey where I grew up in the late 1970s and early 1980s, a spate of antisemitic incidents of vandalism shocked the community. They may have been provoked by the TV series that also introduced me to Holocaust history in 1978. The appearance of swastikas galvanized local educators, supported by members of the local synagogue, to do something. They decided to bus students to a large hall at nearby Brookdale Community College in Lincroft. The assembly featured a Holocaust survivor. I remember the gathering—not a very intimate one, with hundreds of students from the region in the lecture hall fidgeting, snickering, and eyeing one another. But the "goofing around" came to a halt shortly after this elderly woman began to speak. I do not remember her exact story or her name, but I do recall the atmosphere.[7] Students listened respectfully, and this small woman's stature rose with each word. Her story was beyond our worst nightmares, but undeniable because there she was in person to prove that it happened. This gathering coincided roughly with the founding of Brookdale's Holocaust Educational Center in 1979, the first of its kind in New Jersey, and among the first in the United States. Its mission is "education about historical issues of the Holocaust and genocide; elimination of racism, antisemitism and all forms of prejudice that damage our society; and development of creative programs and activities regarding these crucial human issues."[8]

To accomplish these ambitious goals, the center sponsors many programs and has developed its own education resources. Foremost among these is arranging for survivors to visit schools, a common practice of the numerous centers of its kind that have sprouted across the United States in the past two decades.[9] An office, or speaker's bureau, which also exists at the U.S. Holocaust Memorial Museum, maintains contact with a network of survivors willing to speak at schools and other educational venues. The bureau works with educators and survivors to arrange these visits. The development of such speakers programs targeting middle and high schools took off in geographic areas where survivors had settled, such as New Jersey, whereas university programs depended mainly on a particular faculty member's interest, usually in literature, German history, or Jewish studies. Only more recently have academic, research-oriented centers been more firmly established both at the U.S. Holocaust Memorial Museum and in universities around the United States. The most visible, indeed most popular, of all survivor speakers who has long been a presence on college campuses is the Nobel Peace Prize recipient Elie Wiesel, a voice of moral authority speaking at graduation ceremonies, museum openings, and other events drawing large crowds. In April 1996, close to 2,500 Nebraskans (very few of them Jews) gathered to hear Wiesel in the University of Nebraska's performing arts hall in Lincoln; hundreds had to be turned away for lack of space. They waited patiently for more than an hour, as Wiesel's flight was delayed, and welcomed him with an ovation. Clearly this scene is unlike the intimate experience of having a survivor in a classroom with about thirty students, but it epitomizes the prominence of Holocaust survivors as conveyers of historical lessons and ethical messages that we seek to draw from this tragedy.[10]

Despite the existence of receptive audiences, most survivors have not felt prepared to speak in classrooms. In 1982, when Helen Tichauer was first asked by Professor Henry F. to speak in his class, she asked him, "What shall I say?" He told her to just talk about her experiences at Auschwitz. Helen agreed but had some reservations. She "did not want be like a patient on a couch" or "participate in some emotional sharing."[11] For some Holocaust survivors, recounting and in a sense reliving the past was much too painful, could not be articulated in public, let alone to students who might ask unanswerable questions. As scholarly studies of survivor testimonies have demonstrated, there are layers of memory that are laden with psychological trauma; survivors experienced and witnessed happenings for which language is lacking to express or recount them. And for those survivors who are very articulate, those who are listening may not accept or might distort what they are saying. On the receiving end, students and teachers might be overwhelmed by the challenge to integrate a survivor's highly personal experiences and reflections into the framework of higher learning with its expectation to problematize and critique. Empathy, instead of facilitating discourse, can be a conversation stopper. For Helen, her first classroom experience was a disaster; afterward she told herself, "Never again shall I do that." She had spoken to the students for about forty-five minutes, tracing her biography during the wartime. She prepared her presentation as a logical narrative, a chronological story. But at the end of her presentation, no one asked a single question. She was insulted and discouraged. She doubted herself, and questioned, "Was I such a bad presenter that I did not generate any questions?"[12]

According to the students' written evaluations of her presentation, Helen was not emotional enough. The students expected tears and not a didactic lecture. One disappointed student wrote that Zippi "did not share her personal feelings, and how she has been affected." In a similar vein, another student wrote that Zippi "did not seem to be hurt now." Another dismissed the entire encounter with the comment "I really was not moved or touched by her story," because Helen was too cool and detached in her narration of what happened. This apparent lack of emotion led one student to doubt her story, stating, "I was skeptical about most of what she said, hard to believe this could happen." Eight years later Helen returned to Professor F.'s classroom and discovered that student opinions of her presentation had not changed. But in this set of evaluations one student (out of fourteen) came to Helen's defense, writing that it is hard enough for her to speak at all, and we must be grateful that she does. Thus it seems that the lack of emotion in Helen's presentation style was viewed with suspicion. Perhaps if she had been less factual and more visibly traumatized, in other words, if she had been less of a teacher and more of an eyewitness, then many students would have viewed her account as authentic, compelling, and true. Helen was dismayed. She wanted the students to learn, not criticize her lecture style or cynically question what she had experienced.[13]

In the years that followed, as Helen avoided the classroom, she observed how other survivors told their stories. She was deeply bothered by presentations that distorted events or attempted apparently contrived connections between their own experience and the general history. She rethought her approach. She would speak with students, but only in a question-and-answer format, as a group interview. As she explained in one interview with students in 2003: "I have conditioned myself. I don't talk on a daily basis and so I like to share my experiences because I know how it was, and it is, and I know how very little has been properly explained [about Auschwitz-Birkenau] until now." When a student asked her opinion about survivors who chose not to tell about their experience, she responded:

> Survivors who never talk don't know. They have nothing to talk about. They don't have anything to say. Most people were so busy sleeping, eating, working. There was no time to observe. And not everybody has a memory. And many people who arrived, for example, Jewish people, were arriving from ghettos where they already went through hell. So I think that they really don't know what to say, where to start and where to finish.[14]

Silence is not always rooted in ignorance; it can, in effect, be the choice of a survivor who has spoken but finds his or her audiences unreceptive or attuned to a different story. Primo Levi, also an Auschwitz survivor and an intellectual giant in the field of Holocaust literature, visited classrooms. Levi wanted to impart some of the themes of his writings to youth, but the more he spoke with students, the more disillusioned he became. Students repeatedly asked him questions that bedeviled him, such as why did the Holocaust happen. Levi could only reply with "vague, generic answers, that man is evil, man is good." This left him dissatisfied. He concluded that his own experience could not be easily reduced to life lessons and stopped visiting classrooms.[15] As autobiographical as Levi's deep reflections might be, here he voices an insight into the problem of communicating testimony shared by many survivors. Auschwitz, one should not forget, was not a place of learning abstract lessons but a mass murder site; survivors are not historical sources but human beings. Can survivors as the prime witnesses, who "bring to life" this horrific event, "teach" students the history or impart important lessons of life? Given the aims of Holocaust education, are we expecting too much, especially from survivors and their families?

Like most Holocaust educational organizations, the Vancouver Holocaust Education Center provides teachers with guidelines for integrating survivors, not questioning, but asserting the value of this enterprise. Two aspects of this orientation material are particularly striking: the stress on experience and the distinction between a survivor and historian. The guidelines state:

> Through the recounting of their experiences, survivors frame and make sense of an experience that is hard, even for them, to grasp or believe. Survivors write and record their experiences to preserve them and gather them into a form that confers meaning. The key here is the word *experience*. A video camera may record everything that transpires, but it experiences nothing. Experience belongs to the consciousness of a person; it arises in the encounter between the world of experience and one's thoughts and sense of self. It is the survivor's experience that your students will be privileged to hear. . . .
>
> Survivors focus on their lived experience. What they experienced does not always resemble an historian's view of history. Students are encouraged to ask survivors questions that are different from those that they would ask of historians. The survivor knows what was in his/her gaze, within his/her realm of experience, what he/she felt and observed.[16]

A 2006 study titled "Best Practices in Holocaust Education" also emphasizes the power of "experience." The report was based on interviews with leading Holocaust professionals in the United States and Israel, and evaluations of the guidelines, mission statements, programs, and other published reports of a sampling of Holocaust education centers around the United States.[17] The study found that the "primary educational benefits" of using survivors were the following:

1. The immediacy of firsthand experience to convey the reality of the Holocaust;
2. The possibility of personal interaction with survivors; and
3. The emotional power and connection with individuals who experienced the Holocaust[18]

These two examples manifest the growing emphasis on the emotional, experiential exchange that occurs between the survivor and the student. This "affective

revolution" that privileges feeling over thinking has its roots in education theories of the 1930s such as those presented in John Dewey's *Experience and Education*
(1938). It is the idea that profound learning happens as a "sense experience," that
one learns by doing or by a "direct encounter with the phenomena being studied rather than simply thinking about it."[19] A highly publicized program at one
institution takes this to an extreme. It reaches out to schoolchildren who wish to
"adopt a survivor" so that they can learn "of the survivor's attitudes and feelings
towards these events to understand precisely what the survivor experienced." In
this manner, the "life and legacy" of the survivor is extended, suggesting that the
intimate exchanges with students will be inherited, palpable even after the survivor generation has passed.[20]

So what does the trend of experiential learning have to do with Holocaust survivors in the classroom? The notion of secondary witnesses described by
Elie Wiesel and others[21] implies a certain transference of experience between the
survivor and the student, an appropriation of a highly complex and fluid set of
personal knowledge and feelings that, given the limits of intersubjective processes
involved in remembering, representing, and receiving, can never be fully successful. As a pedagogical aim, its problems are apparent; still, this idea has motivated
educational use of Holocaust survivors, particularly at the secondary level. Based
on a pool of solid knowledge, survivors and students might indeed feel they are
part of a shared classroom experience. But when the survivor's visit replaces a con-
tent-driven lecture or critical analysis of a text, when the survivor's singular story
is the only piece represented in the vast mosaic that constitutes the Holocaust in
Europe, then educational standards have been not enhanced but diminished.

Roger Simon and Claudia Eppert, educational theorists working in Holocaust studies, recently argued for an ethical understanding of what it means to
listen to another person's tragedy. We "assume that history becomes meaningful
when seen through the lens of personal experience." As modes of instruction, survivor testimonies "carry the injunction 'listen and remember.'" We have a responsibility, they argue, to understand our position as the recipient of testimony from a
firsthand witness within a larger "chain" of recording and retelling.[22] As students
of this history and "transmitters" of survivor testimony, we have an obligation not
only to take care that the testimonies are preserved but also to study them in all
their aspects—facts, distortions, ambiguities, utterances, lapses, idiosyncrasies,
and omissions.

The pioneering work of Lawrence Langer and Geoffrey Hartman, among
others, has provided us with the intellectual foundation for understanding and
utilizing testimony within the limits of what is possible on both the remembering and the receiving end. Rather than promote passive listening, or a student-
consumer who takes in the survivor's dramatic story as a purely sensory experience,
both students and teachers should endeavor to write down what is told, or record

it, to consult Holocaust literature and other sources to ensure that the most substantive testimony is understood and contextualized. Aiming for an authentic personal "experience" might make the survivor's visit memorable to students, but this
cannot replace teaching the content and meaning of the survivor's story, not to
mention a critical understanding of the history of the Holocaust.[23]

With the passing and aging of survivors, where will these classroom
developments lead? Some scholars, such as Ernst van Alphen, have observed that
the second generation, the descendants of survivors, will continue to offer that
emotional and "human" connection to the Holocaust. He questions the assumed
continuity of experience and witnessing, between what Geoffrey Hartman terms
primary and secondary witnesses. One can envision teachers showing video testimony to students of a deceased survivor combined with a classroom visit of
that survivor's child, who will "authenticate" and personalize that story on the
screen. But many descendents of survivors did not learn the details of a parent's
story of suffering and survival. What will they have to say? Should they be
"briefed" by scholars on the history and details of a parent's testimony to prepare
them to continue the parent's act of bearing witness? Some have recommended
this approach and are actively pursuing funding to train second-generation speakers. Others are more cynical about what we can learn from the next generation
who are not witnesses but are granted some stature due to their familial ties to
this past.[24]

Helen's Unfinished Interview: 2000, 2003, and 2006

It is against these developments that I would like to explore what happened when
Helen Tichauer agreed to reenter the classroom in 2000, 2003, and 2006. My first
contact with Helen was in the autumn of 1994, when I telephoned her at the rec-
ommendation of Joan Ringelheim, then director of the Department of Oral History
at the U.S. Holocaust Memorial Museum and one of Helen's most long-term confi-
dantes. I was employed as a researcher in the museum's exhibitions department and
looking for more information about the Feldafing displaced persons camp, Helen's
immediate postwar "home," which was featured in the museum's exhibit Liberation 1945. Since then, Helen and I developed a friendship over the years, and a
working relationship of sorts not unlike that between her and the other contributors to this book. Routine telephone calls often combined warm exchanges about
family with abrupt turns to discussions of recent Holocaust literature, conferences,
and, of course, the history of Auschwitz. As I pursued my dissertation on Holocaust history and started to develop my own syllabus to teach the subject, Helen
was a constant source of insight and information.

Zippi always challenged me and questioned me, but she also came to trust me. In 2000, I began teaching the subject at Georgetown University and then, as of 2004, continued at Towson University. One of my course aims was to introduce students to the variety of sources on the Holocaust and to teach them how to analyze, interpret, and combine them. I was delighted when Helen Tichauer, among the most knowledgeable and keen eyewitnesses of Auschwitz-Birkenau, agreed to speak with my students. However, she insisted that her approach be different from that of other survivors. Above all, she wanted her presentation to be "unrehearsed," and she wanted the students to prepare questions. For the remainder of this chapter, I would like to describe and analyze the interviews that my students conducted with Helen and assess these interviews in light of the larger development in the past thirty years whereby Holocaust survivors have become "teaching tools." The essay will conclude by returning to the theme "lessons of the Holocaust" and specifically what students learned from their exchanges with Helen.

To start, there were some logistical, technical issues to prepare. Over the years Helen's health deteriorated, but her acumen and intellect remained intact. In addition to having failing eyesight and hearing, she had been confined to her apartment in New York City for more than a decade while she cared for her husband. Because she could not travel to my class in the Washington, D.C. area, we arranged for her to talk with students over a speakerphone, which we set up on a conference room table. The audio exchange was unusual but in many ways advantageous. Though one could not see her expressions as she reacted to questions, there were no distractions. Everyone gathered around the table listened intently to her incisive responses. For those survivors who cannot travel, use of audio communications offers an option to continue to bring their voices into the classroom, especially in regions in the United States where survivors did not settle.

Students were prepared for the interview from the first day of class. Helen appeared on the syllabus, and the interview event was deliberately scheduled toward the end of the semester. Students were given a handout that Helen wrote about her experiences, entitled "Ladies First."[25] They were also provided with the published chapter of Helen's interview with David Boder, as well as a layout of the Auschwitz-Birkenau barracks and facilities.[26] As the interview date neared, students had read (presumably) and written papers on standard works by Raul Hilberg, Marion Kaplan, Christopher Browning, Tadeusz Borowski, and Primo Levi. We discussed the topic of survivor testimony and its importance as a source. They had acquired some basic knowledge of the camp. After the interview session, the next class was devoted to an open discussion based on a rough interview transcription. Then I collected more questions from the students and telephoned Helen to find out additional information. I reviewed the transcript with Helen and added footnotes and corrections. The final document was provided to all the students, who were required to incorporate the interview in their research papers and final exams.

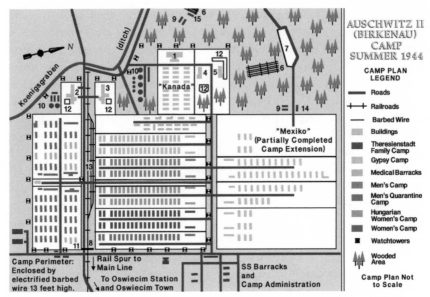

Auschwitz II (Birkenau) camp, summer 1944 (courtesy United States Holocaust Memorial Musuem)

About one week before the interview, each student submitted possible questions. I removed duplicate questions and provided the students with a master list of questions for the interview, with each student's name assigned to his or her question. Helen did not want to know the questions in advance, though I offered to share them with her. Once we were gathered and the technical audio setup was established, each student was called upon to pose his or her question. After conducting these interviews with Helen over the years, I of course noticed some overlap in the questions, but her responses always contained new information, a different facet of the same core problem. Above all, Helen sought to challenge students' preconceived notions or to test what they had learned. Students had to sort through the history they had absorbed in the books, what I told them in lectures, Helen's published testimony, and the unknown and surprising details and images that emerged during the interview.

COMMON QUESTIONS AND THEMES IN THE INTERVIEWS

Most students wanted to learn about Helen's initial deportation to Auschwitz in March 1942.[27] Simona S. from Georgetown asked, "What did you think about your future as you traveled there?" (with all the back-shadowing that is implied), or Jason E. at Towson University asked, "How did you end up at Auschwitz?"

Helen started with a mini-history lesson, in a manner that established her authority and general knowledge. At the same time she was very personable, asking the students to call her "Zippi" instead of Ms. Tichauer or Helen. She explained that she was from Slovakia, and that between 80,000 and 90,000 were deported from her country. She excused herself for speaking in numbers "because we use numbers referring to people [and] it is hard to believe that we are talking about people in numbers as if they were potatoes or apples." On another occasion she started with the Wannsee Conference and then linked that to the appearance in Bratislava of posters calling for young single Jewish men and women to appear for agricultural work in the East. Helen elucidated her mind-set and the predicament she was placed in at the time of her deportation, March 1942:[28]

> Helen (2000): We had no idea in those days why every day, every hour brought with it new restrictions. . . . The war was going on and we figured what's the difference if we spend two or three months (as they had promised) to go somewhere to work assuming that we would return home. . . . We thought we would do something useful. We had no experience with the brutality and killing of Germans. We could never imagine what lay ahead.

> Helen (2006): The Slovakian government offered their Jews to the Germans. We were more or less "invited" to report on a certain day and place. . . . If you don't report, then we will take instead your parents. . . . We were transported in cattle cars to Auschwitz. . . . We were lured into something.

Rohit P. at Georgetown and Carmen B. at Towson asked: How did you receive your privileged position in the office of the women's camp at Birkenau?

> Helen (2000): Three groups of people arrived to Auschwitz these first weeks in March 1942. Among them were thousands of German non-Jewesses who had been transferred from Ravensbrück. They were mainly political prisoners who were brought there to establish the administration of the women's camp. They had experience in this; some had been in the Nazi camp system for several years. I had knowledge of the German language from school. I approached a German female political prisoner who was a *Lagerälteste*, her name was Eva Weigel.[29] I said to her that I was a trained graphic artist, I have been injured and I do not want to go out anymore to that work [demolishing war-damaged houses]. I asked her if she could help me. She had connections to the top in the SS hierarchy, the top management there. She was in charge of professional placement in certain jobs.

At this time the camp was just being organized. She said that she knew what my profession was. Just stay in your barrack, and if one of the SS women asks you why you are not at work, just tell them to talk with Eva Weigel about it, just say that I had Eva's permission. After two days, Eva Weigel came to me and said suddenly, come with me. She led me to a leading SS man named Hans Aumeier, an ugly one. He asked me, do you know how to mix paint from raw materials? It was something I actually knew very well. I went to a professional school for this. I was a sign writer by profession. I was one of the few women in my country to be board-certified in this.

As they developed a policy in the women's camp at Auschwitz that women would run the system, anything a woman could do was assigned to a woman in that camp. When absolutely no female could be found then a man would be brought in from the man's camp.... They asked me to paint red stripes on every incoming inmate. The stripe ran down the back. We were running out of the old Russian uniforms. We had enough civilian clothing from the Jewish arrivals.[30] ... We marked the civilian clothing with a red stripe so that when the prisoners worked in the fields and places outside of the camp, they were easily spotted. They could not run away. We had no hair, but that did not mean that one was automatically recognizable as a camp inmate. In those days, shaven hair was not an uncommon sight, with the illnesses, lice, skin rashes. The next day I received in abundance painting supplies, all that I had asked for including the necessary brushes. I started painting those red stripes and did this for weeks and weeks. After the new inmates had those red stripes then they were allowed to go out to their work detail, whatever was necessary. So I started my "career" there as a painter.

I developed many contacts in the camp because I spoke German. People from all walks of life would meet and talk. Somehow by sheer luck, one of my Slovakian friends, an accountant, was selected to establish a roll call system in late autumn 1942. As you know, the roll call in a military environment is very important, but in a concentration camp the roll call was everything. The SS guards in charge of that did not know how to count from one to five. They were very primitive people. They needed the inmates to help them to count and annotate certain things, basically to do their jobs. There was no system, and it was very hard to conduct the roll call. People were very restless, they did not know how to behave. They were asked to stand in rows of five, but they constantly shifted. They could not be counted, and it took hours and hours. My friend asked me if I could help her design forms for this. I always liked systems, and to be efficient especially if it could actually save lives. By cutting down the roll call time from four hours to forty minutes you saved lives. People moved indoors rather than stand outside in the cold or rainy weather. So I helped design a little system that was suitable.

The camp administrators made a little room available to me, as part of the camp office, they called it the drawing room. . . . I was asked to produce those armbands [for camp functionaries], that was another function that I had. . . . Then the influx of newcomers became very big. There were people coming from Greece, everywhere, you name it, eighteen different nationalities, Jews and non-Jews alike. I was designated to attend to the registration of incoming newcomers . . . the Jewish and non-Jewish prisoners (excluding the German nationals) were tattooed in the numbering system. The same number on your tattoo was then printed on a rectangular piece of white linen. . . . I had to print the numbers on that little white strip of cloth sewn onto the dress [or uniform]. There were not always new arrivals, so I continued to work in the camp office as a painter . . . [and] in the drawing office, making diagrams, monthly reports, . . . drawings of the camp roads, maps. Then I started to play in the camp orchestra, the mandolin. So I had three rations—the regular camp ration, the camp office, and the orchestra ration. As you can see, I became a very rich girl.

Eric H. at Towson and Patrick L. and Lauren E. at Georgetown asked: Did you interact with the SS or other German personnel? What was your impression of them? Did you ever encounter Mengele?

Helen (2003): I tried to stay away [from the SS] as good as I could. And I had not been watched by the SS, nor by the camp office, [I was] not really under supervision. We were left more or less alone because the SS had no idea [about our] administrative matters. . . . It was only during roll call, daily roll call twice, that we had to report to the superior, and that was always an SS person. And they accepted what we did. Bookkeeping, incoming inmates, new transports, outgoing transfers, dying people, transfers to hospital, transfers to other camps; these were the daily activities where always an SS person must have been involved to sign papers or to accept what we presented. That was the general rule. But if you want to know about details then you must ask me about details.

   . . . simple SS men went out, for example, to work with inmates in the field, but it was work outdoors, they were watching, supervising and abusing, . . . but [abuses] never happened in a setup of an office or another workplace where they needed those inmates to do the job for them.

   [Mengele] was in a uniform and he was a hunter. And I'll tell you why. You see, most people encountered him because he was very visible, and he was not the only one who participated in the newcomer selections. There were fourteen others. But today people are . . . everyone for them now is Mengele. What I am saying is the following: we had all of those top-notch people coming into our camp office from time to time. He arrived mainly when newcomers arrived because he was always interested in…actually his selection was not the way people are describing him, that he was standing there. He was more interested in professionals, like, for example, health professionals, wherever they needed some specialty, a nurse or a dental hygienist for the SS dental department. Or anything in connection with his experiments on twins and midgets, he always selected medical personnel. And that was mainly why, the reason why he appeared at selections. That was what people don't know. And that is the truth. So he came often to the camp office, so he informed us, or advised us, we had a professional card system established…I would mention [who was trained in the] medical, or health profession, to inform him. So that was the main reason why he always appeared at new arrivals, or from time to time among the people, you know, the camp office, to ask for health professionals.

Lauren E. asked:
Were you aware at the time that Mengele was conducting medical…[experiments]?

> Helen (2003) My connection to him was the following…if I had my drawing office and he noticed that, he became a little bit interested in my services. He told me that he needed a microscopic draftsperson. Because in prior years they did not use photography, but they used the naked eye, for drawings, they were done by hand. So that was a profession of a microscopic draftsperson. So he wanted me to become his microscopic draftsperson, and I was fighting…with my superior inmate [prisoner supervisor] and superior SS woman, not to be taken out of my job because I have never been trained for that. And that was the only encounter I had personally with him.

> Helen (2006): I started to build a model of the camp, a three-dimensional model in my free time. And they [German SS personnel] would always ask me, what kind of profession do you have? I could not explain it to them, because they did not know what it was. I would answer that I have the same profession as your Führer. And that was the end of the conversation, and questioning.[31]

Michael B. at Georgetown and Ian M. and Steve F. at Towson asked:
Did you have any free time, time to reflect, think about all that was happening around you?

> Helen (2003): [Ordinary inmates who worked outside] had no time to think. People were sleeping as much as they could. . . . You had no

time to think because you constantly had to follow certain orders, good ones, bad ones, silly ones, you name it. Then comes the next step, maybe you are busy with performing your . . . my God, that was always a horrible thing. You had to stand in line, and then wait for that little bit of food that they supplied you. So you had no time to think. You were pushed around. Then comes work back again, and then the marching home to the barrack. There was no time to think because it was a very unpleasant situation without shoes. Summer and winter you had to carry your shoes in your hand. Now, arriving at the camp again, you arrived in your barrack, where you had to wait until some bread was distributed. That was another time-consuming business. Then finally you had a piece of bread, . . . you were exhausted, tired, were happy to go to your bunk where you were falling asleep. There was no time to think! We were better off at work in places like I did, I had time to think because my work was not an ordinary administrative business. When you think, you think like any other human being during work hours and you could analyze the daily happenings in your mind, and no matter how you felt, good or bad, you could think. And to think, it was important to think. And so people who like me, who could think, could remember too, and memorize. So there are a group of people who could not think, who had no time to think and there are people who had the time, or a chance to think. They are the people who could memorize. The others are only today trying to memorize or compare what they are reading. Those survivors who were not able to think are depending now on stories by hearsay and are giving us sometimes accounts of their experiences falsely, because they didn't have the time to observe properly.

Helen (2006): We did have free time at night, from time to time. We spent our time in the beginning by killing the lice. . . . [During the day in the printing office] that was creative work, and when I did it, then I sometimes forgot where I am. . . . While playing music [in the camp orchestra], while drawing in the office . . . I was my own master. I could forget many times where I am. It was so therapeutic, it is hard to explain.

Sara T. at Towson and Erin J. and Michael B. at Georgetown asked: How did you survive? What strategies among the inmates improved one's chances to survive?

Helen (2000): There was not much to adapt to. We were aware of one thing, that we must survive. We learned to eat everything that was given to us immediately. Because if you did not eat it right away, then somebody who was hungrier than you would steal it. . . . In the beginning (three to four months) we had no soap, no water, no under-wear. Women menstruated. We had no toilet paper. People had diar-rhea, stool and urine running down. Smelly and dirty, horrible. You could not adapt to this. So you turned into an animal-like being. Those who were luckier like me who had indoor work, office work, were spared many tortures. First we heard rumors, like in three months we will go home. . . . But then the time would pass and nothing hap-pened, we were there, more months passed. Then *we* were spreading rumors ourselves to keep up the morale, and even invented a date when we were going home. It kept people somehow alive. . . . It is hard to believe that we were so crazy to have hope . . . in the middle of this nightmare . . . living hell. Even sometimes at night during all the gas-sing and burning pit fires, the burning of bodies, we still had hope. Were we crazy?

I had more to eat, and I could share with my friends. Plus the new arrivals were always supplying me with new information about life outside of the camp. . . . there was a lot of camaraderie.

Helen (2006): I never looked an SS man in the face. That was one of my strengths. You could not live in Auschwitz alone. You could not survive, you could not even eat your own food alone. You had to share . . . to stick together and try to comfort each other. Somehow we developed a tendency each of us to have a camp sister with whom you could share your rations . . . we all had some connections to people prior to our Auschwitz relocation, people from the same schools, class-mates, you name it. I even met . . . my own schoolteacher.

Yes, there was one moment when I thought that I will not survive. I was among a very heavy indoor selection [not done upon arrival]. At the end of 1942, there was a big influx of new arrivals. And every time that they needed room for the new arrivals, an amount of people had to be killed. So there were daily, large killing activities. They were taking people, whole barracks were loaded onto trucks and off to the crematoria. On one occasion I was very sick and had to be hospitalized and the whole infirmary, the whole barracks was to be gassed. I was selected out as the only person because of my activities, and the camp management, they wanted me to live. I was there among all of them, but taken out from the group of people being loaded onto the truck. I was the one saved out of 10,000 due to my skill. And even then I did not know if I would survive, but it happened. . . . So many things happened to me, and I survived, they were miracles, those moments.

Alicia W. at Towson and Andrew L. at Georgetown asked:
Did you witness any resistance activities, and if so, what kind?

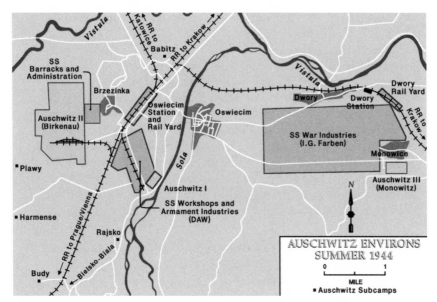

Auschwitz environs, summer 1944 (courtesy United States Holocaust Memorial Museum)

Helen (2000): We did not witness any resistance activities. Once you were engaged in resistance, you became very invisible. Can you imagine, once you openly resisted you were in deep trouble. It was very secret. You might have even been a part of it and not have known it.... So I would never say that I did something, but I know exactly that resistance groups used my office and used me. But questions were never asked what is this or that for. And that's why we know so little.... if everyone knew that they were at the time working in the resistance then things would not have functioned.

Helen (2006): That is another invention. Today if you speak with people, everyone was in the resistance. The resistance in Auschwitz was very strong, but they were not our people [in the women's camp]. The blowing up of the crematorium, the stealing of the gunpowder from the munitions factory, all of that was resistance. Unfortunately they were wiped out. I knew the people. I know the story.

Kiki K. and Kerry N. at Towson and Stella C. at Georgetown asked:
What image of the camp has stayed in your mind all these years, or in what ways is the camp experience still with you? We have heard about survivor's guilt. Do you experience that?

Helen (2000): The living hell. Dante's *Inferno*. You know that in the middle of 1944 there were so many Hungarian Jews arriving that four crematoria were not enough to burn all the bodies. So they were burning the bodies in open pits. At night the sky was red from the flames. There was a curfew. No one was allowed to go out, but being a worker in the camp office I could move freely, from one place to another, from one barrack to another. I was out in the late evenings while they were burning bodies, with those flames high in the sky. The red was all around you. I thought I was in the living hell. That will never leave me. I have been in hell. Very few people had a chance to go out and witness that. I think that there, there was a living hell, and that hell exists as well as the devil. I started to believe in the devil. Isn't that strange. I have nothing more to add.

Helen (2006): Guilt! There was no guilt. The Germans should have guilt. If anybody should have "survivor's guilt" then I don't. What do you mean by guilt? Do you have guilt if you survived the Twin Towers? Do people who did survive, did they develop a guilt complex? . . . I never felt guilty in my life for anything [related to the Holocaust]. If I would have done something wrong, then maybe, but that is something which is not for us to discuss, the guilt complex. I think that not the survivors, but the professional psychologists who have developed that, invented it! I went voluntarily to Auschwitz to avoid having my parents taken then, but they were taken anyhow.

In addition to these questions, students asked Helen about the bombing of Auschwitz, the persecution of homosexuals and lesbians, food rations, relations between Jewish and non-Jewish inmates, and her view of human nature. These themes reflect individual students' knowledge of the Holocaust, their intellectual curiosity, as well as their expectations. Students sought new information and wished to obtain special, insider knowledge of Auschwitz that one had not read or seen in movies or documentaries. As a historical source and informed eyewitness, Helen could share her special knowledge and grant students some measure of expertise. Furthermore, when asking about how Helen ended up at Auschwitz, students wanted to define turning points in her biography. One student, Simona S., sought to capture Helen's frame of mind as she was deported to the camp, drawing a line between a pre- and post-Holocaust world, which of course Helen certainly could not do herself until later. In comparing the Slovakian government's demand for work in the East to a summer work project, "like joining the Peace Corps," Helen tried to connect with her young audience. When she entered Auschwitz, Helen was of university age, unsure of what would happen next, but, as she stated, she had "the best of intentions." But then Helen quickly dispelled any romanticized or nostalgic notions of her "coming-of-age" in Auschwitz. The call for labor in the East was for Jews obligatory, and if one did not appear, then one's parents would be taken instead. Once she arrived at the camp, she was shocked by the conditions and the "walking skeleton" prisoners.

Students tried to establish the level of Helen's self-awareness while caught up in this horrific maelstrom, asking her if she realized that she was entering hell, or if she had time to reflect. As Helen stressed, the ability to observe, grasp, and memorize the scope of the Nazi system at Auschwitz was possible only for those who were in a "privileged" or secure position. Being among the few Jewish prisoners with this vantage point who survived the war, Helen was able to explain the structure of the women's camp administration, and as a "survivor in the classroom" she came across as a credible source of Auschwitz-Birkenau history. Her unrehearsed, question-and-answer approach was also more persuasive than a precomposed narrative. Interviewing an expert-survivor such as Helen forced students to become directly engaged with the history in a manner that was more challenging than passively listening to a life story that seemed as if it had been told before or followed a predictable narrative construction.

But not all students embraced this challenge, either out of shyness, ignorance, or disinterest. Some posed questions to affirm certain preconceived notions, values, or biases. Survivors relate painful stories of personal losses and suffering, but one usually anticipates a "happy ending" to their story, one of liberation by American soldiers and emigration to the United States. Some students associate themselves with the survivor, believing that they could have masterminded an escape, carried out an act of resistance, secured a hiding place, or managed to obtain a privileged position. Thus many questions tried to ascertain Helen's survival strategy and her connection to the resistance. Her answers to these questions were usually the longest in the interview session but not equally forthcoming. Helen interwove her personal story of survival with the history of developments in the women's camp. Her changing tasks and duties paralleled the growth of Birkenau. Helen's account seemed to confirm Raul Hilberg's statement that in many ways Auschwitz was a camp in search of a mission.[32]

As Helen described how her survival was linked to the expansion of the camp and its forced labor and killing operations, students began to realize the moral predicaments and gray zones of the history and her place in it. The halo effect of her victimhood and the heroism of her survival became muddied by the very facts that she presented. Helen referred to her "career" at Auschwitz as a painter, as a producer of armbands, and as an illustrator in the graphics office. Helen had to make herself useful and valuable to the SS without compromising her integrity and humanity. She used her position to help others, for example, by helping to drastically cut the time spent with roll call. This was an achievement that Helen proudly and deservedly credits with saving lives.

Regarding resistance, Helen was more guarded in her responses. She pressed the students who raised this topic to be more precise. The students assumed that Helen was in a position to sabotage the system and provide information or support to underground plots, such as the blowing up of crematoria in autumn 1944. Helen admitted that she knew the people who were in the resistance, and she stated bluntly, "I know the story." But Helen's curt tone discouraged follow-up questions by students. She criticized the broadening definition of resistance, spurning those who now claim a place in the resistance as inventors of their own heroism. Resistance was such a secretive act, she explained, that one could not witness it. The real resisters were "invisible." Helen will not state that she was part of the resistance or that she did something, but she asserted "that resistance groups used my office and used me." Is it possible that Helen is still operating today under that code of silence and fear that governed resistance activities in Auschwitz? She certainly grieves the deaths of those who died for the resistance. More than any other fellow Jewish inmates mentioned by Helen, Roza Robota figured in each of Zippi's exchanges with students.[33]

Students often want to hear about the Nazi perpetrators, especially famous ones such as Josef Mengele. Posing questions about German personnel and encounters with famous Nazis seemed to be the students' attempt to connect Helen's singular experience with the more familiar and predominant images of Nazis found in history books, documentaries, and television broadcasts such as the History Channel. It is also a way of injecting agency and causation into her story by trying to place her experiences at the receiving end of Nazi-initiated policies, orders, and the powerful individual perpetrators who controlled her destiny. Helen surprised them by asserting that she did not have much interaction with the Germans, since the "SS had no idea about administrative matters." She presented the SS personnel at the camp as shadowy figures to whom reports were sent, but who were generally absent. Mengele came by Helen's office because he needed a draftsperson, and he was interested in using her for medical drawings. There is a certain incongruity in her characterizations. On the one hand, she seemed chummy with powerful SS leaders (including Maria Mandel), but on the other, she constantly feared them.

In a rare moment during the Towson interview of 2006, Helen lashed out at a student's question. When Helen was asked about whether she experienced survivor's guilt, her friendly tone quickly turned to outrage. Upon this, students shrunk in their chairs, and an awkward silence followed. The dialogue broke down. Some display of emotion was important for establishing that the survivor experienced the trauma. But the transmission of it had to be coherent and understandable in the classroom setting. Such outbursts changed the dynamic. The survivor could not teach, and student empathy turned into feelings of helplessness, and in some cases aversion. I was reminded of this situation a year later when a professor at Johns Hopkins University explained to me why he does not bring survivors into his classroom. The one and last time he tried this, he explained, the survivor had a breakdown in front of the students. No one knew what to do. All were ill prepared and not equipped to deal with the survivor's trauma, and the survivor went home feeling humiliated and ashamed.

Helen's otherwise cool composure was not a sign of detachment. She is not a professional speaker who has honed a performance. Her answers were substantive and varied. But in them one also detects limits. She signals that she knows more but does not offer to share it, unless she is pressed and believes that her questioner is knowledgeable enough to grasp the details she can divulge. Why this guarded approach? Perhaps there are deep memories that are too upsetting and potentially overwhelming. Perhaps the details that she safeguards are embarrassing, shameful, or dishonorable. Perhaps she still feels the need to keep certain things secret. Maybe she fears that her memory is fading. As a survivor in the classroom, Helen navigates a course of labels and expectations, being referred to as a "victim," "survivor," and "eyewitness," as a transmitter-witness, a vessel of history, and an expert on Auschwitz. Above all, Helen is conscious of her audience. Her answers and demeanor catered to college-aged youth. Afterward, Helen was always eager to evaluate the interview and find out how students had reacted, and to determine what they had learned. As we discussed how everything went, she usually asked me: "Wendy, am I a good teacher"?

Concluding Observations

As I looked over the series of student interviews with Helen, some gaps were evident. Many questions were not asked and many periods in her biography not dealt with in her responses. Students were perhaps sensitive enough or too uncomfortable asking her to relate what violence she had witnessed or experienced. Helen did not speak in detail about the extreme suffering and deprivation she endured in the death march or during her time at Ravensbrück at the end of the war, though, as she would state, "well, nobody asked." She also did not explain to students that she was a *Geheimnisträger*, a bearer of secrets, producing reports on the number of gassed (*sonderbehandelt*) prisoners from the women's camp, actually two years of reports with eighteen curves showing the fates of registered prisoners subjected to "indoor selections" or transfers.

As close as Zippi and my students might have felt during the interview sessions, those were distant encounters within a format oscillating between a personal conversation and a seminar source analysis. We were short on time in these interviews, and I had the benefit of following up with her, editing the texts, and adding footnotes as she elaborated certain points. Sometimes she would return to these pieces of her story unexpectedly, months later during a casual phone call. Her interviews remain unfinished. When she later spoke to me about those graphs with the prisoner numbers, she explained that she tried to disengage herself from the figures, to forget them after reporting them: "to try to remember them would have driven me crazy."[34] But Helen deliberately made a second copy of those reports and secretly hid them to document the crimes for postwar justice. She has asked many scholars to find them, but they have not turned up. Though she tried to forget those figures, I think that those charts and graphs that she drafted for reports to the SS headquarters in Berlin are still etched in her mind.

If Helen had any goal when she agreed to speak with students, it was not to teach lessons of the Holocaust or establish any personal legacy. Instead, she wanted to uphold the truth, to impart some piece of the concrete reality of Auschwitz-Birkenau as she observed it in her unique "privileged" position. Given her unusual activities in the camp, she is a "bearer of secrets" not to be kept secret. She has knowledge to share, beyond her life history; yet how well her story resonates with students remains unclear, partly as a result of her insistence on facts. She rarely relates how she felt, and she is not interested in how the students feel, but only in whether they have learned something new. Though she maintained a remarkably cool tone that seemed detached, one senses there were some boundaries to her telling. Her tone of voice changed, she became indignant when one student asked about "survivor guilt." There were limits to what she shared about resistance. She tends to focus on administrative details of the camp; as she stated, she is fascinated by systems, especially the development of efficient ones. Her answers to my students' questions attest to her preoccupation with orderly, businesslike, almost managerial effectiveness and efficiency. She was operating in that "gray zone" of the camp as an administrator of a system that she herself could fall victim to at any time, and that was devouring her own people in this "living hell." She could take pride in her work there, even find moments to escape in her drawing office or in the orchestra, but Helen saw and understood the operations of the camp as a whole.

Would students remember their interview with Helen? Some may keep the formal transcript that we created. But as is more often the case, class notes and other materials from courses disappear or get thrown away at the end of the semester or after graduation. Students may not feel the responsibility or obligation to transmit her story as "secondary witnesses" on a chain of witnessing, described by Wiesel and educational theorists; then again, given Zippi's conviction that only those who were there can bear witness, she might find the notion of "testimony by proxy" presumptuous if not bizarrely presentist. As much as we would like to create unbroken links between telling and retelling, we are bound to lose proximity to the events and, in the process of representing them, invariably replace these gaps in the chain with our versions of the story.

To determine more precisely if students had retained any information from their encounter with Helen, I decided to contact students who had taken my Holocaust history course at Towson in spring 2006. There were thirty students in that course, but only about half of them could be found, and from among those, seven responded. I asked the students if they remembered any aspects of the interview with Helen, of her experiences at Auschwitz-Birkenau, and of her persona. I was pleasantly surprised to learn that certain details did stick in their minds. Everyone recalled that Helen had a special position in the camp administration, some even that she was a graphic artist and that she had developed a lifesaving roll call system. Two students remembered that she played in the camp orchestra. One student reflected that "her answers didn't seem rehearsed . . . because she didn't speak in public her answers may have been more genuine, rather than what she thought we wanted to hear." All respondents mentioned how Helen reacted to the question about guilt, and one concluded that Helen "seemed to embrace the life that she has had the opportunity to live." Students wondered about the future of Holocaust memory with the passing of survivors. Indeed, as one student had asked Helen during an interview, "What in your opinion do you think is the greatest obstacle that future generations face in preserving the memory of the Holocaust?" On this issue intensely discussed by Holocaust pedagogues and scholars, Zippi should have the last word:

> People forget very quickly, but you cannot tell people "you must remember." It must come from the people, just like you have chosen to take your course. Nobody asked you to do so. . . . I am not in the Holocaust business, but I realize that I have been in a position to observe, that I am a good observer. . . . There is so much unsaid up 'til now, and even though we are dying out, there's always something we will find of interest which we can analyze and discuss. But you cannot force anybody to become aware of what happened.

| Conclusion |

What Have We Learned?

People today, Zippi insists, do not understand Auschwitz. With this sweeping yet clearly legitimate assertion from which she does not exclude scholars such as the contributors to this volume, Zippi refers to the huge gaps in our knowledge about the daily goings-on in the camp. We might know about Auschwitz as today's icon of modern man's technological capacity to commit mass murder, about the origins of the camp, about the aim its creators had in mind, or about the size and composition of those groups murdered on arrival; we have but a faint idea, however, what those who were lucky enough to get registered as prisoners went through during the days and nights, the weekdays and the weekends in Auschwitz. To be sure, terms like "selection" and "special treatment," "Kapo" and "Kommando," "roll call" and "Rampe" are well known; yet, what they meant in the camp and how their usage changed over time is rarely addressed in what we read or hear about Auschwitz. The reasons for this relative lack of knowledge are clear: few survived to tell the story, most were completely overwhelmed by being thrown as fuel into a death factory, and many came to Auschwitz too late during the war to know how the key elements dominating the life of inmates had evolved.

But does it matter when Zippi tells us in intricate detail about the camp system to mark new arrivals with color stripes, triangles, and numbers? Is it not sufficient to know that those not gassed on arrival were registered, and does it not deflect from broader issues of death and survival if we focus on the nitty-gritty of prisoners' camp life? Do we need her matter-of-fact account when we have highly insightful reflections from other Auschwitz survivors, most notably Primo Levi and Jean Améry, who pose profound existential questions? For the historian, the answers to these questions are clear: it does matter, detailed information is essential, and, as Raul Hilberg put it, "Any source may have significance."[1]

We can never know enough about what happened in Auschwitz; every voice helps us understand better, especially one that speaks on the basis of vast personal experience and deep practical knowledge. Nothing attests more fittingly to the crucial importance of concrete events and factual detail than the stubborn attempts by Holocaust deniers to substantiate their lies with manufactured forensic evidence, be it a chemical analysis of the Auschwitz remains or the historical authentication of wartime documentation. Inside and outside courtrooms, denial of the Holocaust cannot be refuted by abstract assertions about Auschwitz, as learned and profound as they may be. Only hard evidence will do.

Denial has as little to do with the history of the Holocaust as antisemitism has to do with Jewish behavior. For those eager to learn, the unsettling quality of survivor testimonies, particularly detailed accounts such as Zippi's, derives partly from the fact that they confirm again and again the unbelievable nature of manufactured mass murder, not only in its totality—who can grasp the meaning of millions murdered on a routine basis?—but in its crucial parts and mechanics, its organization and administration. To implement the inconceivable, the rules of causality applied. Registration, dehumanization, and exploitation through numbering, torture, and forced labor were part of a process designed to produce the result envisioned by the camp's planners and rulers: morphing a mass arrest site into the location of unprecedented crimes.

Zippi insists that Kapos or other privileged inmates could decide whether they wanted to behave like devils toward their fellow prisoners or try to improve their fate. For the overall process of destruction driven by outside decisions, this made no difference; for individual prisoners, this room to maneuver, if ever so small, could mean life or death. Zippi's testimony corroborates that even within what Primo Levi called the gray zone, the area of unclear responsibilities and choiceless choices, different shades of gray existed. In Auschwitz, order and chaos, self-sacrifice and betrayal, death and normality formed a bizarre homogeneous unity that each prisoner experienced differently. Not one story, be it by an eyewitness or by a scholar writing after the war, can properly convey all the variations to the theme. Because the transformation of Auschwitz since the end of the Second World War into a synonym for the Holocaust, or still more generally a symbol of human inhumanity, has led away from the actual history of the camp complex, the crimes perpetrated by Germans and their helpers, and what happened to the men, women, and children tortured and killed there, we need as broad a mosaic of sources as we can get to paint a purposeful, that is to say nuanced, clear, and comprehensive, picture of the past.

But what if survivor accounts do not fit into the picture historians and others paint by using more or less colorful documentation? In her conversations with the authors, Zippi again and again stresses the importance of a victim's vantage point during the Holocaust for what he or she could later attest to. The ability to observe and reflect, the time of arrival to a specific camp or ghetto, the duration of incarceration, the degree of depravation, the position in the prisoner society, and the proximity to the perpetrators—all these factors greatly influenced what survivors could remember after the war. There are thus differences in the insights—be they historical, psychological, or of another type—that testimonies can covey. The issue of how much and what we can learn from survivors is further complicated by their personal or political interests, changes in their memory, the incorporation of acquired knowledge into one's personal story, and our preferences and interests as users and recipients.

We know that survivors can and do change their stories; as long as these changes can be traced, they present fewer problems than chances for further research, if only by raising the question what is it that makes a person retell his or her story differently. In this respect, Helen Tichauer's remarkably consistent story has very little to offer. What we have seen in this book, however, is how outside intervention can significantly transform testimony in its content and connotations. Scholars can detect and explain the inherent evolution of survivor accounts, but do they—and the authors of this book include themselves in this question—reflect sufficiently on the effects of their own transforming (by way of translating, editing, or annotating) of these very accounts?

In deciding how to use Holocaust testimony, we are, in this as in any other research project, guided by scholarly as well personal and societal considerations and factors. What makes sense to the readership of a Holocaust book in the early twenty-first century might have been met by earlier audiences with disbelief or skepticism; because progress is not linear, the opposite also applies. Since the 1990s, the Holocaust has become a staple item on the media agenda; survivor testimonies abound in films, museums, and books and on the Internet. Not surprisingly, the decision about what to publicize is often driven by the urge to depict new, dramatic, or otherwise moving stories; behind these present-day priorities and the powerful images they produce, the complexity of historical reality can vanish from sight. But even where we do get closer to the personal meaning of the Holocaust by approaching one of its survivors, we might in the end find that the distance that separates those who experienced genocide from those who did not remains cannot be bridged.

As much as we like to extract positive lessons from the accounts of survivors, there are stringent limitations. Whether it is the story of one survivor or thousands, no single story can speak for those millions who perished during the Holocaust. In concluding his analysis of the testimonies of 173 survivors of the Starachowice camps, Christopher Browning states that "the suffering of the victims, both those who survived and those who did not, is the overwhelming reality. We must be grateful for the testimonies of those who survived and are willing to speak, but we have no right to expect from them tales of edification and redemption."[2] Our gratitude to Helen Tichauer for her willingness to share her story and our ambition to convey this story accurately are great; so is our skepticism that we have succeeded in getting it right. Her story can be read and interpreted in more ways than those presented in this book.

| APPENDIX |

English Translation of an Interview Conducted by David Boder with Helen Tichauer; Recorded in DP Camp Feldafing, Germany, September 23, 1946; Translated February 1956

Edited by Jürgen Matthäus[1]

MRS. HELEN TICHAUER[2]

/Spools 149, 150, 151/

{p. 1/2044}

BODER: /In English:/ We are starting again. Munich, Septem-...Germany, September the 23rd in camp Feldafing...camp Feldafing, near Munich, a camp for about four thousand and several hundred DP's. The camp is located on a large compound of about fifteen to twenty acres, covered with armory-like buildings, which was a camp of the Hitler Youth. /One sentence is omitted for reasons of uncertainty./ The interviewee is Mrs. Helena Tichauer, sometimes, as she says, known in Auschwitz and here as Zippy. She is married to Mr. Mack...to Mr. Tichauer who was our interviewee on Spool 146, 147 /these numbers are incorrect/. Mr. Tichauer was called in our spools Irving. /In German:/ Now then, Mrs. Tichauer, will you please tell me how old you are...your full name and how old you are, if one may know.

TICHAUER: /In German:/ Tichauer, Helena, nee Spitzer.

BODER: Spitzer.

TICHAUER: Spitzer.

BODER: Yes.

TICHAUER: Born in November, the tenth of November, 1918.

BODER: Where?

{p. 2/2045}

TICHAUER: In Bratislava in Czechoslovakia.

BODER: So then you are a Czechoslovakian subject.

TICHAUER: Yes.

BODER: I see you have here a tattoo number. Where is it from?

TICHAUER: My number, 2286, belongs to the first numbers of the women who, in the year '42, March '42, arrived in Auschwitz.

BODER: Aha. Now, will you tell me how . . . from the day of the day of the action brought you to Auschwitz and what happened further?

TICHAUER: Now the action, how they actually came to Auschwitz, is in this case also interesting.

BODER: Yes.

TICHAUER: The Slovakian country was given by Hitler its independence. As a price the then Minister-President Votetch Tuka gave sixty thousand Jews . . . he put them at the disposal /?/ of the Germans. That is Erret /?/ KH /or KA? A few words giving apparently the meaning of these letter are not clear/.³

BODER: Well. How were these Jews taken?

TICHAUER: These Jews were 'invited.' First of all women were 'invited.' The young ones, that is girls up to forty-five years, to present themselves voluntarily to an assembly point in Bratislava. That was the Patronka. Not much was told to them, but / they were informed/ that most of them are assigned to agricultural labor in North Slovakia. The transports arrived, that is, the people assembled in the lager, and to . . . to . . . the first transport of one thousand girls departed on the 26th of March from the city of Poprateck /?/.⁴

{p. 3/2046}

BODER: '42 {in German interview correct: "[19]43?"}.

TICHAUER: '43 {in German interview correct: "[19]42"}.

BODER: '43 {in German interview correct: "[19]42"}.

TICHAUER: A day later the second transport departed, again of a thousand women. We traveled all night.

BODER: In what transport were you? In the second transport?

TICHAUER: In the second transport.

BODER: All right. Now tell us what happened. You assembled. What did you have with you?

TICHAUER: With /two words not clear/. We assembled. Immediately the same day we had to surrender our identification papers, and we had to commit ourselves ... the things ... that means, fifty kilos we were permitted to take with us, and we had to commit ourselves to put at the disposition of the state the things that we have left behind.

BODER: Hm.

TICHAUER: We were actually forced to comply with this form- ... form- / formality/.

BODER: Now, how did you put that /the things/ at the disposition of the state?

TICHAUER: Of course we don't know any more what became of them since a week later we were transported away from the assembly point, where we had been cut off from the whole world, with our fifty kilos.

BODER: Now one moment. Where were your father, your mother, and ...

TICHAUER: My parents were /remained/ still at home. In general all parents remained still at home. The first transport consisted of unmarried girls who were called upon to cooperate /?, to do 'nothing' to avoid compliance/ in coming. And in case they were not to come, measures would have {p. 4/2047} been ... /she seems to be cautious about her High German grammar/ measures would be taken, and the parents be taken instead /in retaliation/. For this simple reason no girl dared not to come, because for everyone the parents ... the parents were to be considered /?/. Since one had the worst premonitions about these matters, one was ready to sacrifice himself.

BODER: Nu.

TICHAUER: Nu. We were then, after one week, exactly after . . .

BODER: Now let us not go so fast. Who guarded you?

TICHAUER: We were then guarded by the Grinka /?/ garrison.[5] These were the counterpart of the SS that time in Czechoslovakia, called SS, corresponding to the German SS.

BODER: So they were not Germans themselves.

TICHAUER: No. The Germans themselves took over this assembly lager the last day, got people up, and conveyed them with the transport.

BODER: Aha. Now wait . . . go on.

TICHAUER: The trip lasted a night and a day.

BODER: Now then, in what kind of rr-cars were you embarked?

TICHAUER: These were <u>normal</u> cattle cars.

BODER: What does that mean? Are there <u>not-normal</u> cattle cars?

TICHAUER: Yes.

BODER: For example?

TICHAUER: For example, cattle cars which at times have no tops, which are without roofs.

BODER: Aha. Open rr-cars.

TICHAUER: These were closed cattle cars. These were closed and were supplied, {p. 5/2048} of course, with proper locks so that we were unable to see the daylight, nor did we have an idea in what directions we were exactly traveling.

BODER: Did you have a toilet in the rr-car?

TICHAUER: A toilet, no. But there were buckets which served for that purpose.

BODER: How many people to a rr-car?

TICHAUER: There were about sixty to eighty people embarked in each car.

BODER: In your case only women, is that so?

TICHAUER: In our case women only.

BODER: Only younger . . . /?/

TICHAUER: Only girls up to the age of 45.

BODER: Then there were no married women?

TICHAUER: No married couples, because these followed only two months later.

BODER: But were they married women?

TICHAUER: Married women, no.

BODER: Now go on. Neither small children?

TICHAUER: Small children neither. At the border, approximately … The next morning early we noticed that we are somewhere in a strange region. After prolonged guessing whether here or there, it occurred to us that we had traveled in the direction of Upper Silesia. We were at the railroad station /word not clear/,[6] and we knew that we are traveling in the direction of Poland.

BODER: You were told where you are going.

TICHAUER: No. About that we were given no information. Most to the contrary.

BODER: Yes, but you were told at the start that you were going to Slovakia.

TICHAUER: At the beginning we were just told that /we would go/ to North {p. 6/2049} Slovakia for work in the fields. But when we saw that we arrived in Poland, we were of the opinion that we possibly may go to work in the fields in Poland, because there were already earlier circulated rumors that field … field laborers are needed partly in Poland, partly even in the Ukraine. We did not think much of it, because we were promised our return home within two months. And we were gladly ready to work up these two months only to protect in this manner our parents.

BODER: Did you in general know already what is happening in the lagers? Were these things known in Hungary … /correction/ in Slovakia?

TICHAUER: Actually no, because concerning women hardly anything was known. We knew about the German concentration camps for the simple reason that a large part of the immigrants, the German immigrants principally, were at that time tolerated in Slova- … Czechoslovakia, and …

BODER: Those were people who had run away?

TICHAUER: ...who partly were permitted to leave. Part had run away. And most German Jews knew what a German concentration camp was. But never in life had we dreamed that we, completely harmless /people/ will be put in a concentration camp only because we are Jews. Now then, the next day, it was on a Sunday {in German interview correct: Saturday} afternoon, at about five o'clock the train stopped at the station Oswiecim, Auschwitz. And in some way...

BODER: Where is that about? Near what big city is it?

TICHAUER: Well, that is...Auschwitz by itself is a big city. However, it is located between Katowice and Krakow.

BODER: Yes. /In a low voice:/ Please speak in this direction.

TICHAUER: We were unable to orient ourselves, because Auschwitz was completely {p. 7/2050} unknown to us. That is, in general, Auschwitz was known /to us/ not as a concentration camp. We arrived as I said already by five o'clock in the afternoon. The train stopped. We were received in kind of a strange <u>tone</u> /manner/. We only heard a howl, because the rr-cars were locked. Faster and faster <u>out</u>, and so on, and on. When the turn came to our rr-car we were chased down. Before us stood people in uniform, the kind we did not know before, because in Slovakia we had no opportunity to see actual 'skulls'.

BODER: You mean the men had skulls /emblems/?

TICHAUER: They had skulls...

BODER: Describe please the uniform.

TICHAUER: The uniform was a normal SS uniform, dark green, half high boots, a kind of German boots, Wehrmacht boots. The flaps /?/ on the...What do you call it?

BODER: On the...on the coats.

TICHAUER: On the tunics were marked with SS, and on the cap, on the helmet /?/,[7] which they mostly wore, one saw a skull.

BODER: With two bones?

TICHAUER: No, a skull, /just/ a skull. That was the insignia of the...of the skulls. That is, that was /a regiment/...

BODER: Yes.

TICHAUER: This is known. Now then, we were chased out...

BODER: What does that mean, 'chased out'?

TICHAUER: With a, 'Out, out.' With /words not clear/ so we understood that we have to get out. We were hurriedly lined up in rows of five and /led/ in {p. 8/2051} the direction of a door /gate?/.

BODER: And your things?

TICHAUER: No, the things were not given to us. And the things we never saw again.

BODER: Did not see again?

TICHAUER: Never seen again.

BODER: Remained in the rr-car?

TICHAUER: Remained in the rr-car. On the way we saw something that I hardly could describe any more today. It was a most peculiar sight. Half-finished stone blocks /buildings/ surrounded with barbed wire. On the roofs, at the windows, stood striped, living corpses. I can't express myself differently. People without faces, /without/ facial expressions, like...like made of stone. Next to them stood...today we know they were sentries, sentries so to speak, who guarded these prisoners, and / word not clear/ who...these were men. When they saw us, they were....when they in some way directed their attention at us, they were yelled at, so that they would not dare any more to turn their head/s/, and continued with their work. At that time, as I understand it now, the lager Auschwitz was being constructed for us, for the women...to complete it, so to speak, because most of them were up on the roofs.

BODER: /Words not clear./

TICHAUER: Correct. It was...the men's lager was completed already since 1940 or '39, but for the women, who were just now expected, ten blocks were assigned. These were stone blocks one story high with basements and attics. We were a thousand girls. We entered the lager. That means in front of {p. 9/2052} the lager was the gate with the inscription which gave us something to think /about/. 'Work makes free'/<u>Arbeit macht frei</u>/.

BODER: Just the same as in Dachau.

TICHAUER: Yes. Naturally we were of the opinion that we /have come to/ a work lager. But not so from the gate on the left side. If one would turn somewhat to the left one could see in the German language in printed block letters the sign <u>Concentration Camp Auschwitz</u> which, so to speak, aroused in us some obscure uneasiness. The thousand girls who came to the lager saw before themselves, before the last block, it was block ten, a crowd. We did not know at the first moment whether these are girls or women or humans altogether. They stood there in old Russian uniforms, the hair /heads/ shorn bare, wooden slippers on their feet. And so they stood and stared at us. Then suddenly there were heard some calls. Certain girls had recognized girl friends, sisters, or the kind, and after long . . .

BODER: You said they were there?

TICHAUER: They had arrived a day earlier.

BODER: They had the naked heads?

TICHAUER: They were already, so to speak, established /?/ prisoners.

BODER: Yes.

TICHAUER: And so . . .

BODER: They had already their hair shorn?

TICHAUER: . . . had their hair shorn already. We could not talk much, because we were surrounded by SS, but we understood that these are our women neighbors from Slovakia, and the conditions in which they find themselves. That was enough for us. It did not take long. That means . . . We had {p. 10/2053} arrived. What we still had left, an overcoat, clothes /?/, shoes, stockings and such, was taken away, and in groups of a hundred we came to a block which was called the shower. That was a bathhouse.

BODER: The what?

TICHAUER: The shower.

BODER: Yes.

TICHAUER: It was a bathhouse where the women were bathed, were their . . . that is our hair was shorn. We were given the Russian uniforms.

BODER: Men's uniforms?

TICHAUER: Russian men's uniforms, old ones. And in a few hours we were made equals to the arrivals who preceded us.

BODER: Now wait a moment. This we want. Your things that you had with you were taken away, correct?

TICHAUER: Yes.

BODER: You were then taken to a bath?

TICHAUER: Yes.

BODER: Then your hair was cut.

TICHAUER: Yes.

BODER: Where?[8]

TICHAUER: Where? One moment. Before the first Jewish transports arrived from Slovakia, there arrived a thousand Reich-German prisoners from Ravensbrück.

BODER: Men or women?

TICHAUER: Women, because in the women's lagers there were only women. We had no contact with men. This was not permitted at all. These were women prisoners who were already for three or four or five years imprisoned, and {p. 11/2054} as punishment were transported from the concentration lag/er/... from the concentration camp Ravensbrück. These women then clothed us, bathed us, shore our hair, handed us over to the SS. These prisoners, those Reich-German prisoners...

BODER: When you were shorn and bathed...

TICHAUER: Yes?

BODER: ...did any SS men come in?

TICHAUER: There came in at that time the lager leader {missing here: "Höss"},[9] the then lager leader of Auschwitz, Superior Storm Division Leader Ohmeier /?/,[10] and many others whose names are today not known to me...and to inspect us like cattle. It was going on like a cattle show. They turned us here and there /right and left/.

BODER: While you were nude?

TICHAUER: Nude. Besides there was the SS physician Dr. Bodeman,[11] that time the lager physician /?/ who looked us over, and... I don't know, inspected us, and put us through the normal process of bathing and hair shearing.

BODER: The men were present?

TICHAUER: The SS men, yes. The first night...

BODER: The hair was cut only from your head?

TICHAUER: The hair was cut from all places, wherever there was hair on the body /word not clear/, our eyebrows and also on . . . [12]

BODER: With scissors or with . . .

TICHAUER: Partly with electric machines, such shearing machines, and when these failed /got out of order/ scissors were used which most often were half dull. A few weeks later, after thousand of prisoners were brought {p. 12/2055} during these months from Slovakia, from Poland. From Poland the first prisoners came to /from?/ prison in Auschwitz. In order to have somehow an orientation, they started to proceed with the tattooing. The early methods were . . . have in fact failed. The early methods corresponded to a stamp. They arranged needles in the form of numbers, simply pressed it on the arm, and simply spread over India ink. But in a few days the tattoo was gone. Then followed the normal tattooing with the double needle which was applied to the left elbow of every prisoner in consecutive numbers beginning with one.

BODER: How was that done? Did they scratch it?

TICHAUER: No, just by touching. That is a double needle. One needle longer, the other shorter. And this was dipped in India ink, and then stamped /pricked/ . . .

BODER: Does that hurt much?

TICHAUER: Hurt? We did not feel pain any more, because the clothes /a few words not clear/ as such, the removal of hair from the head of a woman, all that /she appears very emotional/, the whole transformation which occurred at that time has hurt much more, so that we did not feel anything any more. Because we were like . . . like transformed into stone. Yes? I don't know how to say it exactly.

BODER: Yes, yes.

TICHAUER: But it did not affect us, nothing whatever they did to us. When our /finger/ nails, our toenails . . . or whatever, nothing affected us any more. {p. 13/2056} Because we knew that now we are completely /?/ cut off from civilization, from mankind, and that we were /now/ on the 'other side' of life, on an 'other side' where, however, people still live. /Pause./

BODER: Nu . . .

TICHAUER: Nu. The first night we were lodged in this stone block, crowded together, first of all, because it was . . . The lager in fact was not exactly ready. There were old straw sacks from the men's lager thoroughly rotten. These were spread out on the floor . . .

BODER: After all that washing?

TICHAUER: After that whole procedure /to-do/ . . . just in part, because there were then not even enough straw sacks available. And one lay down wherever there was room. Fixed up with a piece of bread, we spent the night. The following day began for us something entirely new.

BODER: Who tattooed you, men or women?

TICHAUER: There were . . . This tattooing was really performed two months later.

BODER: Oh yes.

TICHAUER: The thorough tattooing. The first /tattooing/ was also performed by the prisoners,[13] prisoners who . . . then . . .

BODER: Men or women?

TICHAUER: Men. Always men. Now . . . /pause/

BODER: Yes.

TICHAUER: Yes. /A few words not clear./ The next day—it was still dark—we were aroused by whistles and yelling. We heard the word <u>appell</u>. <u>Appell</u> was for us something completely unknown. At the moment we thought <u>appell</u> is something for soldiers, appell is somewhere . . . pertaining to soldiers. {p. 14/2057} So maybe they want to make soldiers also out of us. We got up, were chased out, and . . .

BODER: What do you mean? Who . . .

TICHAUER: Chased out by SS women into the yard. We did not know exactly what to do. Then came . . .

BODER: Did they beat you?

TICHAUER: During the first hours I could not about . . . I don't want to talk about it at all. Then it was for us . . . we had . . . in fact, we were really unconscious /in a daze/. Yes?

BODER: What does it mean, you don't want to talk about it?

TICHAUER: /Animated and in a high pitched voice:/ I can't talk about it. We were unconscious /in a daze/. I don't know. I don't know whether I sensed a blow or not. It was . . . One thing I know. We were lined up, lined up in a manner so they could count on us, after much fuss. Naturally, it did not come to a count, because...

BODER: Why 'naturally' not?

TICHAUER: Why not? Because there was a terrible chaos. Those SS women who then were in charge of conducting the lager....There was at that time the superior super/visor/...the 'report leader' Margot Drechsel[14] who at the beginning did not know at all what to do. She did not yet have any experience. She had the people lined up, and as soon as they attempted to re-count us, the number never was the same, because the prisoners in part did not know...one...in one group stood the sister, in the other stood possibly the cousin. People ran from one group to the other. In one group...in one group the strength /number/ was larger, in the other {p. 15/2058} smaller. So that the first days it was totally impossible to arrange a correct appell.

BODER: Now how did they count? Were there /identification/ numbers?

TICHAUER: No. The people were stood up five in a row, one /row/ behind the other, and then they...

BODER: How were the people counted?

TICHAUER: ...were counted by rows /?/.

BODER: Not each person /was counted/?

TICHAUER: No, no, no, no. That was out of the question during the first few days. And in the course of time the prisoners, too, learned how to line up. The 'report leader' also learned how to count correctly, and as soon as the appell was correct we would disperse.

BODER: How long did such an appell last?

TICHAUER: An appell, if performed correctly, yes /you see/?

BODER: Yes.

TICHAUER: /It/ could be over in ten minutes.

BODER: But how long did it actually last?

TICHAUER: And...during the first years appells lasted as long as four hours.

BODER: During the first years or the first days?

TICHAUER: During the first years, I should say, because we had . . . It time
and again depended. There was elected a prisoner who would
assist the count leader, that SS women, that is, worked with
her. The prisoner during the first year was . . . for the <u>first</u>
year I should not say an illiterate, but she could hardly figure.
There was no consideration for efficient work, and she was not
at all interested that the prisoners be counted up promptly.
{p. 16/2059} For the first time, in the year 1943, a Jewish
woman was appointed report clerk. She attracted attention /
by the fact/ that right from the beginning she was appointed
block elder and proved to be good. She was by profession a
clerk /?/. She could figure, could write and read, and was
interested to help her fellow men /a few words not clear/.[15]
And thanks to her, many, many prisoners are alive today from
our country as well as from other countries. She accomplished
that often appells were correctly completed in ten minutes, and
in /cases of/ rain or severe cold the prisoners could disperse in
a few minutes. In two or three months—it was in August—
there arrived daily a thousand girls from Slovakia, partly Arian
prisoners, political prisoners from Poland, from . . .

BODER: Who was called a political prisoner?

TICHAUER: A political prisoner was in the eyes /?/ of the German army anybody who in some manner had committed an offense against the
German power. Even women, women of the German State, who
had but a Polish friend were treated as Poles[16] and designated
as political prisoners. And so in August our number had reached
the number of about seven thousand, and spotted typhus and
malaria their first victims . . . /she is apparently confused by her
own attempt at a 'higher level' of style/. Well, spotted typhus
and malaria . . . when prisoners fell the first victims of spotted
typhus, the Germans decided, the SS lager leaders decided to
have the women's lager Auschwitz moved four kilometers away
to Birkenau. At that time there remained in Auschwitz more
than two thousand prisoners, women prisoners, who in some
way were not well. The rest were relocated in Birkenau.

BODER: Where were the crematories? The crematories were in
Birkenau?

{p. 17/2060}

TICHAUER: Modern /?/. Modern /?/.[17]

BODER: Yes.

TICHAUER: Crematory <u>One</u> was a modern crematory in Auschwitz
which served only to burn corpses. The little white building which stood in Birkenau in the forest was /appeared as/

nothing else but an innocent little 'cottage.' I myself had in the year . . . '43, in the winter between '43 and '44, a chance to step into that little cottage. Because this little cottage has all our Auschwitzian . . . /correction/ Slovakian brothers and sisters on its conscience. This white little cottage had a couple of windows, a large iron door, and a sign, 'To the <u>bath</u>.' People were at that time chased into that <u>bath</u>, according to stories of people, of prisoners, of men whom I encountered <u>above</u> . . . these were men of the special commando. The special commando was the commando which consisted of prisoners. These prisoners were compelled to drive people into the gas chambers, to transport them 'in a state of death' to the crematory, and to burn them.[18] These people had a few months leave according to dictates from Berlin in order to organize /?/ the gas-killings. These people had then in the winter . . .

BODER: What does it mean, they had leave? They were in the general /?/ lager . . . ?

TICHAUER: They were in the general lager, but were sent as a lumber commando. They had to cut lumber precisely around that cottage. And there I had a chance in some way to ask someone from the special commando how the people were gas-killed. And he showed me the iron door and the barred window. The people were driven in. It was one room. The door, the iron door, was slammed shut. Through the iron bars, through the window, gas was {p. 18/2061} passed in, and the window 'automatically' /properly/ shut.[19] After a few moments, a few seconds, a few minutes, whatever the case, until the people were dead. They were put on lories. And nearby there were pits where the people were burned.

BODER: Then they were not burned in the crematory. They were burned in pits?

TICHAUER: Burned in pits, still at that time. I still want to reiterate that in August '42, when the women's lager was relocated to Birkenau and the two thousand sick prisoners had remained in Auschwitz, /they too/ were gas-killed in the little cottage.

BODER: Who, the two thousand?

TICHAUER: The two thousand girls.

BODER: But the little cottage was in Birkenau.

TICHAUER: Correct. They were loaded into trucks and driven over.

BODER: Oh.

TICHAUER: Upon arrival in Birkenau it was constantly heard about trans-
            ports to Lublin. We did not believe in the transport.

BODER: One moment please. Did you work in Auschwitz?

TICHAUER: I worked in Birkenau. I also did work during the first weeks
            in Auschwitz.

BODER: Aha. What kind of work did you do?

TICHAUER: The first weeks I was in the wrecking commando in
            Birkenau.

BODER: What does that mean, wrecking…

TICHAUER: There were still a few shot up /bombed/ houses in Birkenau
            which had to be demolished.

{P. 19/2062}

BODER: Did you live in Auschwitz?

TICHAUER: No…/confused/ we lived in Auschwitz and walked to
            Birkenau for demolition /work/.

BODER: On foot?

TICHAUER: On foot. Barefooted.

BODER: How many kilometers?

TICHAUER: Some four kilometers. /Pause./

BODER: Now then.

TICHAUER: /Long pause./ Now then. In time they directed definite /?/
            attention to me. After the Russian uniforms which we were
            given did not suffice any more, it was decided to give us
            civilian clothes. Civilian clothes were, of course, sufficiently
            available, because the baggage was taken away from all the
            women and the worst clothes selected and put at the dis-
            posal of the prisoners. But in order to distinguish us from
            the civilians /the general population/, that is we did not
            have any contact with civilians at all, but should there have
            come one or another chance to escape, and in order to be able
            to distinguish us, it was ordered by Superior Storm Leader
            Ohmeier /?/{Aumeier} that a black vertical stripe be drawn
            behind, on the back from top to bottom.[20] Since they did not
            want to send painters from the men's lager to the women's
            lager, they were on the lookout for a woman who in some
            way was acquainted with paints. There were dry paints and

the proper oil, and they wanted that the women help themselves to it. I was then the only one who reported for it. I did not know at all for what purpose. They looked for a women painter. And since I am by profession also a script painter, I reported.

{p. 20/2063}

BODER: What does it mean, script...script painter?

TICHAUER: Script painter means sign painting.

BODER: Nu.

TICHAUER: Now I got...

BODER: How old were you then?

TICHAUER: Then I was twenty-two. I got red powder paint and a pot of varnish and brush shoved into my hand. I was ordered to mix the paint. And later prisoners were led before me, and I got the order that a vertical stripe be af-...

BODER: Oh, you had to do that while they had their clothes on them?

TICHAUER: ...to affix, correct.

BODER: Aha.

TICHAUER: Now, so the work started. From dawn to dusk I was fully occupied. I had to make the red stripe, and every prisoner to have the red stripe was so far in good order. He could 'report' and could now be tattooed.

BODER: Oh, that was before the tattooing?

TICHAUER: Yes. Now, however, it was a number /that was/ affixed to our arm, to the left forearm. But in order to still more...in order to recognize us better, and to recognize us adequately in case of a control, they had on cloth...they had printed on cloth in the men's lager, which by that time had already a printing apparatus, the numbers which the prisoners had tattooed on the arm. In order that the men's lager...in order not to be dependent on the men's lager, I was given a printing apparatus, and I printed on tape, on linen tape, numbers from one to seven thousand, about eight thousand. That many we were at that time /in the lager/. I was then shoved into the {p. 21/2064} office, that was the receiving office where every prisoner, newly arrived, was asked for his personal data, and as soon as the prisoner was through with the complete registration, he received automatically a number pressed in his hand, and it was his duty to sew on this number on the dress / the masculine pronoun in the preceding sentences is obviously used to designate both sexes/.

BODER: These were women.

TICHAUER: These were exclusively women.

BODER: Yes.

TICHAUER: The printing of numbers came for me soon to an end, because other painting tasks were given to me. For example, I had to paint signs, numbers on a cabinet for the lager leader. In general various small, nearly useless tasks. When I . . .

BODER: Who gave you the assignments? Who told you what to do?

TICHAUER: The lager leader.

BODER: That was an SS?

TICHAUER: Yes, Stibetz /name not clear/.²¹ At the beginning we had . . . the lager leader was in fact the leader of the women's lager and the men's lager.

BODER: Yes.

TICHAUER: But under him was the head woman supervisor. In the year '42 we had the head woman supervisor Langenfeld.²² When we were already in Birkenau . . .

BODER: How did you behave when she gave you orders . . . the orders?

TICHAUER: All out normally. We had to stand at a distance of three meters. When entering . . . we were called for. In the moment we entered the room of {p. 22/2065} the women lager leader or of the lager leader we had to present ourselves thus, 'Security prisoner twenty-two eighty-six requests permission to enter.' Then the entrance was granted. One received then an order. One was addressed in part by thou, in part by thou/ a slip, apparently intended you/ {Tichauer says "Du"; you} depending on the mood at the moment. The order was chosen /?/, that means it was given, and the prisoner had to reply, 'Security prisoner twenty-two eighty-six begs /permission to/ leave.' That was the pro- cedure. Now . . . in September 1942, I had already fever for two or three weeks. At the time when we were relocated from Auschwitz to Birkenau I had fever too. But we knew, should I get sick . . . that somehow has been whispered into our ear /that/ one <u>should</u> not /has no right to/ be sick. And so in a state of fever I printed numbers, I made /printed/ stripes, and so have taken care of my work. I belonged then to the office of the commander as a draftswoman, was assigned to a block where there were no /not only/ Jews, but also Jews and also Arian prisoners, because the Jews were . . . Now there were in Birkenau two rows. On the left, left of the gate, were stone blocks where before . . . where once before were quartered Russian prisoners of war. From them . . . from the forty thousand who once were there, only thirty-two /thousand?/ remained alive.[23]

BODER: What happened to the others?

TICHAUER: The others had died away /croaked/.

BODER: What does that mean?

TICHAUER: Had died away in the swamp and morass. That I know . . .

BODER: What do you mean? Did <u>you</u> work there?

TICHAUER: We worked . . . That I know from those of the forty-two / thousand/ who {p. 23/2066} were still alive. To the right of the gate were wooden barracks. Those were 'horse-stable' barracks where the Arian prisoners were quartered for the simple reason that these barracks were cleaner.

BODER: The 'horse stables' were cleaner?

TICHAUER: Were cleaner. And there were 'exception blocks' for such prison/ers/ . . . for such prison/ers/ . . . for such Jewish prison- ers who performed certain indispensable work. Because <u>then</u> it was considered indispensable, say to print numbers or to paint a stripe, or to draw eventually a little birthday card. So then these prisoners . . .

BODER: A little card?

TICHAUER: A little card. Yes. So these prisoners were assigned to the Arian block. Every night, I had every night the shivers. This was noticed by my Arian supervisor, the State German {word in German: "Reichsdeutsche"} and she compelled me to present myself to the sick ward of the lager. That was the hospital. When the acceptance was completed, after three weeks in bed, without treatment, without medicines, there came for me a most strange day.

BODER: /in English:/ This concludes Spool 149 with Helena Tichauer reporting. We are going over directly to Spool 150. Germany,

September the 23rd, 1946, at Camp Feldafing, a large instal-
lation of the former Hitler Youth. And here in the room with
bare walls, apparently the paintings and the like have been
covered, /i.e./ the wall decorations. But the floor is of hard-
wood which could adorn any fine American home. I estimate
fifteen or twenty acres of land, all with large barracks, which
the Hitler Youth occupied, and which is now occupied by
about five thousand Jewish displaced persons. An Illinois
Institute of Technology wire recording. We are going over to
{p. 24/2067} Miss Elena Tichauer's /Mrs. Helena Tichauer's/
report which will be taken on another spool. /End of Spool
149./

BODER: /In English:/ The interviewee is Mrs. Helena Tichauer, con-
            tinuing from Spool 149. This is Spool 150. Mrs. Tichauer is
            continuing her report on her camp in Birkenau. /In German:/
            All right.

TICHAUER: Now then. In the year 19 . . .

BODER: Well, in the year . . .

TICHAUER: In the year 1943, in September,[24] that's when I came into
            that sick ward of the lager, that is in the hospital. It was an
            isolated block. It was block 27, a stone block, where only
            Jewish prisoners were located, without treatment, without
            medicines, because medicines were not made available to
            Jews. One was three weeks here almost without a drop of
            water, without normal nutrition to live on.

BODER: Please /?/ describe the beds in the sick ward.

TICHAUER: In this Jewish stone block there were no beds. There /were/
            the so-called <u>cots</u>.

BODER: How is that written /spelled/?

TICHAUER: K-O-J-E-N.

BODER: <u>Kojen</u>?

TICHAUER: <u>Kojen</u>, correct.

BODER: <u>Koyki</u>, like they say it in Polish.

TICHAUER: Yes.

BODER: Yes.

TICHAUER: Within a height of three meters or three meters–twenty /
            centimeters/, {p. 25/2068} were located three such holes, so

to speak. These were simply caves where room was found for five people when things were bad. When things were good /laughter—she apparently means when things were thriving for the hospital/ there were many more /laughter again/. This about describes it.

BODER: Yes. Were these wooden scaffolds?

TICHAUER: The block was about twenty-seven meters long. These were stone scaffolds.

BODER: /With surprise:/ Stone scaffolds?

TICHAUER: Stone scaffolds, vertically. Horizontally they were wooden scaffolds. In length such a cut was about two meters.

BODER: Oh, these were a kind of plank bed.

TICHAUER: Correct.

BODER: <u>Polati</u> /wooden sleeping platforms/ in Russian /?/.

TICHAUER: So that one could lie down. In width it was two, about two, meters. In height, well, two times two, a square hole. Three such holes were above... one above the other.

BODER: Yes.

TICHAUER: That is three times. The one on top was at the most advantage, because on top there was air and room up to the roof. The people were located there according to demand. If there were more sick ones, then five, six, up to eight persons lay on such a cot.

BODER: All one next to each other?

TICHAUER: All next to each other like herring. If there were more room, then three or four could lie /on one cot/. Now then, so we lay there com- {p. 26/2069}pletely abandoned. People lay, lice-ridden, starved, and unattended. The first of October, 1943,[25] came. Through the window—there were a few windows—through the windows one could see trucks going and coming. Later we learned that nearby, behind the block 27 was located block 26, and behind block 25. Block 25 was the famous isolated.../correction/ isolation block. There were assembled the half-sick, half-exhausted, almost completely exhausted girls, and every day departed a transport of trucks full of such girls. It was said they were going... they go to Lublin. But since within an hour the same clothes, that means the old uniforms with the numbers, with the sewed on numbers, would come back, we knew exactly that people were not transported to Lublin in the nude, and it did not take long before we got word that, /from/ men of the special detail, that the people were gas-killed. On the first of October all sick prisoners who were located in block 27, where I too was, were dragged out before the block. They were instructed to sit down next to each other. There were that time seven hundred girls in the block, sick part with spotted typhus, part with malaria, with infections, and whatever else may have occurred.

BODER: What did you have?

TICHAUER: I?

BODER: Yes.

TICHAUER: I had come down that time with spotted typhus. I . . .

BODER: With other people nearby who had what?

TICHAUER: They . . . malaria and . . . and small infections.

BODER: All in the same plank bed?

{p. 27/2070}

TICHAUER: All in the same block.

BODER: No. On the same . . .

TICHAUER: All from the same cot, correct. So we were instructed to assemble before the block, half exhausted. Cold it was. Three or four hours long we were sitting. Meanwhile before us passed trucks <u>by the dozens</u> /loaded/ with girls through the gates.

BODER: <u>White</u> /a confusion of the ending <u>–wise</u> or <u>dozenwise</u>, 'by the dozen'/trucks?

TICHAUER: No. Trucks. These were normal . . . .

BODER: Oh, <u>dozenwise</u> /by the dozen/?

TICHAUER: <u>Dozenwise</u>, yes. Through the gates, in the direction of the white house. At that time already two crematories of modern construction were completed and in action. In the course of the following months all the regular . . . two, as a matter of fact, three /crematories/ were completed and which worked later on day and night on 'double steam' /to utmost capacity/ when later on the Jewish transports proceeded to arrive from all lands of Europe.

BODER: Now have you seen such a crematory?

TICHAUER: Yes, but...

BODER: /Hesitantly:/ How many people could be burned at one time in one...

TICHAUER: One thing I know. At our gate passed...if a transport arrived with a thousand people, and it always so happened that only ten per cent would get into the lager, that is one hundred out of a thousand. And nine hundred consisting of mothers with children, whether young or old...that was all the same. Whoever /?/ led a child by the arm or by the hand was considered as {p. 28/2071} a mother.

BODER: As what?

TICHAUER: As a mother.

BODER: Yes.

TICHAUER: Mother, child. Older person, sickish person. I should like later to return to...to <u>how</u> /the method by which/ such a sorting out, selection, was proceeding, because I.../Pause./

BODER: Yes. Let us return to what happened to you.

TICHAUER: Let us return. On the first of October passed <u>dozenwise</u> /by the dozens/ these automobiles before our eyes. Only later, when I...

BODER: Now let us stick to that. What happened to you?

TICHAUER: Good. Correct. Then came our turn. There came Ohmeier /?/ {Aumeier}. The name of the lager leader...his name was Mueller.[26] So Mr. Mueller also came over and said that <u>everything</u> /a frequent attitude of <u>deanimation</u>, of treating people in terms of discarded objects/ that he has delivered up to now is still too little for him /to satisfy him/. This I have heard with my own ears. I was that time not any more unso-phisticated[27] with reference to all these things, because dur-ing the time when I was still not lying in the sick ward, I had been working in the office, and I only know that death lists arrived constantly and especially of those who were loaded on automobiles and then were never to be seen again. At that time he only said...it was...Ohmeier said it was not enough for him. Block 25 was emptied out. Healthy women in my estimation above about three thousand in number, who were then /transitorily or slightly?/ sick, were shipped away /?/ in this manner. Now came our turn.

{P. 29/2072}

BODER: Healthy women were shipped?

TICHAUER: Healthy women, yes. Mr. lager leader Mueller was alerted by
           his woman secretary who then worked for him, for reasons of
           race pollution—she was a prisoner and her name was Anny
           Meier . . . Anny Meier[28]—that I, too, was among the prison-
           ers who were here in block 27. And I, before my illness,
           painted for the lager leader a few numbers on a box and was
           unable /then/ to finish them. So he came up to me, and asked
           me what I was doing there. I replied that I was free from
           fever and would like to work again. So he said to me, 'Good,
           then you /the courtesy form of you/ go over there. That is the
           Arian "ambulance" /infirmary/. Let them measure your /c.f./
           temperature, and if you /c.f./ have none, you remain, and if
           you /c.f./ have any, you /c.f./ go with them.' Often . . . on the
           Arian ambulance then a sister /nurse/worked . . .

BODER: By 'ambulance' you mean a clinic /ambulatorium/?

TICHAUER: Yes. That was a wooden barrack, a little one /a shack/.

BODER: Yes. You see, we call an 'ambulance' a vehicle.

TICHAUER: Well, a clinic, so to speak.

BODER: Yes.

TICHAUER: There worked a German nurse, a German 'political' /pris-
           oner/ who was there already about eight years,[29] with whom
           I previously had a little contact. She worked there. She knew
           exactly what it was all about. And she assured me when she
           said, 'Zippi, even if you had 43 degrees /109 degrees Fahr-
           enheit/ of fever, I shall say nothing.'

BODER: What did she call you, Zippe?

TICHAUER: My name was Zippi. That is what I was called.

{P. 30/2073}

BODER: Z . . . ?

TICHAUER: Z-I-P-P-I.

BODER: Yes.

TICHAUER: Her name was . . . /recollecting/. The name escapes me for a
           moment. I shall later come back to it. And indeed, in five
           minutes Mr. Mueller came, and she reported that I was free
           from fever. I had to . . .

BODER: Were you?

TICHAUER: I was not free from fever. I was given <u>valeriana</u> in order to calm myself and had still to sit there for three hours and wait.

BODER: Outside?

TICHAUER: In the room. I saw then through the window how all my … my girls, with whom I lay together sick, were chased up the truck and driven out through the gate. I was immediately instructed to begin with my work in the office. Feverish, half blind, half deaf, after typhus, I began with my work. I weighed then barely seventy pounds. Now I weigh fifty-two.

BODER: Fifty-two kilo?

TICHAUER: Fifty-two kilo, and that means one hundred and four pounds /115 pounds nearer correct/. The idea that I was on that day the only remaining survivor out of four thousand girls gave me the strength and faith for further endurance. I was a hundred per cent sure that the girls were gas-killed for the reason that we in the office have established, besides the card index by names, a <u>number book</u>.

BODER: A number book?

TICHAUER: A <u>number book</u>. And every prisoner who had passed … died was marked up with a black … a red cross, every number. And prisoners who were gas- {p. 31/2074}killed /were marked up/ with a black cross. This way I had /in/ black and white /a record of/ what happened. Weeks later I recuperated. Meanwhile still daily departed transports of the girls from the lager. And in February, 1943, when the number, the number of prisoners, of the last prisoner, of the last arrival had reached the count of thirty-three thousand,[30] of whom there were already more than twenty thousand Jews, there remained after a large selection, in February /one/ thousand five hundred.

BODER: February of what year?

TICHAUER: '43. /One/ thousand five hundred Jewish prisoners, women prisoners.

BODER: When?

TICHAUER: In February '43. The total number amounted then /to/ about seven thousand. <u>That</u> /inanimate designation/ which was not gas-killed, perished from typhus, without treatment, without medicines, perished in part from starvation. There was then even a large <u>selection</u> of non-Jewish prisoners.

BODER: What is a <u>selection</u>?

TICHAUER: A selection is a sift, a 'natural' sift, which was designated by the foreign term /Latinism/. That was not a 'natural' selection. It was a selection /choice/ of the SS. Now then...

BODER: How did they choose those people?

TICHAUER: They judged according to their whim, according to appearance whether one is still fit to work, fit to live or not. There was a <u>general</u> appell on that...I think it was the nineteenth of February {1943}. A <u>general</u> appell was an appell at which the whole lager was assembled on a nearby meadow.

BODER: Who /?/?

TICHAUER: Women only, and were then one by one returned to the lager. To the {p. 32/2075} right and to the left. This...this selection was attended at that time by superior supervisor Maria Mandel and the then labor service woman leader Hasse, the sister of the woman supervisor Franz /?/ Coupulett /?/ in the lager Muehldorf,[31] in the women's lager Muehldorf. The going was to the right and left. And <u>everything</u> that went to the left went to the block 25. That time not only Jewish women went. A large part of those who went were Yugoslav women. Even <u>state</u>-German /Footnote 1: State-German—actual citizens of the German Reich as distinguished from Folk-German, citizens of invaded countries who collaborated with the Nazis and claimed privileges on account of alleged German ancestry./ women thieves' accomplices /?/,[32] state-German political prisoners, state-German asocial prisoners, Russian /women/, everything that was still on hand. Indeed, no consideration was given whether Jewish or not Jewish. But it was then that the last Arian was gas-killed /the last time that an Arian was gas-killed/. Then further orders arrived from Berlin, because the women supervisors or the SS people made 'special actions' only then when Berlin would order to proceed with a selection. I want to give a little example. There were about two thousand typhus cases in the hospital. The lager inquired in Berlin whether it would be permitted to gas-kill the girls of the two thousand typhus cases, that is of the two thousand Jewish typhus cases. In about three months came the reply, '<u>Yes</u>.' Meanwhile, however, forty per cent of these girls had gotten well. But the number two thousand had to be gathered up. So they took all Jewesses from the hospital who lay there, without exception, whether they had scabs or any other little thing. And so the rest which was {p. 33/2076} missing from the two thousand, that is the rest who were discharged who were

already well, was by ... was replaced in a manner that they
went through the blocks. That is, the SS went through the
blocks. And this time, for example, they took a fancy to the
barracks service detail who looked well. So they took the
healthy barracks service detail. They took girls who at the
moment were running on the road to the toilet. They took
<u>whatever</u> got in their way. The number two thousand was
reached. But that was not enough for them. They took this
time advantage of the 'special action,' and raised the number
to three thousand. And these girls went all[33] into the gas. I
know that, because I marked their numbers in the <u>number
book</u> with <u>black</u> according to a list which we received.

BODER: Well, but it never said in the number book what black
means.

TICHAUER: It did, indeed. We knew: SB—<u>Sonderbehandlung</u> /special
treatment/.

BODER: Hm. That was the name /for it/?

TICHAUER: That was the name.

BODER: It did not say <u>gassed</u>?

TICHAUER: No. Always and again: <u>special treatment</u>. The commando /
detail/ who worked <u>at it</u> was also called <u>Sondercommando</u>.
And according to orders from Berlin only such Jews could/
or could <u>not</u>? See footnote 2/ be gas-killed, who came with
RSHA transports, that is verlockte /Footnote 2: This word
presents a great difficulty for the translator. It has two most
distinct meanings, and unfortunately there is no clue in the
context. <u>First meaning</u>: enticed, allured, trapped. <u>Second
meaning</u>: covered with locks, with long, curly hair, possibly
due to neglected appearance, or due to religious traditions of
the Khasidic sect. In general it seems that the recollections
are deeply affecting her mood. She loses control, in places at
least over the process of verbalization, causing substantial
contradictions and instances of confusion in the narrative./
Jews.[34]

{P. 34/2077}

BODER: What does it mean, RSHA?

TICHAUER: Main Superior Security Office /<u>Reich's Sicherheit Hauptamt</u>/
Berlin.[35] Jews who came to prison were treated as card-regis-
tered /exact translation: cardwise; from <u>karteimaessig</u>/ Jews.
They were entered in the card index. Their clothes ...

BODER: What does that mean, <u>kartei-</u> ...

TICHAUER: Card-indexed, a card index, no? Their clothes were card-indexed, which they, however, never saw again, and /they/ were protected against gas-killing, against the 'special treatment.' /Footnote 3: It is, therefore, not clear whether these prisoners were or were not the same as the <u>curly</u> or possibly <u>trapped</u> Jews. See footnote 2./ That was the /their/ only advantage. But if by some mistake such a Jew from such a transport would go to the gas /chamber/, then a death certificate was simply made out, a <u>normal</u> death certificate—acute intestinal inflammation, etc.

BODER: Now then, the card . . . What did you say . . .

TICHAUER: Card-indexed Jews, and for that reason . . .

BODER: Card-indexed Jews were such who were <u>not</u> gas-killed?

TICHAUER: Who were <u>not</u> to be gas-killed. And that is to a large extent the {p. 35/2078} reason why we today possibly see weak older people who are today alive. /This is/ thanks to the fact that they were card-indexed, that means prisoners from jail. These were privileged. Indeed, it was paradoxical.

BODER: What . . .

TICHAUER: The people who came from the prison have definitely consciously committed something. The others came into the lager harmless and innocent, only because they were Jews.

BODER: So then the criminals, so to speak, have remained alive.

TICHAUER: Correct. A large part of them. Or they were at times whipped to death, were killed at work. That was already . . . That happened not only to Jews. So were . . . so found their end many others, thousands of others, non-Jewish prisoners. /In a low voice:/ Do you have, <u>please</u>, any question? /She apparently searches for suggestions for a new topic./

BODER: Now what followed? How did you fare? I want to know everything.

TICHAUER: And so I worked then in the office. My work consisted . . . Because I, after my illness, had completed for the lager leader the few numbers on his wardrobe, and I as a single one out of four thousand got out /was saved/, they /the Germans/ took notice of me. The SS /woman/ who then was dismissed or transferred, and a new one came . . . /the latter/ knew always from the others: This prisoner was favored by Mr. Mueller /the deficient syntax is, as always, that of the original/. They did not know why. And when it subsequently came to any kind of selections, so they used to 'forget' about me. Besides, I performed, in the course of time, tasks which no other woman was /capable of/ doing, because I was a professional. They were pleased /?/[36] by a properly looking card index, with little things {p. 36/2079} that I did for them time and again according to instructions, exactly like any other prisoner who had to do work that was assigned to him.

BODER: Now then, how was it . . .

TICHAUER: Later on I worked as a prisoner in the office, doing always what was indispensable /to do/. Then came the superior storm leader Hoefler /?/,[37] that Hoefler who was hanged in / by sentence of/ the Bergen-Belsen trial. He became our lager leader.

BODER: In . . . in Birkenau?

TICHAUER: Yes. I want to say a few more words in connection with Hoefler. At the selections which were performed at the arrival of a transport, of which I already mentioned that ninety per cent went into the crematory, Mr. Hoefler was also present. At times Mr. Hoefler, at times Dr. Mengele,[38] at times Mrs. Upper supervisor Mandel, at times Mrs. Upper supervisor Drexel. It depended, alternating. That went on automatically, left, right, left, right. Whoever had luck got into the lager. And only those who got into the lager were tattooed, got their number, and were entered in the card index. Mr. Hoefler, too, took part in these selections exactly like all the others belonging to the SS. But thousands of male and female prisoners could possibly be thankful for their lives to Mr. Hoefler, because he was the one who undertook a most radical campaign of delousing. In all lagers, men's lager and women's lager, the typhus louse had disappeared. And in this manner prisoners were spared by typhus.

BODER: How did he accomplish that?

TICHAUER: He ordered the clothes to be put into steam boilers where the typhus louse was killed. The eggs, the larvae were killed. Often the prisoner {p. 37/2080} was shorn, the hair, wherever he had hair, was taken through a bath, a cleaning. He went as far as to provide enough water and soap, and such delousings took place every month. Thus there was /at that time?/ not a single prisoner in Auschwitz or Birkenau who was not submitted once a month to a delousing.

BODER: Aha.

TICHAUER: And so Hoefler, exactly like the others, took notice of me as the draftswoman of the lager, put paints at my disposal, and arranged for me a small room next to the office where I worked. I got then the first, larger task to draw up a diagram, a diagram of the labor force, that is, of everything that took place in the lager, the daily changes in the /labor/ force, the daily additions, the labor force in the communication /? she says richtung/ industry,[39] in agriculture, and wherever else prisoners worked—to present that monthly in the form of a diagram which would then go to Berlin. I made that diagram once /one copy/ for him, and once /one copy/ for myself. And the last day, on the 18th of January '45, I threw a roll of duplicates of the diagrams behind the bookcase in the Birkenau lager, section /one word not clear/ 2B. I think it has fallen into the hands of the Russians.[40]

BODER: You don't know into whose hands it fell.

TICHAUER: No.

BODER: Why could you not take it yourself /?/, afterwards?

TICHAUER: I could not . . . Why? I . . . we had to evacuate.

BODER: Oh, you were evacuated?

TICHAUER: Yes, and precisely before all papers, all the 'principal' books, {p. 38/2081} everything was burned. And about these diagrams nobody knew anything. I threw them behind the bookcase.

BODER: Where did you throw the diagrams behind the bookcase? / Apparently some trouble with the recorder./ Now go on.

TICHAUER: Yes. In order to kill time in some way, I undertook in this little room to reconstruct the Birkenau lager in plastic / a plastic model/. I obtained the proper tools /?/ and all that was needed for it.

BODER: You slept in a general block?

TICHAUER: I slept with all prisoners together. I was not privileged / officially/. I was not a band carrier /apparently a band on the arm to designate a trusty/. I was simply recognized as draftswoman of the lager.

BODER: What did you get to eat?

TICHAUER: To eat? Exactly the same as any other prisoner. In the morning there was coffee. Then we /I/ got daily five hundred grams . . . no, I don't know exactly, but it was . . . it was a quarter from a five pound bread. That still means about 500 grams.

BODER: That is then from a bread of two kilos?

TICHAUER: No, two pounds. From <u>one</u> kilo of bread, 250 grams.

BODER: Grams.

TICHAUER: Indeed, it constantly changed. One time the bread was for four /people/. Another time it was for five.

BODER: What kind of bread was it?

TICHAUER: It was <u>Wehrmacht</u> /soldier's/ bread.

BODER: Was it baked / a long time/ before?

TICHAUER: It was baked every day. Auschwitz, the men's lager Auschwitz, had a {p. 39/2082} bakery.

BODER: Yes.

TICHAUER: The Auschwitz lager as such was autonomous. The most diverse shops...

BODER: Was there a...a...a gas factory nearby, in the proximity?

TICHAUER: A factory which manufactured <u>these</u> gases?

BODER: A gas factory...

TICHAUER: No. The gas was /came/ in cans and was called Cyclon.

BODER: Yes, now then.

TICHAUER: These cans were seen now and then, because they were also used on occasions of delousing. However, for delousing there was more economy with gas than in gas-killing of people. That we know.

BODER: More economy?

TICHAUER: More economy. Everything was always calculated. But it happened to be sufficient for the lice.

BODER: Yes.

TICHAUER: Now where was I?

BODER: Now. Then...

TICHAUER: Yes. I have decided to mount in plastic /a model of/ the lager Birkenau. And indeed, after three months of this work with another prisoner who /a female/ had assisted me with it, we have presented the lager Birkenau on a surface 2 meters times 80 /centimeters/. Afterwards it was placed under glass and was carried over to the commandant's office, /number/ 2. I still have this plan in my head. Because the construction authority, although they processed at that time the plans in a professional /form/, were always so busy, and the gentlemen of the lager, the lager {p. 40/2083} leader, the report leader, constantly wanted schematic plans. They understood, of course, more readily the schematic plans. And so they came to me, and in this manner they kept me regularly /?/ occupied.

BODER: How did you draw, with India ink, with ink, or...?

TICHAUER: I always provided myself with most necessities. Everything was available, because there came also with the transports draftsmen. There came also artists who were not so lucky to get into the lager, but their things remained, and these were /gathered together/ in one lager. That was the 6th lager Brezinki,[41] near... there was one lager in the midst of all crematories, camouflaged with trees, barracks... where there were barracks which... in which the clothes and everything that the people brought with them was piled up. And precisely from here I fetched the things.

BODER: Now then, where did you go to from Auschwitz?

TICHAUER: There came the 18th of January.

BODER: '45?

TICHAUER: '45. From afar we heard already detonations. We knew exactly those were the Russians. The last crematory blew up in the air, on orders of the SS, because the first four /her speech becomes hesitant/ were by the prisoners themselves, who there... by the special detail /Sonder-commando/, who all the time had to burn the people. The crematory... the crematories were demolished.

BODER: Were they ordered to do so?

TICHAUER: /It/ was ordered from Berlin. The nearer the Russians came, the faster they worked. And on the last day there was no more time. We had to leave, and the crematory blew up in the air.[42] The prisoner...

{p. 41/2084}

BODER: When did they stop gas-killing people?

TICHAUER: They stopped gas-killing people at the end of October, '45.

BODER: '44.

TICHAUER: '44, on orders /from/ Berlin. And the subsequent transports which afterwards...which afterwards arrived, no matter whether children or old people, were not gas-killed anymore. There are still today entire families who had the fortune to come that time and to survive. Mostly Slovakian transports arrived at that time. And the last transports /narrative becomes ambiguous/ where I myself...had little children from my family, were not gas-killed and remained /alive/.

BODER: Now then, did your family survive?

TICHAUER: No. These were just relatives.[43] My...of my own parents I know through people who came afterward /after my own deportation/ to us, with the subsequent transports in the year '43, that they /her family/ were shipped off with the 'family transport' to Lublin. And of this 'family transport' we know for sure that nobody lives. In /from/ Czechoslovakia, that is in /from/ Slovakia, sixty thousand Jews were deported. Of these sixty thousand there are living /a/ hundred fifty men and four hundred fifty girls.

BODER: From Czechoslovakia? How...

TICHAUER: From Slovakia.

BODER: ...do you know these numbers?

TICHAUER: How? Well, all the girls came with me. The Lublin transports did not survive it. And all the other transports came to us. And the count...we of course made daily count reports by nationalities, which I in part...in {p. 42/2085} part had to regis/ter/...to assemble, yes? The count, in the last month the count stood for the girls at four hundred and fifty, the Slovakian /Jewesses/.

BODER: Now tell me, what happened then? The Russians came nearer. The crematory blew up in the air.

TICHAUER: In the air.

BODER: And what happened then to you?

TICHAUER: And the men prisoners and women prisoners were evacuated.

BODER: And you were among them?

TICHAUER: I was among them.

BODER: Where were you evacuated to? How were you evacuated?

TICHAUER: We went in the direction of Wroclaw.[44]

BODER: On foot?

TICHAUER: In . . .

BODER: Men and women together?

TICHAUER: No. Accompanied by SS. About forty thousand prisoners, to estimate, were then shot down, because . . .

BODER: Where?

TICHAUER: On the road. Because we . . .

BODER: Then how many prisoners have left Auschwitz?

TICHAUER: /In an almost casual manner:/ Over /a/ hundred thousand.

BODER: /With astonishment:/ Hundred thousand, at the same time?

TICHAUER: Yes.

BODER: Now . . .

TICHAUER: And we saw dead prisoners right and left. Ahead of us . . . the men who {p. 43/2086} marched ahead of us were, in large part, shot down, and we just passed the / dead/ people. The SS at that time was especially selected for this transport, a large part Folk-Germans, a large part . . .

BODER: Folk-Germans, who were they?

TICHAUER: Folk-Germans. Folk-Germans are all Germans who are not State-Germans, who <u>feel</u> German by nationality, claim to be such, but are not State-Germans.[45]

BODER: Not born in Germany.

TICHAUER: Thus Yugoslav Germans, Sudeten Germans.

BODER: Aha.

TICHAUER: And Ukrainians.

BODER: Germans.

TICHAUER: Who call themselves Germans, and so forth, so forth. Everybody . . .

BODER: And they belonged /?/ to the SS.

TICHAUER: These SS members of . . .

BODER: Yes.

TICHAUER: Folk-Germans were in the large majority worse than all the others. We were chased by them, now north, now south, now east, now west. We could not explain to ourselves the chase here and there, because it was important that we get ahead, because they chased /us/ away from the Russians. But when we were in the one place it was told that the Russians were five kilometers away, so we had to turn south. When we were here, we had to turn north. And so we arrived after a day and night in the city of Wroclaw {Loslau}, Upper Silesia, where we were confined in rr-cars, in open cattle cars in January, one hundred in each /car/.

{P. 44/2087}

BODER: Now, describe the trip.

TICHAUER: The trip proceeded day and night in a way here and there. Just like the march on foot, so the trip by train, without provisions, in a storm, without toilets, with nothing.

BODER: Still, what kind of guard did you have?

TICHAUER: Guarded by the SS. They traveled with us. We traveled. One did not know exactly where to.

BODER: Still, you were not in fact without any food during that time.

TICHAUER: Without food, because there was an order that among about one hundred persons, one hundred women who were located in the one rr-car, two breads and a can of canned food /?/ be distributed. But that was used ... only about fifty per cent of it was distributed, because the SS themselves were hungry.

BODER: Nu.

TICHAUER: We received the first day a thin slice of bread and maybe one hundred grams /3 ½ ounces/ of meat.

BODER: Each one?

TICHAUER: Each one. The rest consisted of snow which we licked, which happened to fall. Later on, near Berlin, the population did not exactly know who we were, so they brought us hot coffee or hot water.

BODER: The population?

TICHAUER: The population. We ourselves traveled in the direction /of/ Oranienburg. And I was quite well acquainted /with the situation/. I knew exactly where the individual concentration camps were still located.

BODER: How did you know that?

{P. 45/2088}

TICHAUER: How? Because we ourselves at the office have sometimes transferred prisoners. Then there came prisoners from one lager to the other. We always calculated where <u>what</u> is located. I knew exactly. If the road leads to Oranienburg, then the road takes us to Ravensbrück. And Ravensbrück was a famous German concentration camp for women. Ravensbrück... I don't know. I wish, before returning to Ravensbrück, still to mention one episode.

BODER: Yes.

TICHAUER: /Slowly:/ There were prisoners in Auschwitz who were assigned for experimental ... for experimental purposes. That means they were forced ...

BODER: /Words not clear, possible: Where?/

TICHAUER: There were ... in the men's lager, in the men's lager. There was one block; that was block <u>ten</u>. Block ten was located near block eleven, the so-called bunker where thousands of executions had taken place, which I could once observe through the crack of some wooden boards.

BODER: For instance?

TICHAUER: It was then ... when we were in Auschwitz it was thus. One could see it. The prisoner was chased out, to the left. Then one heard a report /detonation, shot/. We learned afterwards it was a neck shot /occipital shot/, and to the right one can ... one could see through the crack mountains, piles of warm human corpses. At that time Main Squad Leader Mr. Barich did the shooting.[46] His neighbor /co-worker/ was Mr. Stivitz in block ten.[47] I myself was not there at the time when experiments were performed. Block <u>ten</u> had the purpose of bringing about artificial insemination. Shall I tell/?/?

BODER: Yes.

{P. 46/2089}

TICHAUER: I hope you will be able through personal witnesses to learn something about block 10.

BODER: /Words not clear./

TICHAUER: Now...Ravensbrück. When I arrived in Ravensbrück, I heard something different, and it is correct. Women, mostly Polish, were also placed in an isolation block, from whom then ribs were removed, who were converted into cripples, in order to implant them /the ribs/ in German war wounded.

BODER: Now how can women's ribs /be grafted/ on men?

TICHAUER: It may not have been ribs. It may have been bones, a shin-bone. It would have been another part of the body. At any rate, that is correct.

BODER: Yes.

TICHAUER: However, the women were then not any more released as cripples. Ravensbrück, too, had its crematory. There were also other means to kill a person. There were syringes. There were various other things of which you will learn from other witnesses, possibly from physicians who worked there. Ravensbrück made on me personally the impression like possibly Auschwitz in 1942, cold,[48] disorder, dirt, famine. A chase / pushing around/. They[49] did not know whatever to do with us. We are again transported away to smaller lagers, which were planned for /a/ thousand people. And there came three thousand. One can imagine how the conditions for living and nutrition looked about, up to the day of liberation. Then...

BODER: Where you were liberated from?

TICHAUER: One moment /wait/. On the day of liberation...it was the 3rd of May.

{P. 47/2090}

BODER: /In English:/ This concludes Spool hundred and...hundred and fifty. Miss Elena Tichauer...Miss Elena...Mrs. Elena Tichauer. She started her record...her report on 149, and we are going over to the third...we are going over to the third spool of her report. /End of Spool 150./

BODER: /In English:/ Germany, September the 23rd, 1946. Feldafing Camp, about 30 kilometers or so from Munich, a camp for displaced Jews. Block buildings /?/ on about a 20 acre or so reservation, if we could call it /that/. Full with two-story buildings, now with additional temporary buildings also, in which Hitler Youth was getting its preliminary training. The interviewee is Miss Helena Tichauer, otherwise Zippi genannt /called/, and we are now discussing here the final wandering which so often came through, where...where prisoners of war or concentration camp inhabitants were carried around and chased around /by the Germans/ from one place to the other for some reason . . . so that they should not get into the hands either of the Americans or the Russians. / In German:/ And so where did you come to after these wanderings, Mrs. Tichauer?

TICHAUER: The last lager after Ravensbrück was a small work lager, Meistro/? name not clear, but sounds like: <u>Meistro</u>/.[50] But it did not last long any more, because one week before . . . two weeks before the end of the war the Red Swedish Cross . . . correctly, the Swedish Red Cross sent autobusses and officially removed the prisoners. I don't know /her speech becomes fast and erratic/ what influenced them /the Nazis/, whether the international /word not clear/ was broken.[51] I don't know what motivated them that they altogether set some prisoners free, and that aroused in us a bit of hope. {p. 48/2091} There was . . .

BODER: But you did not get out yet?

TICHAUER: I remained there. There came the first of May. The first of May was celebrated in our heart as the day of freedom. And the first of May we were, indeed evacuated from the lager Meistro /?/. And we knew . . .

BODER: Wait /?/. By whom? By whom were you evacuated?

TICHAUER: By the SS. That was up /north/ in Mecklenburg. And we had an inkling, we knew, that this road may, indeed, lead to freedom, and they /the premonitions?/ did not disappoint us.[52] Behind the city of Goldberg . . .

BODER: How many days were you en route?

TICHAUER: One day and one night.

BODER: Yes. Nu.

TICHAUER: There were on the highway people, soldiers, prisoners, how[53] . . . whatever still had hands and feet /endeavored/ to go in the direction of Lübeck. I personally, together with two girls, made ourselves disappear in the crowd, tore ourselves away. Before /escaping/ we rid our clothes from the red stripe /she says: We removed our clothes from the red stripe/.

BODER: From the red stripe?

TICHAUER: From the red stripe, yes.

BODER: How did you do that?

TICHAUER: I myself . . . I myself as a painter was always 'prepared for it' in painting my stripe not with oil paint but with simple red water color which, however, was adequate, and with a light /word not clear/ brush the stripe could be easily removed. And that, indeed, I did en route. I have . . .

BODER: And your girl friends.

{p. 49/2092}

TICHAUER: As well. We mingled with the crowd. That was not difficult, because there was too big a confusion /?/, too great a state of nervousness /excitement/ among all /of us/, even among the SS. And in the afternoon I found a little farm house lying aside, to be exact, a farm where I saw that the Germans were moving out. That was the German Wehrmacht. And so I went to that farm and went to sleep in a barn. At night . . .

BODER: With whom /were you/?[54]

TICHAUER: With the two girls. But here we found already others roaming /?/ through the fields. That is people who had arrived exactly at the same /idea/. These were mostly French war prisoners, some Russians, even members of the SS who have thrown away their insignia and did not want to continue / with their duties/. There was a conglomeration of people. The night was passed in a barn.

BODER: What were you talking about?

TICHAUER: Talking? There were debates about it. Should we move on? Why then move on? We were driven /chased/ towards the Americans. Why should we not be liberated by the Russians? For us prisoners that should be all the same, whether we are liberated by the Americans or by the Russians, or by the English. We want to be liberated. And it is a pity to give away still our last strength, because we are almost too exhausted to be /able/ to continue ahead, at a running pace. We knew that the day of liberation through the Allied / forces/, no matter by what nation, /will/ be our day, yes? And . . .

BODER: And what did the SS say, the German?

TICHAUER: They have . . . they were ready to remain here and to let themselves be {p. 50/2093} taken prisoners. There were also two Danes, or /maybe/ Dutchman, at any rate from the Northern countries, two tall men who were quite undecided and did not know what to do. They wanted to get away. And with quite strong persuasion I told them that it was not worth-while, because eventually they could be shot by the Germans as well. They remained. And indeed, at night we heard in the forest, in the proximity of the forest, the thunder of cannon. Possibly these were even *Katiushka*. We were, of course...

BODER: What is <u>Katiushka</u>?

TICHAUER: <u>Katiusha</u> /a different form from <u>Katiushka</u>/ is a Russian special weapon.[55] We were women and had no special knowledge, but we reasoned in a way /?/ that on the <u>upper</u>...on the upper {Northern} front the Russians used mainly the *Katiusha*, and at about three or four o'clock /a.m.?/ silence settled in. In the morning we were hungry. There were potatoes in the yard /on the farm/. We boiled for ourselves some potatoes because we were hungry, and all at once we saw a soldier, that is, one in uniform. The Frenchmen /prisoners/ had retained their uniforms. We did not care any more about uniforms, because by now there was a conglomeration of every /kind of people/. And he greeted in Russian, <u>Zdravstvuy</u>.[56] So then I asked him, 'Who are you?' He does not answer me. I noticed...I noticed on his cap the Russian Soviet star.[57] And I ask him, in some manner, in a broken Russian, 'Are you a Russian soldier?' So he answered, 'Yes.' 'And are the Russian here already?' So he says, 'Yes.' 'And are we free?' So he replies, 'Yes.' And there was a Russian detail, an advanced detail /some words not clear. She may be talking about a single soldier/ {p. 51/2094} who looked /?/ around and inspected the whole site and wanted to ascertain what was going on. In about ten minutes appeared on the highway several tanks, horses, marching /?/ soldiers, automobiles, and moved forward /?/. Since they knew that we were prisoners they supplied us with provisions, candy, and the kind.

BODER: Did they have the provisions with them?

TICHAUER: Yes. They had already provisions from...where from I don't know. However, about that they had no qualms /they did not bother about the Germans/. They knew that prisoners were on the road. There were prisoners all along the road. They had no qualms when occupying a city or a village to requisition things and to give them to us. Because the prisoners were half naked, half starved, and were in need of the things. The same night I decided...yes, the same night I decided to go homeward, and one day...

BODER: To Slovakia?

TICHAUER: To Slovakia, correct. It was the third of May. Within a few hours the American and Russian troops decided to meet /?/.

The same night I stopped an automobile which was going back /to a place?/ about two hundred kilometers from the front in order to fetch /something/. There was a Russian captain. I asked him to take us with them.

BODER: All three /of you/.

TICHAUER: All the three. He . . .

BODER: Were these Jewish girls /? the spool becomes very indis-
            tinct for long stretches. Apparently some disturbances in the
            power supply/ . . .

TICHAUER: No. There were two Polish girls present /with me/.

BODER: Yes.

{p. 52/2095}

TICHAUER: He took us as far as the city of Waren, where he let us off and
            brought us food and provided us with lodging.

BODER: /Not clear, but possibly: In a camp?/

TICHAUER: No, a /private/ dwelling. And he told us we should . . . we
            shall rest up for a few hours, and /that/ any automobile had
            orders to accept prisoners and transport them wherever they
            wanted /possibly: if on their way/. We arrived, and there
            were in the city of Waren . . .

BODER: Where is that?

TICHAUER: A German city of Mecklenburg. We met with various prison-
            ers of all nations. For the first time /I/ saw . . . I saw strangely
            uniformed /dressed/ . . . that is newly uniformed who were
            still unknown to me.[58] They had in their formation carts,
            horses, and bundles like all the others. And I asked them who
            they were. And to that they replied they were American
            war prisoners who now, too, were liberated, that they now
            were liberated,[59] and that their aim /destination/ was the
            American zone. And so they asked . . . they asked me about my
            nationality. /Her speech becomes animated and excessively
            rapid./ And I told them /?/ . . . I told them that I was[60] from
            Slovakia. And so they had one . . . one among them whose
            parents years ago had emigrated to America who, too, was
            of Slovakian origin, and even from nearby my home town of
            Bratislava. He was introduced to me, and he still knew a bit
            of broken Czech. We chatted for a while. Then we took
            leave from him and endeavored to get ahead /with our jour-
            ney/. On the road we met a great variety of people, and all
            were nice, and brought us . . . we understood each other, and

they /apparently also the Germans/ helped us wherever / with whatever/ they could. On the 28th of May we arrived home already through {p. 53/2096} Poland.

BODER: Not by train?

TICHAUER: No . . . . by train only from Poland. All the time just however it would happen. Times on horses, times on foot, times by automobile . . . by automobile. To us it was all the same. We wanted /to get/ ahead. We wanted /to get/ home. We knew that we should find nothing at home, but of course the first victory[61] /the spool becomes very noisy and the speech indis- tinct. About two sentences, one Q-n. {question by Boder} and one Tis. {answer by Tichauer} are indistinct./

TICHAUER: I arrived home and right the first day I found my brother, the only one remaining from three. He himself was sentenced to two years in the prison of Bratislava beginning with January '42. Then he was sent to a Jewish distribution camp, from which he fled, and put himself at the services of the parti- sans. A year and a half he spent in the hills. He survived, and we found each other on the 27th of May /possibly a slight inconsistency in the dates/, the only one who returned.

BODER: Did you return to your apartment? What did you find there?

TICHAUER: The apartment was for a long time rented /to others/.[62] We did not possess much before the war, and . . .

BODER: What was the occupation of your parents?

TICHAUER: My father was a master tailor. The possessions which I left behind in clothes and sundry things were taken by my mother—she was my second mother—my master, my teacher, that is my boss for whom I last worked . . .

BODER: As what did you work there?

TICHAUER: As letter painter. There was no argument /?/, because he who saved my things for three and a half years brought them back to me and returned {p. 54/2097} them to me, without demands on my part.[63] I came . . .

BODER: He was of course, a Christian? A . . .

TICHAUER: He is a Czech.

BODER: Yes.

TICHAUER: I came home without shoes /?/. I came home without clothes. The only thing that I brought with me from Germany was a map and a.../word not clear, but sounds like: my sorrows/.

BODER: Nu...of how many people did your family consist?

TICHAUER: My family consisted of father, mother, and three brothers. One of the brothers I found.

BODER: And what did he say about the others?

TICHAUER: He could not know anything, since he was there behind bars. But I know, through reports of others, that my parents...eye witnesses who saw my parents transported away, in July of '42. And that the transports are not alive /?/.[64]

BODER: And the two brothers?

TICHAUER: The two brothers went with them. One was fourteen. The other was[65]...the one brother /pause/...

BODER: The one who you found?

TICHAUER: The oldest one.

BODER: Now, you were...you had two brothers.

TICHAUER: Three.

BODER: Three brothers. And the third brother?

TICHAUER: Two went with the parents to Lublin.

BODER: Yes. And the...the one who survived is the third,

{P. 55/2098}

TICHAUER: That is the third, and he came back.

BODER: With what partisans was he?

TICHAUER: He was in...with the Slovakian partisans, with the Slovakian forces /?/ of Mikolash /?/.

BODER: Mrs. Tichauer, could you possibly tell me about some more details, about the life in the lager or other events which you actually have witnessed or experienced by way of proximity?

TICHAUER: Well, about the life in the lager I can certainly tell you, because I lived in the midst of it. But about particular impressions or particular atrocities, so to speak, which possibly happened, which I still have experienced, about these / words not clear/.

BODER: Well, it is... Well then, tell me what you still have to tell.

TICHAUER: What I, for instance, am unable to forget is the fire by day and night. Four hearths /ovens/...

BODER: Four chimneys?

TICHAUER: Four chimneys were day...

BODER: Speak louder /?/[66]

TICHAUER: ...were active day and night. And the pits which were installed in the year 1944 when again Hungarian transports were arriving, not /word not clear/ transports[67] were arriving, rendered a sight which does not yield to description, because one imagined himself in a living hell. One was encircled all round by fire. Our own lager... at our lager there was just wire fence, and thirty meters beyond was the crematory /number/ two. And so it was not far. And one could see if he <u>wanted</u> to see. There were cases when one could see people stride in on automobiles or even on foot, {p. 56/2099} and a few minutes later one saw naked corpses being carried out on litters from the bunkers. And what could one think about it / on such an instant/? One saw fire and smoke. One saw among the silhouette little figures, children—those must have been children—in pits. One saw only...one could...one can imagine how in the devil.../corrects herself/ how in hell the devils treated their sacrifices /burned offerings/.

BODER: Now tell me this. You worked in the office as a clerk.

TICHAUER: Yes.

BODER: Did you hear anything about the Gypsies?

TICHAUER: Of course.

BODER: Now then, please tell me about it as extensively /with as many details/ as...

TICHAUER: Even most extensively...

BODER: Yes.

TICHAUER: The Gypsy lager, the so-called Gypsy lager, was established in the year '43. From...known from...from sources...from certain sources why actually Gypsies were brought to Auschwitz, from reliable sources, I may say the following. Hungary, the land which retained its Jews up to the year '44, had possibly no interest...well, it just did not hand over the Jews. And Germany did not know by what means to 'obtain' the Hungarian Jews. In the year '43, at the beginning of '43, I was told . . . I was told by a /woman/ employee who worked close to the lager leader that she has heard some whispers. That was Mrs. Wagener. That now Gypsies from Hungary will be brought in, not only Gypsies from Hungary, but Gypsies of all over Europe,[68] in order to assemble them here, and afterwards to hand them {p. 57/2100} over to Hungary, because in Hungary supposedly Gypsies are living in large numbers, but that in exchange Hungary should hand over to us /to Germany/ the Jews. At that time that was rather unclear, because nobody knew about it. I myself had the opportunity . . . not only I. Then there were months when it was officially permitted to write home. I directed one card /post card/ to a friend /woman/ who had relatives in Hungary. Through the flower /through metaphoric, disguised wording/, they understood that Hungarian Jews are to be expected. At the beginning of '43, that is, in the middle of '43, I had written about it, not officially, but of course through the flower.

BODER: What does that mean, 'through the flower'?

TICHAUER: I for example . . . for example . . . I really don't have to use the /hypothetical / example, because the mail that I had sent home is now at my brother's. I wrote for example thus / here follows a mixture of German with Hungarian/. The friend's name was Grete /?/. At home she was called /name not clear/.[69] I am /called/ Ilonka in Hungarian. So I wrote thus: 'Gitti /?/ that is Ilonka's friend, Gitti has relatives in Shuran.'[70] Shuran is a Hungarian town. 'I have heard that they have the intention to join Ilonka. I would disadvise you to do so, because you have no chance to live there.' I could not write to her differently.

BODER: Yes.

TICHAUER: But she knew exactly that I was Ilonka, she was Gitti /?/, and Shuranians are Hungarians, Hungarian Jews. No man, no devil could then imagine that there was indeed the intention to bring over the Hungarian Jews. But fate came to be thus. Hungarian Jews came without Gypsies {p. 58/2101} /in return/. Then Hitler had occupied Hungary and took / the/ Jews by force, that is, they were forcibly taken, and the Gypsies, German Gypsies, half-breed Gypsies, Gypsies from Poland, from Czechoslovakia, from all other countries . . . I don't intend . . . I do not speak now /only/ of the roaming Gypsies, but also of the settled Gypsies, about the educated people /Gypsies/ of the half-breeds.

BODER: Educated /?/ for what? /Sentence not clear./

TICHAUER: Office workers, trained musicians, completely intelligent elements, that is, real /worthwhile/ people, who possibly have served mankind a great deal and still could serve, were now lodged in the Gypsy lager with /their/ families.

BODER: They lived /there/ women, men, and children together?

TICHAUER: Correct. And the Gypsy lager was the sector B2E. The layout was thus: S- /word not clear/[71] was the women's lager. That was located horizontally, and along the street were located sector A, that was the quarantine lager for the men, B sector 2, that was the former Czech lager—about this a great deal also could be said—sector C there followed the lager street, a street. Sector D was the men's lager Birkenau, Sector E the Gypsy lager, sector F the men's sick-building, sector B2G ...

BODER: Well ...

TICHAUER: ... was Brzezinki /Birkenau/ the lager in /at/ the crematory. The Gypsies had witnessed the procession of all the Jewish transports into the crematory. They witnessed the burning. They were located within about 200 meters. And when they were invited /ordered/ to mount the trucks ...

BODER: How come? Was it decided to annihilate the Gypsies?

{P. 59/2102}

TICHAUER: Berlin had decided to annihilate the Gypsies. Thus, young Gypsies were assembled. They were embarked in rr-cars in front of the Gypsy lager. The rails were laid up to the crematory. And the Gypsies saw that their relatives were journeying in the opposite direction. And indeed these women Gypsies I happened to meet again in the year '45 in Ravensbrück. But what happened to the others, that nobody knew, because the young were transported away, young men, too, but only a percentage /fraction/ of them, a small percentage, and young women. And the rest were invited /ordered/ to mount the automobiles /trucks/. They hesitated /were unwilling/ and replied, 'We don't want to be burned with the Jews.' They were given peace /were let alone/ for about two, three weeks. And then they were deceived /she uses a makeshift verb; sounds like: reduced/[72] by the /manner of/ transport of the young people. On the same day when the young Gypsies were loaded in the rr-cars and sent off in the direction of the rr-station Auschwitz, that is, in the opposite direction of the crematory, the old Gypsies then regained a bit of hope, and said that they too will be shipped away ... but the transport went to the crematory. And what happened that night /she chokes with tears/,[73] about that was told by the prisoners who worked in 2B, that is, in the lager of Brzezinki. Frightful scenes took place there. A day later the lager, the Gypsy lager, was empty, and the following Hungarian Jew transports of men who arrived were lodged in that lager. /See the story of Kaletzka-Kovitzka, Volume II, Ch. IV, pp. 245–275; also in *I Did Not Interview the Dead*, pp. 1–25./

BODER: Now, it is true that the Gypsies were not even gas-killed?

TICHAUER: Still, why not? The Germans had no interest to make their labor {p. 60/2103} more difficult. On the contrary, indeed. The gas-killing proceeded with great courtesy. The SS were comparatively courteous and calm /?/, because they did not want that confusion should occur. They wanted that the people.../they/ treated the people with calm /or: they calmed the people/, and the like, because they themselves did not want to be disturbed in their work. They enticed the people /into the gas chambers/ in the most crafty /perfidious/ manner. And since we are talking about the Gypsy lager...not far from the Gypsy lager was also located the Czech lager, the lager[74] consisting of Czech Jews, who 'automatically' were sent with their families from Theresienstadt.

BODER: Why...

TICHAUER: Theresienstadt. /See Schlaefrig, Volume VII, Ch. XXVI, pp. 1135–1204./

BODER: I know about Theresienstadt.

TICHAUER: Theresienstadt had transports /sent to/ Auschwitz. Then...it was said that nothing happens to the people in Auschwitz. They were kept together with their families. They could write letters. They could send packages. And what happened after six months? Exactly after six months it happened so with the first, the second, and the successively following transports. When the six months were over, there...For example, of a transport the 19th of February the whole Czech lager was, without exception, young and old, well and sick, were gas-killed. One day before...

BODER: February '44?

TICHAUER: '44. For example, a day before they were compelled to write to Theresienstadt, in general to Bohemia and Moravia, with a date one month {p. 61/2104} ahead, and when London immediately reported /over the radio/ the gas-killing of Theresienstadt.../corrects herself/ the Czech lager in Birkenau...

BODER: What did they...

TICHAUER: London reported /broadcast/. The Germans denied it /say-
            ing, 'How come? The mail has arrived a month later still from
            Birkenau to their acquaintances, to their relatives, from those
            whom you consider dead.'

BODER: They had to date it /the mail/ a month ahead?

TICHAUER: They had to. Correct. One month ahead.

BODER: Yes, yes.

TICHAUER: If they were gas-killed in February, they were compelled to
            write *March*.

BODER: Yes.

TICHAUER: And because of that the Jews of Theresienstadt were deceived
            /she uses the word <u>irritiert</u> apparently falsely assuming a der-
            ivation from <u>Irre</u>/. There came further transports. They were
            again permitted to stay together with their families for six
            months, /and were/ again gas-killed. And the last... /with/
            the last transports there came from Theresienstadt in part,
            young girls, already sorted out in Theresienstadt. Of those
            some are today alive, and the final transport was treated com-
            pletely 'normally,' just like the others. Of these /two words
            not clear/ transports 90 per cent, too, were sent into the gas,
            and 10 per cent went into the lager.

BODER: Hm.

TICHAUER: Such was the end of Theresienstadt /she either means the end
            of the prisoners sent from the Theresienstadt to Birkenau, or
            lacks complete {p. 62/2105} information; again see Schlae-
            frig, Volume VII, Ch. XXVI, pp. 1135–1204/. I personally,
            in collaboration with a Mr. Schoehn,[75] who was already for
            years in the concentration camp, a Czech prisoner, in cooper-
            ation with a /several words not clear/[76] Czech woman Lotte
            Batja, a Czech Jewess,[77] we have smuggled out plans /?/ of
            the crematory to Theresienstadt, so that people should come
            afterward would know where... where the road leads to.

BODER: Now then, you say that you have sent to the transports 'infor-
            mation'... to Theresien/stadt/.

TICHAUER: Sent information. /The spool becomes indistinct; her voice
            fades./ Unfortunately the leadership in Theresienstadt has
            incriminated itself very, very /much/.

BODER: The Jewish leadership?

TICHAUER: As well. They were afraid for themselves. Because after-
            wards I met a gentleman who came from Theresienstadt,
            and who knew much about Theresienstadt. That was a Doc-
            tor Vollmeier[78] who only heard something whispering, but
            could not learn much more. He was.../about 8 words not
            clear/. And to prove that these transports actually went to
            the gas /chambers/ I can only refer /? to the fact/ that I had
            to prepare the diagrams, yes? And if just from one day to
            the other the population would fall by the thousands, went
            away in transports...there always went transports from /
            this/ lager to a work lager.

BODER: /Not clear./

TICHAUER: /One word answer not clear./ And besides, the fact that
            one sole prisoner got out of the transport, that was /I/, the
            draftswoman for Dr. Mengele[79]...or there were twins.
            There were twins who were saved, because Dr. {p. 63/2106}
            Mengele studied /did research on/ various pairs of twins,
            etc. And still in connection with this /her narrative becomes
            syntactically almost incoherent/, with the deception about
            work transports and transports of others to the gas /cham-
            bers/, I want to mention still a little event. One evening
            there were transferred to us from the isolators...from the
            isolation lager[80]...two thousand women. All of the two
            thousand were bathed, dressed and prepared for...prepared
            for transport. We in the office knew that only one thousand
            women were to be transported to a work lager, because we
            had written off at our appell this force /number/ until the
            lager reported that the transport was ready. The other two
            /?/ thousand were marked as 'SB treatment.'

BODER: Sonder Behandlung /special treatment/...

TICHAUER: Sonder Behandlung. And how actually proceeded the trans-
            port and the deception? Thus: There stood before, the lager
            rr-cars. And there stood trucks behind the rr-cars. First there
            stepped out one hundred girls. It was evening. They were
            driven into the rr-cars. The next hundred on trucks, the third
            hundred in to the rr-cars, the next, the fourth hundred, on
            the truck.

BODER: Where stood the truck?

TICHAUER: Behind the rr-car, parallel.

BODER: So that...

TICHAUER: So that the prisoners in the rr-cars did not know where the
            autos were going, and those in the autos did not know where
            the rr-cars were going, and...

BODER: But they did not have to go through the rr-cars.

{P. 64/2107}

TICHAUER: No. Two /rr-cars/ were disconnected and there was a free passage. And then it started. The rr-cars went actually 'to transport' into another lager, and the other thousand were gas-killed. First, the same clothes came back, and second, we had to check-mark: <u>Sonder Behandlung</u>. So, one never knew how he stands. Never. /Pause./

BODER: Well. Now tell me what kind of, so to speak, home /shelter/ or lager do you have here. Give me a brief description. What do the people have to do here /occupy themselves with/?

TICHAUER: Camp Feldafing is a lager which right after the liberation / was founded/ by Lieutenant Smith.[81]

BODER: Now is that the UNRRA?[82]

TICHAUER: No, at that time still by Lieutenant Smith, /from/ the army which had conquered the lager, that means, which had conquered the region. This lager was seized by the Lieutenant, because he was a witness that thousands of prisoners stood half starved in rr-cars, without knowing where to /what next/. This here is a former state school of the Hitler Youth. The lager here was seized, the people /prisoners/ relieved from their clothes, /placed/ in requisitioned . . .

BODER: What kind of . . . from their prisoners . . .

TICHAUER: Relieved of their prisoner's clothing. That is these were taken away and /people were/ clothed in pajamas. The Lieutenant Smith . . .

BODER: Where did they get the pajamas?

TICHAUER: The pajamas were found here in the lager.

BODER: Oh, from the Hitler /Youth/?

TICHAUER: Correct. Lieutenant Smith quickly created a block for the under- {p. 65/2108}nourished. That is mostly . . . everybody was undernourished.

BODER: You, of course, were not here?

TICHAUER: I was not here, because I . . . When I returned home, my first wish was to come here /?/ and to search for the rest of my family. And I found nobody here, but for my husband whose acquaintance I made here.

BODER: Now then, what did Smith do?

TICHAUER: Smith started /feeding/ the people very gradually. That is, he proceeded with the nourishment of the people gradually, starting with gruel and ending with the most solid things /foods/. The nourishment stood under control. The people were starved, were undernourished, and it was difficult to get the people back on their feet.

BODER: So you were from the south, and other regions...

TICHAUER: Assembled and lodged here.

BODER: Who actually was Lieutenant Smith?

TICHAUER: In the army.

BODER: But... but a...

TICHAUER: A Jew.

BODER: Yes.

TICHAUER: An American Jew.

BODER: Do you know his first name?

TICHAUER: Yes. Irving.

BODER: Irving.

TICHAUER: Irving Smith.

BODER: Yes.

TICHAUER: When the army... and the lager Feldafing was at the time the only {p. 66/2109} lager with the least cases of death. Day and night, in cooperation with my present husband and others as well, he worked day and night for the good of the people here. The people became... after weeks they recuperated, and as said /before/, Feldafing had the smallest death [rate] among all other camps which were then installed. Meanwhile a year has passed. Afterward the UNRRA took over the lager.

BODER: Now how was the lager maintained until UNRRA?

TICHAUER: Through the army.

BODER: Through the army /word not clear/.

TICHAUER: Yes.

BODER: And then the UNRRA took over.

TICHAUER: UNRRA took over. And the people, in spite of maintenance, in spite of lodging, in spite of everything, are already very impatient, because everyone has only one single aim in view, to leave the country which once was hell for him.

BODER: And where do they want to go?

TICHAUER: Go? They have one aim. Out of Europe. In part...

BODER: Are there many[83] who want to go to Palestine?

TICHAUER: Of course. There are people, young...mainly youth, who want to readjust, want to learn, and who /would/ feel at home, let us say, in a national Jewish State. Mostly the youth.

BODER: Hm.

TICHAUER: There is also a part of Jews who have a relative in America and have lost their whole European family and are assembling now the rest of such a family who want to spend their life with them. Also with the intention to {p. 67/2110} learn near them a trade, to re-adjust, free...as free workers...free workers...in an American state /country/, so as to live...

BODER: Tell me, do you have any contacts with the Germans around here?

TICHAUER: /Hesitantly:/ Contact with the Germans? No. Actually no, because the Germans of Upper Bavaria have no desire /interest/ to establish a contact with us. They have no intention whatsoever to feel in some way guilty, although we know exactly that Upper Bavaria <u>has</u> very few people, /they/ have very few relatives who were /? were not?/ in /belonged to/ the /Nazi/ Party. Upper Bavaria was the center of Party conventions. We have Nuremberg.[84] We have Munich.

BODER: That is <u>they were</u> all in the Party?

TICHAUER: To a large extent. And I can say only one thing. The German population in other lands /states/ of Germany behaves completely different.

BODER: Better?

TICHAUER: Better than the Upper Bavarian /?/ population. And precisely for that reason one cannot demand from our people that we should have any sympathy...

BODER: /Two words not clear./

TICHAUER: ...or should establish any contact with those people. We understand. There are children, innocent German children, who are as innocent as were our children, who also /the following words are not clear due to the affective tone of voice/ who also perished /?/ in multitudes. And ...even have composed a song about it. All hatred must be brought about / cultivated/,[85] but we experience no hatred whatsoever. But we feel that we are actually still hated. Still hated!

{p. 68/2111}

BODER: Now, and you yourself, where do you want to go?

TICHAUER: I myself /here follows a brief silence on a wire, 4 to 5 seconds, possibly due to failure of equipment/ ...

BODER: With your husband?

TICHAUER: By myself. Not with my husband, who actually comes from /is originally from /Berlin, /and/ is a German Jew, but considers himself now actually stateless. I presume, had I not found this man, I should have liked to live in Czechoslovakia, would have liked to live there very much, because I felt there always very well /I used to be always very happy there/. I know that nation. I feel a bond with Czechoslovakia.

BODER: Otherwise you want to go to South America.

TICHAUER: Otherwise /a few words not clear/. Otherwise ...

BODER: Yes.

TICHAUER: For the reason that my husband has the rest of his family in South America. In Germany we shall never feel well. In this country there is nothing /?/ for us[86] ...

BODER: /In English:/ We regret to have to finish the interview.[87] This concludes Spool hundred and fifty-/one/ ...

/*Note:* February 23rd, 1956. The wire apparently has run out in the middle of the sentence/.

| NOTES |

INTRODUCTION

1. Her birth certificate identifies her as Helene Spitzer; in Slovak her name was Helena Spitzerova. Her Jewish first name, Zipora, served as the basis for her nickname, Zippi, by which she was known in Auschwitz and later in Feldafing (telephone conversation with Helen Tichauer, April 4, 2007). Throughout this book and in accordance with her preferences, the authors use both names, Helen and Zippi, interchangeably. The introduction and the conclusion to this book represent a collective effort by its authors; the responsibility for errors and omissions is with the volume editor.

2. From a rapidly growing literature, see Lawrence L. Langer, *Holocaust Testimonies: The Ruins of Memory* (New Haven, Conn.: Yale University Press, 1991); Dominick LaCapra, *Representing the Holocaust: History, Theory, Trauma* (Ithaca, N.Y.: Cornell University Press, 1994); LaCapra, *History and Memory after Auschwitz* (Ithaca, N.Y.: Cornell University Press, 1998); Geoffrey H. Hartman, ed., *Holocaust Remembrance: The Shapes of Memory* (Oxford: Blackwell, 1995); Henry Greenspan, *On Listening to Holocaust Survivors: Recounting and Life History* (Westport, Conn.: Praeger, 1998); Annette Wieviorka, *The Era of Witness* (Ithaca, N.Y.: Cornell University Press, 2006).

CHAPTER 1

1. Telephone conversation with Helen Tichauer (subsequently: HT), May 15, 2007. I thank my wife, Jane Sydenham-Kwiet, for her translation work, encouragement, and advice; my friend and colleague Lucy Davey for her invaluable support; Stephen Tyas for his help with background research; my long-standing and close friend Jürgen Matthäus for guiding me through the process of writing this essay; and Helen Tichauer for her unflinching eagerness to share her memories.

2. HT, February 9, 2007.

3. See the contribution by Jürgen Matthäus to this volume.

4. HT, December 6, 2007; May 5, 2007.

5. HT, January 6, 2008.

6. For more background on Helen Tichauer's upbringing, see the contribution to this volume by Nechama Tec.

7. See Richard Newman and Karen Kirtley, *Alma Rosé: Vienna to Auschwitz* (Portland, OR: Amadeus Press, 2000).

8. HT January 2 and 5, 2008.

9. See the English translation of Helen Tichauer's interview with David Boder in the appendix to this volume (interview minute 102).

10. See Yehuda Bauer, *Rethinking the Holocaust* (New Haven, Conn.: Yale University Press, 2001), 186–196. For other rabbinical and theological responses to the Holocaust, see Steven T. Katz, Shlomo Biderman, and Gershon Greenberg, eds., *Wrestling with God: Jewish Theological Responses to the Holocaust during and after the Holocaust* (New York: Oxford University Press, 2007); Esther Farbstein, *Hidden in Thunder: Perspectives on Faith, Halachah and Leadership during the Holocaust*, 2 vols. (Jerusalem: Mossad Harav Kook, 2007); David G. Roskies, *The Literature of Destruction: Jewish Responses to Catastrophe* (Philadelphia: Jewish Publication Society, 1988), 381ff.

11. Gershon Greenberg, "Ultra-Orthodox Reflections on the Holocaust: 1945 to the Present," in Konrad Kwiet and Jürgen Matthäus, eds., *Contemporary Responses to the Holocaust* (Westport, Conn.: Praeger, 2004), 93–94.

12. HT, September 9, 2007.

13. HT, February 2, 2006; October 6, 2006; July 30, 2008.

14. See Livia Rothkirchen, "The Situation of Jews in Slovakia between 1939 and 1945," in Wolfgang Benz, ed., *Jahrbuch für Antisemitismusforschung* 7 (Frankfurt am Main: Campus, 1992), 46–70.

15. See Eduard Nižňanský, *Z dejín Holokaustu a jeho popierania* (Bratislava: Stimul, 2007) (in Slovak, with articles in German and English). On the German-Slovak relationship during the war, see Tatjana Tönsmeyer, *Das Dritte Reich und die Slowakei, 1939–1945: Politischer Alltag zwischen Kooperation und Eigensinn* (Paderborn: Schöningh, 2003).

16. Helen Tichauer, "Ladies First," *Voice of the Woman Survivor* 6, no. 2 (1989): 1.

17. See the contribution to this volume by Nechama Tec.

18. From the massive amount of literature on Auschwitz, see Yisrael Gutman and Michael Berenbaum, eds., *Anatomy of the Auschwitz Death Camp* (Bloomington: Indiana University Press, 1994); Sybille Steinbacher, *Auschwitz: A History* (London: Penguin, 2005).

On the early Slovakian transports, see Yoshua R. Büchler, "First in the Vale of Affliction: Slovakian Jewish Women in Auschwitz, 1942," *Holocaust and Genocide Studies* 10 (1996): 229–325.

19. HT, September 15, 2005; April 20, 2006; October 7, 2006; October 14, 2006.

20. See Franciszek Brol, Gerard Wloch, and Jan Pilecki, "Das Bunkerbuch des Blocks 11 im Nazi Konzentrationslager Auschwitz," *Hefte von Auschwitz* 1 (1959): 7–85.

21. See her interview with David Boder (appendix to this volume).

22. HT, January 10 and 11, 2008.

23. HT, April 20, 2006; May 28, 2008.

24. See Nechama Tec, *Resilience and Courage: Women, Men, and the Holocaust* (New Haven, Conn.: Yale University Press, 2003), 168–169.

25. See Lore Shelley, ed., *Secretaries of Death: Accounts by Former Prisoners Who Worked in the Gestapo of Auschwitz* (New York: Shengold Publishers, 1986).

26. HT, November 12, 2005.

27. HT, October 26, 2007.

28. See Michael Berkowitz, *The Crime of My Very Existence: Nazism and the Myth of Jewish Criminality* (Berkeley and Los Angeles: University of California Press, 2007), 83; Konrad Kwiet and Helmut Eschwege, *Selbstbehauptung und Widerstand. Deutsche Juden im Kampf um Existenz und Würde* (Hamburg: Christians, 1986), 272.

29. Tadeusz Iwaszko, "Deportation to the Camp and Registration of Prisoners," in Franciszek Piper and Teresa Swiebocka, eds., *Auschwitz: Nazi Death Camp* (Oswiecim: Auschwitz-Birkenau State Museum, 2004), 54–69.

30. HT, April 5, 2007.

31. Teresa Swiebocka, *The Architecture of Crime: The Central Camp Sauna in Auschwitz-Birkenau* (Oswiecim: Auschwitz-Birkenau State Museum, 2001).

32. HT, October 20, 2005; November 11, 2005; June 15, 2007. Sokolov survived Auschwitz and migrated to Australia in 1949. He lived in Melbourne and died in 2007; see Angie Fox, "The Auschwitz Tattooist," *Australian Jewish News*, December 19, 2003, 17.

33. See Helen Kubica, "Children and Youth at KL Auschwitz," in Piper and Swiebocka, *Auschwitz*, 123–139.

34. HT, July 6, 2007; December 6, 2007.

35. HT, October 20, 2005; April 7, 2007; April 8, 2007; March 3, 2006.

36. HT, October 20, 2005.

37. HT, April 20, 2006.

38. HT, October 20, 2005.

39. See Hans-Jürgen Hahn, ed., *Gesichter der Juden in Auschwitz: Lili Meiers Album* (Berlin: Verlag Das Arsenal 1995), 172–174.

40. See Lucyna Filip, "Frauen im KL Auschwitz: Opfer und Täter," in *Auschwitz Information* 61 (2003), 4–12.

41. HT, March 31, 2006; April 24, 2006; February 8, 2008.

42. HT, October 12, 2007.

43. Steinbacher, *Auschwitz*, 36.

44. HT, November 20, 2007; see also Boder, *Topical Autobiographies*, 2081.

45. HT, September 20, 2007; February 12, 2006.

46. HT, February 10, 2008.

47. HT, February 9, 2008.

48. HT, November 20, 2005.

49. HT, November 20 and 22, 2005.

50. HT, September 20, 2007; February 10, 2008.

51. Eugen Kogon, *The Theory and Practice of Hell: The German Concentration Camps and the System behind Them* (1950; New York: Farrar, Straus and Giroux, 2006), 312–313.

52. See Piper and Swiebocka, *Auschwitz*, 302, 308; Filip, "Frauen im KL Auschwitz," 4–12.

53. Daniel Patrick Brown, *The Beautiful Beast: The Life and Crimes of SS-Aufseherin Irma Grese* (Ventura, CA: Golden West Historical Publications, 1996); Brown, *Camp Women: The Female Auxiliaries Who Assisted the SS in Running the Nazi Concentration Camps* (Atglen: Schiffer, 2002).

54. Irmtrud Wojak, ed., *Auschwitz Prozess 4Ks 2/63 Frankfurt am Main* (Cologne: Snoeck, 2004); HT, February 7, 2008. I thank Dr. Irmtrud Wojak for this information and further biographical data on the career of Josef Erber, who died in 1987.

55. HT, April 4, 2006. I found Zippi's affidavit, dated February 1, 1971, at the Bundesarchiv Ludwigsburg, B 162/9441 (409 AR-Z 55/1971), pp. 520–525.

56. See Shelley, *Secretaries of Death*; Shelley, *Auschwitz: The Nazi Civilization* (Lanham, Md.: University Press of America, 1992).

57. HT, September 9, 2007; October, 12, 2007; November 11, 2007; November 30, 2007.

58. Franciszek Piper, "The Number of Victims at KL Auschwitz," in Piper and Swiebocka, *Auschwitz*, 190.

59. HT, September 29, 2007.

60. See the account given by Vera Plaskura, in Shelley, *Auschwitz*, 21.

61. Examples of these cards are published in Piper and Swiebocka, *Auschwitz*, 32–33.

62. These claims have been made by Edwin Black in his *IBM and the Holocaust* (New York: Random House, 2001), 351–352, a controversial book.

63. HT, April 19, 2007.

64. HT, October 19, 2007; February 17, 2008.

65. HT, October 19, 2007; February 2, 2008.

66. HT, February 9, 2008.

67. See Boder, *Topical Autobiographies*, p. 2080; HT April 19, 2007; and the appendix to this volume.

68. See Steinbacher, *Auschwitz*; Gutman and Berenbaum, *Anatomy*; Deborah Dwork and Robert Jan van Pelt, *Auschwitz: 1270 to the Present* (New York: Norton, 1996); Lawrence Rees, *Auschwitz: A New History* (New York: Public Affairs, 2005).

69. HT, September 10, 2007.

70. HT, March 23, 2008.

71. HT, April 20, 2006; October 27, 2006; November 10, 2006; November 30, 2007.

72. See the contribution to this volume by Atina Grossmann.

73. See Suzanne Rutland, *Edge of the Diaspora: Two Centuries of Jewish Settlement in Australia* (Sydney: Brandl and Schlesinger, 2001); Rutland, *The Jews in Australia* (Melbourne: Cambridge University Press, 2005).

74. HT, February 23, 2006; November 10, 2006; March 24, 2007.

75. HT, March 27, 2008.

76. Raul Hilberg, *The Politics of Memory: The Journey of a Holocaust Historian* (Chicago: Ivan R. Dee, 1996), 83.

CHAPTER 2

1. From now on whenever I quote without footnoting, the statements come from Helen Spitzer-Tichauer, known as Zippi. I obtained this information from Zippi through two lengthy interviews, which I conducted in her apartment in New York City. I have collected the bulk of the information through our telephone conversations, which began in 1997 and have continued to the present. When talking to Zippi, I would return to the same issues over and over again, trying to make sure that I understood her explanations. In this essay, I have tried to stay as closely as I could to what Zippi told me. However, I am reluctant to present all my quotes as verbatim transcriptions.

2. Nechama Tec, *Resilience and Courage: Women, Men, and the Holocaust* (New Haven, Conn.: Yale University Press, 2003), 10.

3. Rafi Benshalom, *We Struggled for Life: The Hungarian Zionist Youth Resistance during the Nazi Era* (Jerusalem: Gefen, 2001); Adina Kochba, "The 'Hehalutz' Underground in Holland during the Nazi Occupation," in Zvi Shner, ed., *Extermination and Resistance: Historical Records and Source Material* (Haifa: Ghetto Fighters' House, 1958), 129–139.

4. Michael Berenbaum, "Preface," in Yisrael Gutman and Michael Berenbaum, eds., *Anatomy of the Auschwitz Death Camp* (Bloomington: Indiana University Press, 1994), vii; Shmuel Krakowski, "The Satellite Camps," in ibid., 50–60.

5. Wolfgang Sofsky, *The Order of Terror: The Concentration Camp* (Princeton, N.J.: Princeton University Press, 1997), 5.

6. Yehuda Bauer, "Discussion," in Yisrael Gutman and Avital Saf, eds., *The Nazi Concentration Camps* (Jerusalem: Yad Vashem, 1984), 38–39.

7. The literature contains many examples of women who were traumatized by the head-shaving ceremony. A particularly devastating reaction is offered by Ruth Nebel, "The Story of Ruth," in Renate Bridenthal, Atina Grossmann, and Marion Kaplan., eds., *When Biology Became Destiny: Women in Weimar and Nazi Germany* (New York: Monthly Review Press, 1984), 343.

8. U.S. Holocaust Memorial Museum Archive (subsequently: USHMMA) RG-50.472, spools 9–149 to 150, interview David Boder with Helen Tichauer, September 1946; see the appendix to this volume for the English translation of the interview.

9. Ian Kershaw, *Hitler, 1936–1945: Nemesis* (New York: Norton, 2000), 129–153.

10. Interview with Anna Palarczyk, USHMMA, RG-50.030*0376, tape 1. See also Walter Laqueur, "Foreword," in Danuta Czech, *Auschwitz Chronicle 1939–1945* (New York: Holt, 1997), xv–xxi. He estimates that 13,000 Soviet POWs were brought into Auschwitz, and only 92 were alive when the camp was shut down.

11. Tec, *Resilience and Courage*, 161–162; Nechama Tec, "Jewish Children: Between Protectors and Murderers," (Washington, D.C.: USHMM Occasional Paper, 2005), 1–22.

12. Tec, *Resilience and Courage*, 175.

13. USHMMA, RG-50.0300*0446, tape 2 (of 5), joint interview with Palarczyk and Tichauer.

14. Ibid.

15. Ibid.; Józef Garliński, *Fighting Auschwitz: The Resistance Movement in the Concentration Camp* (Greenwich, Conn.: Fawcett, 1975), 157.

16. USHMMA, RG-50.0300*0446, tape 2, interview with Palarczyk and Tichauer.

17. Member of the Bund (abbreviation of *Algemeyner Yidisher Arbeter Bund in Lite, Poyln un Rusland* [General Jewish Workers' Union in Lithuania, Poland and Russia]), Jewish socialist party founded in Russia in 1897; see Moshe Mishkinsky, "Bund," in Michael Berenbaum and Fred Skolnik, eds., *Encyclopaedia Judaica*, 2nd ed. (Detroit: Macmillan Reference, 2007), 4:278–284.

18. For a brief discussion of this revolt, see Czech, *Auschwitz Chronicle*, 724–726.

19. The execution of the four Jewish women (Ella Gartner, Roza Robota, Regina Safir, and Estera Wajsblum) is described in ibid., 775.

Chapter 3

1. Telephone conversation with Helen Tichauer (subsequently: HT), October 26, 2006.

2. For analyses of interviews and changes in their recounting over time, see Henry Greenspan, *On Listening to Holocaust Survivors: Recounting and Life History* (Westport, Conn.: Praeger, 1998); Greenspan, *The Awakening of Memory: Survivor Testimony in the First Years after the Holocaust and Today* (Washington, D.C.: USHMM occasional paper, 2001). Also Lawrence L. Langer, *Holocaust Testimonies: The Ruins of Memory* (New Haven, Conn.: Yale University Press, 1991); Geoffrey Hartman, ed., *Holocaust Remembrance: The Shapes of Memory* (Oxford: Blackwell, 1995).

3. See Greenspan, *Awakening of Memory*; Annette Wieviorka, "On Testimony," in Hartman, *Holocaust Remembrance*, 23–32.

4. See the edited version in the appendix to this volume; for the audio recording of the original interview and the German transcript see the Web site of the Illinois Institute of Tehnology (IIT) at http://voices.iit.edu.

5. David P. Boder, *Topical Autobiographies of Displaced People*, vol. 11 (Los Angeles, 1957), chap. 43, pp. 2043–2111. The series comprises sixteen volumes published between 1950 and 1957.

6. Ibid., vol. 16, p. 3161. For a short sketch on Boder, see "Voices of the Holocaust," at http://voices.iit.edu. Alan Rosen's biography of Boder, titled *"That Great Mournful*

Past": David Boder and the Ethnography of Holocaust Testimony, is forthcoming in 2009; see also his "Evidence of Trauma: English as Perplexity in David Boder's Topical Autobiographies," in Rosen, *Sounds of Defiance: The Holocaust, Multilingualism, and the Problem of English* (Lincoln: University of Nebraska Press, 2005), 21–33.

7. Ernest Taylor (Ernie) Pyle, a newspaper correspondent and author of such popular wartime books as *Ernie Pyle in England* (1941), *Here Is Your War* (1943), and *Brave Men* (1944), was killed in April 1945, when accompanying a U.S. landing party on the island of Okinawa.

8. Boder, *Topical Autobiographies*, vol. 16, p. 3161.

9. See ibid., vol. 8, pp. 1367–1404. On Jewish DPs, see the contribution in this volume by Atina Grossmann; also her *Jews, Germans, and Allies: Close Encounters in Occupied Germany* (Princeton, N.J.: Princeton University Press, 2007); in general Mark Wyman, *DPs: Europe's Displaced Persons, 1945–1951* (Ithaca, N.Y.: Cornell University Press, 1998).

10. In addition, he conducted 14 interviews in Switzerland and 9 in Italy, bringing the total to 133. Due to the lack of comprehensive documentation on Boder's recordings (i.e., beyond the 70 interviews he selected for inclusion in his *Topical Autobiographies*), multiple recordings, and the inclusion of interview snippets and other audio documentation (songs, conversations, religious services), it is difficult to exactly quantify Boder's project in terms of size. The figures provided here are approximations based on the collection of tapes held at the USHMM Archive (subsequently: USHMMA), RG-50.472.

11. David P. Boder, *I Did Not Interview the Dead* (Urbana: University of Illinois Press, 1949); Boder, "The Impact of Catastrophe: I. Assessment and Evaluation," *Journal of Psychology* 38 (1954): 3–50. A French edition of Boder's book was published in 2007 by Florent Brayard and Alan Rosen with a new introduction under the title *Je n'ai pas interrogé les morts*. On more general psychological issues of survivor memory, see Cathy Caruth, ed., *Trauma: Explorations in Memory* (Baltimore: Johns Hopkins University Press, 1995); Ana Douglass and Thomas A. Vogler, eds., *Witness and Memory: The Discourse of Trauma* (New York: Routledge, 2003).

12. Annette Wieviorka, *The Era of Witness* (Ithaca, N.Y.: Cornell University Press, 2006), 54.

13. Boder, *Topical Autobiographies*, vol. 11, p. 2042 n. 4 (emphasis in the original).

14. Ibid., vol. 1, p. 2.

15. Boder, *I Did Not Interview the Dead*, xii; Boder, *Topical Autobiographies*, vol. 9, pp. 1581–1634 (L. Hamburger); vol. 14, pp. 2533–2570 (K. Eisenberg).

16. See, e.g., ibid., vol. 4, p. 535 n. 2; vol. 8, pp. 1310, 1312.

17. On Boder's use of English, see Rosen, "Evidence of Trauma," 22–25.

18. Addendum to Boder, *Topical Autobiographies*, vol. 16, p. 3161; ibid., vol. 12, p. 2118.

19. See, e.g., Boder, *Topical Autobiographies*, vol. 4, p. 535 n. 2; p. 601 fn. 2; vol. 9 (M. Herskovitz); vol. 10 (S. Isakovitch, I. Unikowski); vol. 13 (A. Krakowski). See also James E. Young, "Between History and Memory: The Voice of the Eyewitness," in Douglass and Vogler, *Witness and Memory*, 275–283.

20. Dale R. Lindsay (Division of Research Grants, Department of Health, Education, and Welfare) to D. Boder, October 13, 1954, Boder papers, M 11, Archives of the History of American Psychology at the University of Akron, Ohio (subsequently: Boder papers). I am grateful to John A. Popplestone, the director of this archive, for providing me with copies from and information on the Boder papers.

21. All remaining recordings of Boder's 1946 interviews are available on high-quality tape at the Performing Arts Reading Room of the Library of Congress (Library of Congress Motion Picture and Sound Division, collection LWO 29916, RWD 7094–7273) as well as in the Archives of the U.S. Holocaust Memorial Museum (USHMMA, RG 50.472). Since 2002, Joan Ringelheim, director of the Oral History Department of the USHMM, and her colleagues have traced twenty-nine participants of the Boder-project and interviewed eleven of them; their video testimonies are available at the USHMM Archive. In summer 2005, David Jacobson, an intern at the USHMM's Center for Advanced Holocaust Studies, surveyed all audiotapes of the museum's Boder collection and could trace additional, uncataloged interviews and testimonial fragments, inter alia by Erwin Tichauer. I thank Joan Ringelheim and her team as well as David Jacobson for their help in the preparation of this essay.

22. Addendum to Boder, *Topical Autobiographies*, vol. 16, p. 3160.

23. Langer, *Holocaust Testimonies*, 21. For a gripping example, see the interview with Roma Tcharnabroda (Boder, *Topical Autobiographies*, vol. 5, pp. 828–864).

24. Addendum to Boder, *Topical Autobiographies*, vol. 16, pp. 3161–3162 (emphases in the original).

25. Letter Helene Tichauer, Brisbane, Australia, to David Boder, December 31, 1950, David P. Boder Papers, Collection 1238, box 22, UCLA Special Collections. I am indebted to Alan Rosen for a copy of the letter and Boder's response, dated January 9, 1951.

26. See Wieviorka, *Era of Witness*, 24–55; David Roskies, "The Library of Jewish Catastrophe," in Hartman, *Holocaust Remembrance*, 33–41; Philip Friedman, "European Jewish Research on the Holocaust," in Friedman, *Roads to Extinction: Essays on the Holocaust* (New York: Jewish Publication Society, 1980), 500–534; Shmuel Krakowski, "Memorial Projects and the Memorial Institutions Initiated by She'erit Hapletah," in Yisrael Gutman and Avital Saf, eds., *She'erit Hapletah, 1944–1948: Rehabilitation and Political Struggle* (Jerusalem: Yad Vashem, 1990), 388–398.

27. See G. W. Allport, J. S. Brunner, and E. M. Jandorf, "Personality under Social Catastrophe: Ninety Life-Histories of the Nazi Revolution," *Character and Personality: A Quarterly for Psychodiagnostics and Allied Studies* 10, no. 1 (1941): 1–22. The study was based on written testimonies provided by German émigrés in 1940 in the form of an essay contest under the title "My Life in Germany before and after January 30, 1933." The contest

contributions are housed at Harvard University's Houghton Library and have partly been published in Margarete Limberg and Hubert Rübsaat, eds., *Germans No More: Accounts of Jewish Everyday Life, 1933–1938* (New York: Berghahn Books, 2006).

28. HT, October 26, 2006.

29. See Boder, *Topical Autobiographies*, vol. 11, pp. 2043–2111; http://voices.iit.edu.

30. See http://voices.iit.edu.

31. Ibid., vol. 1, p. 2.

32. The same caveat raised for the overall number of interviews (see above note 10) applies for the attempt to quantify the languages used. According to the IIT Web site, thirty-seven of Boder's interviewees decided to speak German; nineteen spoke Yiddish (http://voices.iit.edu/profiles.html).

33. Quoted in Wieviorka, *Era of Witness*, 45.

34. See Alan Rosen, "Everything Is All Right, or the Problem of English Writing on the Holocaust," in Rosen, *Sounds of Defiance*, 12.

35. Ibid., 7–11; James Young, *Writing and Rewriting the Holocaust: Narrative and the Consequences of Interpretation* (Bloomington: Indiana University Press, 1988), 160.

36. From Victor Klemperer until today, research has so far focused mostly on the use of German by the Third Reich as a means of mass manipulation and terror; see, e.g., Christopher Hutton, *Race and the Third Reich: Linguistics, Racial Anthropology, and Genetics in the Dialectic of Volk* (Cambridge, Mass.: Polity, 2005). Except for literary figures, the role of the German language for Nazi victims outside the Nazi setting, either in exile or after the war, has not been thoroughly investigated. For aspects of this problem, see Monika S. Schmid, First Language Attrition, Use and Maintenance: The Case of German Jews in Anglophone Countries (Amsterdam: John Benjamins, 2002).

37. Rosen, "Everything Is All Right," 5.

38. Aron Grünhut, *Aufstieg und Niedergang der Juden von Pressburg* (Tel Aviv: n.p., 1972); Eduard Nižňanský, *Židovská komunita na Slovensku medzi československou parlamentnou demokráciou a slovenským štátom v stredoeuropskom kontexte* (Prešov: Universum, 1999).

39. HT, October 18, 2006; April 4, 2007.

40. This mechanism was used during postwar interviews by German-Jewish emigrants in the United States who had experienced massive violence, e.g., in the course of "Kristallnacht"; see Monika Schmid, "'I Always Thought I Was a German—It Was Hitler Who Taught Me I Was a Jew': National-Socialist Persecution, Identity, and the German Language," in Christof Mauch and Joseph Salmons, eds., *German-Jewish Identities in America* (Madison: University of Wisconsin Press, 2003), 141–151.

41. I am grateful to Alan Rosen for this information.

42. Schmid, "I Always Thought," 150.

43. HT, October 26, 2006.

44. Quoted from Wieviorka, *Era of Witness*, 38.

45. Geoffrey Hartman, "Testimony and Authenticity," in Hartman, *Scars of the Spirit: The Struggle against Inauthenticity* (New York: Palgrave, 2000), 95.

46. See Table 1 at the end of this essay on "Themes and sub-themes in Helen Tichauer's 1946 interview and its later versions."

47. Boder, *Topical Autobiographies*, vol. 11, pp. 2043–2111.

48. Ibid., pp. 2045, 2047.

49. "1942" instead of "1943" (p. 2046); arrival in Auschwitz on a Sunday instead of Saturday (p. 2049); "Ohmeier" instead of "Aumeier" (p. 2054); "Poles" instead of "Polen-liebchen" (p. 2059); "Meistro" instead of "Malchow" (p. 2090).

50. "Höss" (p. 2054); "reichsdeutsche" (p. 2056); "Katja Singer" (p. 2059); "Sichel und Hammer" (p. 2093); "Lublin" (p. 2097).

51. "invited" for "aufgefordert" (p. 2045); "helmet" for "Schildmütze" (p. 2050); "a crowd" for "Gestalten" (p. 2052), "shower" for "Sauna" (p. 2053); "where" for "wer" (p. 2053); "organize" for "einzustellen" (p. 2060); "women thieves' accomplices" for "Bibelforscherinnen" (p. 2075); "whipped to death" for "ausgepeitscht" (p. 2078); "neighbor/co-worker" for "Nachfolger" (p. 2088); "cold" for "Chaos" (p. 2089); "rented out" for "arisiert" (p. 2096); "deceived" for "irritiert" (p. 2104); "wish" for "Weg" (p. 2108).

52. Boder refers to the cutting of hair "from all places," including (Tichauer: excluding) eyebrows and eyelashes (p. 2054); to the breaking (Tichauer: striking) of an agreement (p. 2090); to the incrimination of the Jewish leadership (Tichauer: the Jewish leadership letting information disappear) in Theresienstadt (p. 2105).

53. Boder, *Topical Autobiographies*, 2105.

54. Wieviorka, *Era of Witness*, 90.

55. For Zippi's reflections on time and thinking in Auschwitz, see her responses to students featured in the contribution by Wendy Lower to this volume.

56. Jean Améry, *At the Mind's Limits: Contemplations by a Survivor on Auschwitz and Its Realities* (New York: Schocken Books, 1980), 7.

57. Boder's translation in *Topical Autobiographies*, vol. 11 p. 2058: "if performed correctly."

58. Ibid., pp. 2056–2058.

59. Ibid., p. 2065.

60. Boder's translation in *Topical Autobiographies*, p. 2072.

61. Ibid., p. 2107.

62. Ibid., pp. 2076–2077.

63. Ibid., p. 2103.

64. Telephone conversations with Helen Tichauer, 26 October, 11 November 2006.

65. For different examples and interpretations, see Mark Roseman, *A Past in Hiding: Memory and Survival in Nazi Germany* (New York: Metropolitan Books, 2001), 408–412; Rosen, "Evidence of Trauma."

66. See Na'ama Shik, "Weibliche Erfahrung in Auschwitz-Birkenau," in Gisela Bock, ed., *Genozid und Geschlecht. Jüdische Frauen im nationalsozialistischen Lagersystem* (Frankfurt am Main: Campus, 2005), 103–122.

67. Boder, *Topical Autobiographies*, vol. 11, pp. 2055–2057.

68. Ibid., pp. 2084–2085, 2102.

69. HT, November 11, 2006.

70. See Rosen, "Evidence of Trauma," 32–33.

71. See, e.g., Geoffrey Hartman, "Preserving the Personal Story: The Role of Video Documentation," in Marcia Littell, Richard Libowitz, and Evelyn B. Rosen, eds., *The Holocaust Forty Years After* (Lewiston, Me.: Edwin Mellow, 1989), 53–61.

72. http://voices.iit.edu. The IIT is currently preparing a more comprehensive Web site presentation of the Boder interview collection.

73. http://voices.iit.edu/frames.asp?path=Interviews/&page=tisch&ext=_t.html.

74. Donald Niewyk, ed., *Fresh Wounds: Early Narratives of Holocaust Survival* (Chapel Hill: University of North Carolina Press, 1998).

75. Ibid., xi, 1–6.

76. Ibid., 6.

77. Ibid., xi.

78. Rosen, "Evidence of Trauma," 199 n. 3.

79. Jean Améry, "... wie eine Herde von Schafen," 1966 (review of Jean-François Steiner's Treblinka book), in Améry, *Werke, Band 7: Aufsätze zur Politik und Zeitgeschichte* (Stuttgart: Klett-Cotta, 2005), 410–412 (my translation).

80. E.g., "camp" instead of *lager*; "roll call" instead of *appell*.

81. See Table 1 at the end of this essay.

82. Malchow was opened in late 1943/early 1944 as a subcamp of the women's concentration camp Ravensbrück. From autumn of 1944 until May 1945, with the detention of the Hungarian Jews and the evacuation of the concentration camps in the east, about 4,000 women were brought to Malchow. The women were of Polish, French, Hungarian, Czech, Russian, Ukrainian, Bulgarian, Italian, German, and Greek nationality, most of them Jewish. See Irith Dublon-Knebel, "Ravensbrück/Malchow," in *The United States Holocaust Memorial Museum Encyclopedia of Camps and Ghettos, 1933–1945, vol. 1 Early Camps, Youth Camps, and concentration Camps and Subcamps under the SS-Business Administration Main Office* (WVHA), ed. Geoffrey Megargee (Bloomington: Indiana University Press, 2009): 1213–1214.

83. Niewyk, *Fresh Wounds*, 363.

84. See, e.g., Peter Novick; *The Holocaust in American Life* (Boston: Houghton Mifflin, 1999); Tim Cole, *Selling the Holocaust: From Auschwitz to Schindler. How History Is Bought, Packaged, and Sold* (New York: Routledge, 1999); Gary Weissman, *Fantasies of Witnessing: Postwar Efforts to Experience the Holocaust* (Ithaca, N.Y.: Cornell University Press, 2004).

85. For recent examples, see Naomi Seidman, "Elie Wiesel and the Scandal of Jewish Rage," *Jewish Social Studies* 3, no. 1 (1996): 1–19; Susan R. Suleiman, "Do Facts Matter in Holocaust Memoirs? Wilkomirski/Wiesel," in Steven T. Katz and Alan Rosen, eds., *Obliged by Memory: Literature, Religion, Ethics* (Syracuse, N.Y.: Syracuse University Press, 2006), 21–42; Langer, *Holocaust Testimonies*, 58, 210.

CHAPTER 4

1. In 1933, at the beginning of the National Socialist regime, Germany counted approximately 500,000 Jews. In 1946–1947, more than a quarter of a million Jews were gathered in Germany, most of them in the American zone. About 15,000 were German Jews, of whom almost half were in Berlin. The majority were Eastern European Jewish "displaced persons" of whom, however, only a minority were survivors of Nazi camps. The largest cohort, by a substantial margin—and the least studied—comprised perhaps 200,000 Jews who had been repatriated to Poland from their difficult but lifesaving refuge in the Soviet Union and then fled again, from postwar Polish antisemitism, especially after the notorious pogrom in Kielce, Poland, on July 4, 1946, that Jan T. Gross has written about so eloquently in his recent book *Fear: Anti-Semitism in Poland after Auschwitz: An Essay in Historical Interpretation* (New York: Random House, 2006).

2. For detailed discussion, see Atina Grossmann, *Jews, Germans, and Allies: Close Encounters in Occupied Germany* (Princeton, N.J.: Princeton University Press, 2007).

3. I owe a great deal to the workshop on gender and the Holocaust, summer 2004, at the USHMM, in which Joan Ringelheim, at the time the head of the Oral History Department, participated (as did Nechama Tec, who has also contributed to this volume) and at which I presented much of my initial research. The literature on memory and trauma is of course vast and has spawned a whole novel field of "memory studies."

4. Unless otherwise indicated (as in this case, which italicizes the German), all quotes from Boder's interview with Zippi in Feldafing on September 23, 1946, are from Boder's English translation of the original German featured in the appendix to this volume. For a discussion of translation (and other) problems with the transmission of that interview, see Jürgen Matthäus's chapter in this volume. In this essay, I specifically note quotes from Zippi's Boder interview; other quotes refer to my conversations with her, starting in fall 2004 (though verbatim, these quotes are based on my notes, not a recording or transcript).

5. Boder interview, appendix, interview p. 52/2095. In the German transcript, Zippi says, "*Unterwegs trafen wir viele Menschen und alle waren nett und brachten uns . . . hat man uns verstand . . . hat man eben Verständnis für uns aufgebracht*" [were understanding]. On sexual violence by the Red Army in regard to both German and Jewish women, see Grossmann, *Jews, Germans, and Allies,* chap. 3 "Gendered Defeat."

6. The agonized difficulties of trying to connect with family and friends who had not undergone similar camp experiences, the ways in which survivors felt unwanted and felt that they only disturbed others' efforts to rebuild their lives are described for the Czech case in Christa Schikorra, "Rückkehr in eine neue Gesellschaft: Jüdische Remigran-tinnen in der Tschechoslowakei 1945–1948," in Gisela Bock, ed., *Genozid und Geschlecht: Jüdische Frauen im nationalsozialistischen Lagersystem* (Frankfurt: Campus, 2005), 220–238.

7. On the semiclandestine Zionist network that smuggled survivors from Eastern Europe to DP camps in the American zone of occupied Germany for eventual passage to Palestine, see Yehudah Bauer, *Flight and Rescue: Bricha* (New York: Random House, 1970).

8. Description and Smith quote in Katie Louchheim, "The DP Summer," *Virginia Quarterly Review* 61, no. 4 (1985): 703. Numbers reported range from 1,000 to 3,000 in various sources.

9. See Haia Karni, "Life at the Feldafing Displaced Persons Camp 1945–1952" (master's thesis, Baltimore Hebrew University, 1997); also Simon Schochet, *Feldafing* (Van-couver: November House, 1983), for a survivor's account. See also Shlomo Leser's unpub-lished account, "The Displaced Poles, Ukrainians and Jews in the West Zones in Occupied Germany and Austria, and in Italy, 1945–1949" (Haifa, 2008). Interestingly, the same story about an American Jewish DP camp commander's reluctance to reveal his Jewishness for fear of being accused of "favoritism" or, conversely, the expectation of delivering favors, is found in Lieutenant Irving Heymont's letters from Landsberg DP Camp. See Irving Heymont, *Among the Survivors of the Holocaust, 1945: The Landsberg DP Camp Letters of Major Irving Heymont* (Cincinnati: American Jewish Archives, 1982), 25 and postscript, p. 109.

10. Boder interview, appendix, interview p. 66/2109.

11. "Vital Statistics of the Jewish Population in the US Zone of Germany for the Year 1948," issued by Medical Department AJDC-OSE-CC Munich, p. 7, in YIVO LWS 294.1/(folder)272/MK(Microfilm) 488/R(eel)23, 216 (also in AJDCA/417). For the same quote, see Kurt R. Grossmann, *The Jewish DP Problem: Its Origin, Scope, and Liquida-tion* (New York: Institute of Jewish Affairs, World Jewish Congress, 1951), 19. See U. O. Schmelz, "The Demographic Impact of the Holocaust," in Robert S. Wistrich, ed., *Terms of Survival: The Jewish World since 1945* (New York: Routledge, 1995), 44. See, among numerous other sources, Abraham J. Peck, "Jewish Survivors of the Holocaust in Germany:

Revolutionary Vanguard or Remnants of a Destroyed People?" *Tel Aviver Jahrbuch für deutsche Geschichte* 19 (1990): 38; Michael Brenner, *After the Holocaust: Rebuilding Jewish Lives in Postwar Germany* (Princeton, N.J.: Princeton University Press, 1997), 23, and Margarete L. Myers, "Jewish Displaced Persons Reconstructing Individual and Community in the US Zone of Occupied Germany," *LBI Yearbook* 42 (1997): 306–308.

12. Jacob Biber, *Risen from the Ashes: A Story of the Jewish Displaced Persons in the Aftermath of World War II* (San Francisco: Borgo Press, 1990), 49.

13. Edith Horowitz oral history in Brana Gurewitsch, ed., *Mothers, Sisters, Resisters: Oral Histories of Women Who Survived the Holocaust* (Tuscaloosa: University of Alabama Press, 1998), 73.

14. Abraham S. Hyman, *The Undefeated* (Jerusalem: Gefen, 1993), 246, 270, 17.

15. Aaron Haas, *The Aftermath: Living with the Holocaust* (Cambridge: Cambridge University Press, 1995), 102.

16. There are at least five such volumes that all feature the same or very similar images of women pushing baby carriages at the forefront of Zionist demonstrations; none make gender, sexuality, or reproduction central to their analysis. See the poster for the U.S. Holocaust Memorial Museum exhibit Life Reborn, as well as the covers of books by Ruth Gay, *Safe among the Germans: Liberated Jews after World War II* (New Haven, Conn.: Yale University Press, 2002); Zeev W. Mankowitz, *Life between Memory and Hope: The Survivors of the Holocaust in Occupied Germany* (Cambridge: Cambridge University Press, 2002); and David Bankier, ed., *The Jews Are Coming Back: The Return of the Jews to Their Countries of Origin after WWII* (New York: Berghahn, 2005). See also the presentation in the American documentary film *The Long Journey Home* (Simon Wiesenthal Center, Los Angeles, 1997) and in *Ein Leben Aufs Neu: Das Robinson Album. DP-Lager: Juden auf deutschem Boden 1945–1948* (Vienna: Verlag Christian Brandstätter, 1995), as well as the photographs in the 2001 calendar of the U.S. Holocaust Memorial Museum, culled from the exhibition "Life Reborn: Jewish Displaced Persons 1945–1951," and the accompanying volume by Menachem Z. Rosensaft, ed., *Life Reborn: Jewish Displaced Persons 1945–1951: Conference Proceedings* (Washington, D.C.: U.S. Holocaust Memorial Museum occasional paper, 2000).

17. See, for example, Gerda Weissmann Klein and Kurt Klein, *The Hours After: Letters of Love and Longing in War's Aftermath* (New York: St. Martin's, 2000), 272–273.

18. Avinoam Patt has noted the general importance of a rhetoric of responsibility and obligation in DP life and politics; see his "Finding Home and Homeland: Jewish Youth Groups in the Aftermath of the Holocaust" (Ph.D. diss., New York University, 2005; publication forthcoming with Wayne State University Press).

19. See especially Grossmann, *Jews, Germans, and Allies*, 214–216.

20. Karni, "Life at the Feldafing Displaced Persons Camp," 49.

21. Shlomo Leser notes in his unpublished "Displaced Poles, Ukrainians, and Jews" that most Jewish DPs had only civil, not religious, marriages. Zippi and Erwin

themselves married at the *Standesamt* (registry office) in Tutzing. Was this really the general practice? Another question to ask Zippi.

22. Letter to Moe (Moses) Leavitt, from Joseph Schwartz, JDC Paris, November 9, 1946, AJDCA/ 390.

23. Boder interview, appendix, interview p. 67/2110.

24. Grossmann, *Jews, Germans, and Allies*, 169–170.

25. W. Arnold-Forster, "U.N.N.R.R.A's Work for Displaced Persons in Germany," *International Affairs* 22 (1946): 12.

26. For a fine analysis of this literature, see Isidor J. Kaminer, "'On Razor's Edge': Vom Weiterleben nach dem Überleben," in Fritz Bauer Institut, ed., *Überlebt und Unterwegs. Jüdische Displaced Persons im Nachkriegsdeutschland* (Frankfurt am Main M: Campus, 1997), 146–147, 157. On notions of manic displacement, based on a Freudian understanding of trauma expressed by acting out, rather than remembering and working through, see, for example, Ido de Haan, "Paths of Normalization after the Persecution of the Jews: The Netherlands, France and West Germany in the 1950s," in Richard Bessel and Dirk Schumann, eds., *Life after Death: Approaches to a Cultural and Social History of Europe during the 1940s and 1950s* (Cambridge: Cambridge University Press, 2003), 65–92. Kaminer counters that, in fact, "the quick marriages and family formations were an effort to once again join a human community which could even make mourning possible [*die erst Trauer ermöglicht*]. It is a great misunderstanding—if not willful ignorance— by psychoanalysis to interpret these actions as manic defenses [*manische Abwehrversuche*]." See his "Spätfolgen bei jüdischen KZ-Überlebenden," in Dirk Juelich, ed., *Geschichte als Trauma: Festschrift für Hans Keilson zu seinem 80. Geburtstag* (Frankfurt am Main : Nexus, 1991), 28.

27. I am grateful to one of the anonymous reviewers of this volume for supplying this phrase.

28. Patton quotation in Leonard Dinnerstein, *America and the Survivors of the Holocaust* (New York: Columbia University Press, 1982), 16–17. See also Martin Blumenson, (ed., *The Patton Papers: 1940–1945* (Boston: Houghton Mifflin 1974), 751. Also cited in Constantin Goschler, "The Attitude towards Jews in Bavaria after the Second World War," *LBI Yearbook* 36 (1991): 447.

29. I. F. Stone, *Underground to Palestine and Reflections Thirty Years Later* (New York: Pantheon, 1978), 24.

30. Figure from Nicholas Yantian, *Studien zum Selbstverständnis der jüdischen "Displaced Persons" in Deutschland nach dem Zweiten Weltkrieg* (M.A. thesis, Historical Faculty of the Technische Universität Berlin, 1994), 43. Angelika Königseder, *Flucht nachBerlin: Jüdische Displaced Persons 1945–1948* (Berlin: Metropol, 1998), 145 (citing *Undser Lebn*, December 27, 1946, p. 34), describes the case of two DPs in Berlin accused of relations with German women. They had allegedly gotten drunk in local bars, dishonored their Jewish wives, and endangered the community through the possible transmission of venereal disease. Stated punishment ranged from a warning for a first offense to six

months' banishment from camp, although it is unclear whether such sanctions were actually enforced.

31. Meyer Kron, "Through the Eye of a Needle," chap. 10, "Stopover in Germany," in memoir collection, Concordia University Chair in Jewish Studies, Montreal Institute for Genocide and Human Rights Studies, 2001, http://migs.Concordia.ca/survivor.html (accessed July 15, 2008).

32. Schochet, *Feldafing*, 161–162. For frank and unapologetic descriptions of such (usually short-lived) love affairs, see Jack Eisner (whom Zippi remembers fondly as a "good boy"), *Die Happy Boys: Eine jüdische Band in Deutschland 1945 bis 1949*, translated from his English text (Berlin: Aufbau, 2004), 118–120, 163–178. Ruth Klüger describes her complicated relationship with fellow student Christoph (a fictionalized version of German writer Martin Walser) in her *Weiter leben: Eine Jugend* (Göttingen: Wallstein, 1992), 211. The reference to Klüger's German original text (in English *Still Alive*) reminds me that the title of this essay, "Living On," must have been influenced by her German title.

33. Phone interview by the author with A.K, August 5, 2004.

34. On fraternization between German women and African American soldiers, see Heide Fehrenbach, *Race after Hitler: Black Occupation Children in Postwar Germany and America* (Princeton, N.J.: Princeton University Press, 2005); and Maria Höhn, *GIs and Fräuleins: The German-American Encounter in 1950s West Germany* (Chapel Hill: University of North Carolina Press, 2002).

35. See Schikorra, "Rückkehr," and Heda Margolius Kovaly, *Under a Cruel Star: A Life in Prague 1941–1968*, trans. Frances Epstein and Helen Epstein (New York: Holmes and Meier, 1997), on the difficult experiences of Jewish women who did return to Czechoslovakia.

36. See Jürgen Matthäus's analysis in this volume of Boder's mistranslation of Zippi's reference to her husband as the driving force for leaving Europe: The German "In Deutschland wird er sich *nie* mehr wohlfühlen. In diesem Land, wo er alles verloren hat" is rendered by Boder into the more predictable "In Germany we shall never feel well. In this country there is nothing/?/for us…" (see Boder interview, appendix, interview p. 68/2111).

37. Koppel S. Pinson, "Jewish Life in Liberated Germany: A Study of the Jewish DPs," *Jewish Social Studies* 9, no. 2 (January 1947): 117.

38. For a similarly dubious account of a young survivor's take on the appeal of Zionism, see Irene Eber's powerful and beautifully written memoir, *The Choice: Poland, 1939–1945* (New York: Random House, 2004), 167. Of the "glib emissaries from Palestine," she writes, "We were skeptical. It sounded too good—and strangely, not a single one of the emissaries ever talked much about study, learning, making up for years lost, when this was so much on my mind and some of friends' minds as well. How would we ever catch up?" (167).

39. This and the previous quote from Thomas Tresize, "Between History and Psychoanalysis: A Case Study in the Reception of Holocaust Survivor Testimony," *History and Memory* 20, no. 1 (2008): 7, 43 n. 4.

CHAPTER 5

1. Quoted from Simone Schweber, *Making Sense of the Holocaust: Lessons from Class-room Practice* (New York: Teachers College Press, 2004), 154 (Schweber cites Lipstadt's quote in Peter Novick's *The Holocaust in American Life* [Boston: Houghton Mifflin, 1999], 26). I would like to thank my students at Towson University, Maryland, and Georgetown University, Washington, D.C., who participated in my class interviews with Helen Tichauer, and Lisa Zaid, who helped prepare transcriptions of the classroom interviews.

2. For an evaluation of the historical content and moral messages, and various methods to impart them at the high school level, see Schweber, *Making Sense*. Schweber questions whether the Holocaust should "be called so readily into service as moral educa-tion, given the variability of its messages" (147).

3. Christopher R. Browning, "Writing and Teaching Holocaust History: A Per-sonal Perspective," in Samuel Totten, Paul R. Bartrop, and Steven Leonard Jacobs, eds., *Teaching about the Holocaust: Essays by College and University Teachers* (Westport, Conn.: Praeger, 2004), 41–42. The first curriculum plan that incorporated Holocaust units in the public school system appeared in Massachusetts in 1973 (written by Roselle Chartrock). One version of this plan was published in April 1978, to coincide with the airing of the NBC TV series *Holocaust*. Holocaust education at the university and college level has developed independently, not governed by standards and imposed curricular content, but primarily by the will and interest of specific scholars in the field and their resources. See Thomas D. Fallace, "The Origins of Holocaust Education in American Public Schools," *Holocaust and Genocide Studies* 20, no. 1 (2006): 85. The Holocaust Educational Foundation was founded near Chicago in 1976 and undertook as its first main project the collection of testimonials from several hundred survivors in the area, which began systematically in the mid-1980s with the help of scholars (Dori Laub and Geoffrey Hartman) from the Fortunoff Video Archive for Holocaust Testimonials at Yale University (which opened in 1982). The foun-dation's founder, Zev Weiss, an Auschwitz survivor and educational director at Beth Hillel Academy, worked assiduously to bring Holocaust studies into higher education, telephoning history departments and developing relationships with scholars in the field, most successfully at Northwestern University, where a chair was established in his honor.

4. For analyses of early Holocaust teaching at American colleges and universities, and of Holocaust studies conferences that began convening regularly in 1970, see Franklin Littell, "Fundamentals in Holocaust Studies," *Annals of the American Academy of Political and Social Sciences* 450 (1980): 213–217; Henry Friedlander, "Toward a Methodology of Teach-ing about the Holocaust," *Teachers College Record* 80, no. 3 (1979): 519–542; and Stephen R. Haynes, "Holocaust Education at American Colleges and Universities: A Report on the Current Situation," *Holocaust and Genocide Studies* 12, no. 2 (1998): 282–307. According to an internal survey by the U.S. Holocaust Memorial Museum's Center for Advanced Holo-caust Studies, more than 800 university professors from different fields (mostly literature, history, and Jewish studies) offered courses on the Holocaust around the year 2000.

5. Some educators assume that nurturing students' empathy or instilling emotions that identify with the victims is the key to more tolerant attitudes and behavior. This educational trend predated but was later bolstered by subsequent events in what scholar

Thomas D. Fallace argues was an "affective revolution," a term that social studies theorists Gerald Marker and Howard Mehlinger applied retrospectively to educators' intense interest during the late 1960s and 1970s in students' identity, morality, emotions, and values (Fallace, "Origins of Holocaust Education," 81). In several country submissions to the 2006 report of the International Task Force for Holocaust Education, Remembrance and Research, empathy was stressed as a tool of learning; see Karen Riley, "Historical Empathy and the Holocaust: Theory into Practice," *International Journal of Social Education*, no. 13 (1998): 32–42.

6. See Novick, *Holocaust in American Life*; Jeffrey Shandler, *While America Watches: Televising the Holocaust* (New York: Oxford University Press, 1999); Hilene Flanzbaum, ed., *The Americanization of the Holocaust* (Baltimore: Johns Hopkins University Press, 1999).

7. The speaker may have been Hungarian survivor Margit Feldman. Telephone conversation with Dr. Seymour Siegler, cofounder, Holocaust Educational Center, Brookdale Community College, Lincroft, New Jersey, June 5, 2008. In July 2008 the center changed its name to Holocaust, Genocide and Human Rights Education Center at Brookdale Community Center, http://www.holocaustbcc.org/.

8. See http://www.holocaustbcc.org/about.html (accessed June 14, 2008).

9. There are 262 U.S. organizations registered with the International Task Force for International Cooperation on Holocaust Education, Remembrance and Research, www.holocausttaskforce.org (accessed January 2008). The number of centers devoted to Holocaust education has proliferated in the past twenty years, with many organizations expanding from small offices housed in former Jewish community centers or organizations to formal departments and programs with broad agendas of combating racism, preventing genocide, and teaching about human rights. This development has been precipitated by the passing of state legislation mandating Holocaust education in the public schools in California, Florida, Illinois, New Jersey, and New York. Ten additional states have adopted regulations that encourage teaching of the Holocaust, and twelve others have established Holocaust commissions that support its teaching. Altogether forty-eight states have incorporated Holocaust history into their social studies curriculum, though no national standards or strict state oversight exist on the content and methods of teachers to gauge the amount and quality of teaching on the subject. See the country report submitted by the United States to the International Task Force. For the growth of Holocaust centers outside of academe, see the directory of the Association of Holocaust Organizations (www.ahoinfo.org).

10. See Alan E. Steinweis, "The Auschwitz Analogy: Holocaust Memory and American Debates over Intervention in Bosnia and Kosovo in the 1990s," *Holocaust and Genocide Studies* 19, no. 2 (2005): 276–289.

11. Author interview with Helen Tichauer (subsequently: HT), April 10, 2008.

12. HT, January 16, 2008.

13. Student comments, "The Holocaust: The Destruction of European Jews," City University of New York, 1982, 1991; personal papers of Helen Tichauer; HT, April 10, 2008.

14. On the different interview classroom settings from which I quote here and subsequently, see below the section in this essay on "Zippi's unfinished interviews".

15. Quoted from Annette Wieviorka, *The Era of Witness* (Ithaca, N.Y.: Cornell University Press, 2006), 133–134.

16. Survivor Speakers in the Classroom, "An Introduction to Teachers" (emphasis in the original), Vancouver Holocaust Education Center, www.vhec.org (accessed June 14, 2008).

17. The study was completed by the Jewish Education Society of North America for the San Francisco Jewish Community Endowment Fund (subsequently: JESNA study), http://www.sfjcf.org/endowment/grants/programs/SFJCEF-JESNA%20Holocaust %20Education%20Full%20Report.pdf.

18. Ibid., p. 12.

19. See L. Borzak, *Field Study: A Sourcebook for Experiential Learning* (Beverly Hills, Calif.: Sage, 1981), 9. Another foundational study by John Dewey worth noting is *How We Think* (New York: Heath, 1933). Experiential learning theories explore various topics about knowledge and the senses, learning stages and types of learners, and the classroom setting versus the public realm. The field builds on centuries of philosophical work, but its twentieth-century focus is on psychological-pedagogical concepts and academic programs that promote lifelong learning and civic engagement.

20. Irving Roth, director, Holocaust Resource Center, Temple Judea of Manhasset, http://eev.liu.edu/HolocaustReCtr/survivors/index.htm.

21. Roger Simon and Claudia Eppert, "Remembering Obligation: Pedagogy and the Witnessing of Testimony of Historical Trauma," *Canadian Journal of Education/Revue Canadienne de l'Éducation* 22 (Spring 1997): 190. See Shoshana Felman and Dori Laub, *Testimony: Crises of Witnessing in Literature, Psychoanalysis and History* (New York: Routledge, 1992). See Felman's interesting chapter on trauma and pedagogy, "Education and Crisis, Or the Vicissitudes of Teaching," *Testimony*, 1–56.

22. Simon and Eppert, "Remembering Obligation," 176.

23. See, e.g., Lawrence L. Langer, *Holocaust Testimonies: The Ruins of Memory* (New Haven, Conn.: Yale University Press, 1991); Geoffrey H. Hartman, ed., *Holocaust Remembrance: The Shapes of Memory* (Oxford: Blackwell, 1995); Henry Greenspan, *On Listening to Holocaust Survivors: Recounting and Life History* (Westport, Conn.: Praeger, 1998); Greenspan, *The Awakening of Memory: Survivor Testimony in the First Years after the Holocaust and Today* (Washington, D.C.: USHM-Moccasional paper, 2001); Felman and Laub, *Testimony*; Wieviorka, *Era of Witness*.

24. See Ernst van Alphen, "Second-Generation Testimony, Transmission of Trauma, and Postmemory," and Geoffrey Hartman, "The Humanities of Testimony: An Introduction," both in a special volume on testimony in *Poetics Today* 27 (Summer 2006). The JESNA report also noted the current trend, as survivors pass, of teachers utilizing second-generation speakers, artifacts, and video testimony (JESNA study, pp. 13–14).

25. Helen Tichauer, "Ladies First," *Voice of the Woman Survivor* 6, no. 2 (1989), 1.

26. Donald Niewyk, *Fresh Wounds: Early Narratives of Holocaust Survival* (Chapel Hill: University of North Carolina Press, 1998). On the problems with this text in comparison to Helen Tichauer's 1946 interview, see the contribution to this volume by Jürgen Matthäus.

27. The interview from 2000 was completed in a spring seminar on the Holocaust that I offered in the BMW Center for German and European Studies, Georgetown University, Washington, D.C. The students were mostly advanced history, literature, and political science majors, and there was one graduate student. The interview from 2003 was conducted in conjunction with a seminar offered by Professor Leroy W. in the Kennedy School of Ethics, also at Georgetown. The interview from 2006 was conducted in an upper-level history course that I offered at Towson University, Towson, Maryland.

28. These are excerpts, edited versions of Helen's answers. In most places where ellipses appear, Helen repeated phrases, searched aloud for a word, went off topic, or described details that I was unable to include here because of space limitations.

29. Helen later explained that Eva Weigel was a German communist from Berlin who had been interned in Ravensbrück since the mid-1930s and transferred to Auschwitz in March 1942 among the first German female inmates. She was the camp elder of the ten women's barracks in Auschwitz I before the move to Birkenau in August 1942. She was transferred back to Ravensbrück in 1943–1944 and later discharged, since her sentence had come to an end. Meanwhile, her daughter had been forced into a Nazi family as an "adopted child." The daughter later refused to rejoin her mother when she was released. Weigel settled in Berlin and survived the war.

30. Helen later clarified that the belongings of non-Jewish prisoners were stored; if and when these prisoners were released, their belongings were returned to them.

31. Helen is referring to Hitler's failed career as an artist in Vienna. On this episode, see also the contribution by Konrad Kwiet to this volume.

32. Raul Hilberg as quoted in Robert-Jan van Pelt, "A Site in Search of a Mission," in Yisrael Gutman and Michael Berenbaum, eds., *Anatomy of the Auschwitz Death Camp* (Bloomington: Indiana University Press, 1994), 93–156.

33. On Zippi's encounter with Roza Robota, see the contribution by Nechama Tec to this volume.

34. HT, May 24, 2006.

Conclusion

1. Raul Hilberg, *Sources of Holocaust Research: An Analysis* (Chicago: Ivan R. Dee, 2001), 184–185.

2. Christopher R. Browning, *Collected Memories: Holocaust History and Postwar Testimony* (Madison: University of Wisconsin Press, 2003), 85.

Appendix

1. This translation is based on the voice recording of the interview held at the U.S. Holocaust Memorial Museum Archive, RG-50.472 Spools 9-149 to 151; for the audio recording of the interview and the German interview transcript, see the Web site of the Illinois Institute of Technology (IIT) at http://voices.iit.edu.. The aim of this text is to provide readers with a basis for comparing Helen Tichauer's recorded interview with David Boder's translation as published in his *Topical Autobiographies*, vol. 11, chapter 43 (Los Angeles, 1956), pp. 2044–2111. Boder marked his editorial comments with "/.../"; underlined emphases are also by Boder, added by him apparently for the dual purpose of highlighting speech patterns as well as marking linguistic trauma indicators; see *Topical Autobiographies*, vol. 16, *Traumatic Inventory* (Los Angeles, 1957), pp. 3161–3163. While he used *Q-n* for his questions, and *Tis* for Helen Tichauer's answers, throughout this text interviewer and interviewee are identified by name. Minor typographical errors have been corrected here without being noted. My comments and the page numbers in Boder's *Topical Autobiographies* in vol. 11 are in "{...}". I added footnotes to provide basic contextual and editorial information and incorporated Boder's footnotes in the body text marked, analogous to his other comments, by "/.../".

2. Name misspelled "Helena Tischauer" by Boder; corrected here and subsequently.

3. Tichauer refers to the Reich Security Main Office (*Reichssicherheits-Hauptamt* [RSHA]), in charge of deportations of Jews. See Yehoshua R. Büchler, "First in the Vale of Affliction: Slovakian Jewish Women in Auschwitz, 1942," *Holocaust and Genocide Studies* 10, no. 3 (1996): 299–325. From the vast literature on Auschwitz, see for an overview of the camp history Yisrael Gutman and Michael Berenbaum, eds., *Anatomy of the Auschwitz Death Camp* (Bloomington: Indiana University Press, 1994); Sybille Steinbacher, *Auschwitz: A History* (London: Penguin, 2005); Laurence Rees, *Auschwitz: A New History* (New York: Public Affairs, 2005). On the sequence of events, see Danuta Czech, *The Auschwitz Chronicle 1939–1945* (New York: Holt, 1997).

4. Deportation camp Poprad; see Büchler, "First in the Vale of Affliction," 303–305.

5. Wording in German interview: "Hlinka Garde" (Hlinka guard; a Slovak fascist group).

6. Wording in German interview most likely: "Bahnstation Bielitz" (Polish: Bielsko-Biała; industrial town ca. 30 miles from Auschwitz).

7. Wording in German interview: "Schildmütze" (peaked cap).

8. Wording in German interview here and in Tichauer's response: "Wer?" (who [cut your/our hair]?).

9. On Rudolf Höss, see Hermann Langbein, *People in Auschwitz* (Chapel Hill: University of North Carolina Press, 2004), 275–277; Aleksander Lasik, "Rudolf Höss: Manager of Crime," in Gutman and Berenbaum, *Anatomy of the Auschwitz Death Camp*,

288–300; *Commandant of Auschwitz: The Autobiography of Rudolf Höss* (Cleveland: World, 1959).

10. SS Lieutenant Colonel (Obersturmbannführer) and camp commander Hans Aumeier; see Hermann Langbein, *People in Auschwitz* (Chapel Hill: University of North Carolina Press, 2004), 322–323.

11. On Franz von Bodemann, see ibid., 336.

12. Wording in German interview to the effect that all body hair was cut except for the eyebrows and eyelashes.

13. Wording in German interview: "reichsdeutsche Häftlinge" (prisoners from Germany proper, as opposed to ethnic Germans [Volksdeutsche] from non-German territories).

14. Rapportführerin Margot Drexler; see Irena Strzelecka, "Women," in Gutman and Berenbaum, *Anatomy of the Auschwitz Death Camp*, 396–397.

15. Wording in German interview: "Sie hiess Katja Singer" (her name was Katja Singer).

16. Wording in German interview: "Polenliebchen" (sweethearts of Poles).

17. Wording in German interview: "Moment" (just a moment).

18. See Gideon Greif, *We Wept without Tears: Testimonies of the Jewish Sonderkommando from Auschwitz* (New Haven, Conn.: Yale University Press, 2005).

19. Zippi describes here the gassing procedure in bunker 2 in Birkenau, a thatched and plastered brick building also known as the "little white house"; see Franciszek Piper, "Gas Chambers and Crematoria," in Gutman and Berenbaum, *Anatomy of the Auschwitz Death Camp*, 161–164.

20. In the German interview text, Tichauer corrects that the color for the stripe was red, not black.

21. On Friedrich Stiwitz, see Friedrich-Martin Balzer and Werner Renz, eds., *Das Urteil im Frankfurter Auschwitz-Prozess (1963–1965)* (Bonn: Pahl-Rugenstein, 2004), 497–498.

22. On Johanna Langefeld, see Büchler, "First in the Vale of Affliction," 306; Irmtraud Heike, "Johanna Langefeld: Die Biographie einer KZ-Oberaufseherin," *Werkstatt Geschichte* 10, no. 12 (1995), 7–19. For female SS guards who came to Auschwitz from Ravensbrück, see Simone Erpel, ed., *Im Gefolge der SS: Aufseherinnen des Frauen-KZ-Ravensbrück* (Berlin: Metropol, 2007).

23. Note the conflicting numbers of surviving Russian POWs in this interview sequence: Tichauer mentions 32 here and shortly thereafter; Boder in his comments questions her first number, suggesting 32,000 instead, and later puts it at 42,000.

24. Wrong year here and in the German interview; September 1942 is correct.

25. Wrong year here and in the German interview; October 1942 is correct.

26. Camp director (Schutzhaftlagerführer) SS-Obersturmführer Paul Müller; see Irena Strzelecka, "Women in the Auschwitz Concentration Camp," in *Auschwitz 1940–1945: Central Issues in the History of the Camp*, vol. 2 (Oświęcim: Auschwitz-Birkenau State Museum, 2000), 176.

27. Wording in German interview: "naiv" (naive).

28. In telephone conversations on November 11, 2006, and April 4, 2007, Helen Tichauer corrected the name of the woman who helped her to Hanni Jäger, the secretary of Lagerführer Müller. She remembers Elli Meier as the Kapo of a demolition squad in Auschwitz.

29. Reference to a German political prisoner who, before coming to Auschwitz, had been incarcerated in concentration camps since the early years of the Nazi regime. In recent telephone conversations, Tichauer did not recall her name.

30. On January 30, 1943, the numbers issued to prisoners in the Birkenau women's camp exceeded 33,000 for the first time (Czech, *Chronicle*, 319).

31. Wording in the German interview for the last name: "die Schwester der Aufseherin Brandl, die zuletzt im Lager Mühldorf, im Frauenlager Mühldorf, sich befand" (the sister of women supervisor Brandl who had last stayed in the lager Mühldorf). On Maria Mandel, Elisabeth Hasse, and Therese Brandl, see Strzelecka, "Women," in Gutman and Berenbaum, *Anatomy of the Auschwitz Death Camp*, 396–397; Langbein, *People in Auschwitz*, 396, 406.

32. Wording in the German interview: "Bibelforscherinnen" (female Jehova's Witnesses).

33. Wording in the German interview: "auch" (also).

34. On this interview passage and Boder's interpretation of it, see my essay in this volume.

35. See above note 3.

36. Wording in the German interview to the effect that the Germans were crazy about a proper-looking card index.

37. SS-Captain (Hauptsturmführer) Franz Hössler, successor to Paul Müller as camp director; see Langbein, *People in Auschwitz*, 327–329; Strzelecka, "Women in the Auschwitz Concentration Camp," 176.

38. On Josef Mengele in Auschwitz, see Langbein, *People in Auschwitz*, 336–342; Helena Kubica, "The Crimes of Josef Mengele," in *Anatomy of the Auschwitz Death Camp*, 317–337.

39. Wording in the German interview: "Rüstungsindustrie" (armaments industry).

40. Wording in the German interview to the effect that she hoped the diagrams had fallen into Russian hands. So far, these diagrams have not been traced in archives that hold any of the remaining documents generated in Auschwitz.

41. Wording in the German interview: "Effektenlager Brzezinka" (storing site for prisoner belongings, a.k.a. "Canada" section of Birkenau). Brzezinka (also used: Brzezinki) is the Polish name for the village demolished for the construction of the Birkenau women's camp.

42. In the German interview, Tichauer uses the present tense in the last part of the sentence.

43. Not included here is Boder's question in the German interview: "Was hatte Ihre Familie gemacht?" (What did your family do?).

44. Wording in the German interview: Loslau (Polish: Wodisław Ślaski). Boder's translation (Wroclaw) refers to another city called Breslau in German.

45. Wording in the German interview: "Volksdeutsche," usually translated as ethnic Germans. On Nazi policy toward "Volksdeutsche," see Valdis O. Lumans, *Himmler's Auxiliaries: The Volksdeutsche Mittelstelle and the German National Minorities of Europe, 1933–1945* (Chapel Hill: University of North Carolina Press, 1993).

46. SS-Hauptscharführer Gerhard Palitzsch; see Langbein, *People in Auschwitz*, 391–392, 408–411.

47. Wording in the German interview to the effect that Stiwitz was Palitzsch's successor.

48. Wording in the German interview: "Chaos" (chaos).

49. Wording in the German interview: "die SS" (the SS).

50. Malchow, a subcamp of the women's concentration camp Ravensbrück; see Irith Dublon-Knebel, s.v. "Ravensbrück/Malchow," in *The United States Holocaust Memorial Museum Encyclopedia of Camps and Ghettos, 1933–1945*, vol. 1 *Early Camps, Youth Camps, and concentration Camps and Subcamps under the SS-Business Administration Main Office* (WVHA), ed. Geoffrey Megargee (Bloomington: Indiana University Press, 2009): 1213–1214..

51. Wording in the German interview to the effect that she did not know whether an international agreement had been concluded.

52. Wording in the German interview: "Und wir haben uns nicht getäuscht" (and we were right).

53. Wording in the German interview: "Vieh" (livestock).

54. Wording in the German interview: "Mit den zwei Mädchen?" (With the two girls?).

55. The term "Katiusha" refers to Soviet salvo artillery heavily used on the eastern front.

56. Russian: good day.

57. Words added in the German interview: "Hammer und Sichel" (hammer and sickle [part of the Soviet national emblem]).

58. Wording in the German interview preceding the next sentence: "Ich ging auf sie zu" (I approached them).

59. Additional wording in the German interview: "von den Russen befreit" (liberated by the Russians).

60. Additional word in the German interview: "Jüdin" (a Jewess).

61. Word used in the German interview: "Weg" (way, path).

62. Wording in the German interview: "Die Wohnung ist längst arisiert worden" (The apartment had long been Aryanized). "Aryanization" was the state-sanctioned robbery of Jewish property by Germany and its allies.

63. Wording in the German interview: "Es ist Herr Anton [sounds like "Bansemir"], dem ich auch dafür danke, meine Sachen dreieinhalb Jahre aufbewahrt gehabt zu haben und mir ohne Aufforderung dann überbrachte." (It was [her boss] Mr. Anton [Bansemir?] whom I also thank for having kept my possessions for three and a half years and returning [them] to me without me asking for it).

64. Wording used in German interview: "und der Transport ging nach Lublin" (and the transport went to Lublin).

65. Wording in the German interview: "der andere von zwölf" (the other was twelve [years old.]).

66. Word used in the German interview: "geraucht" (were smoking).

67. Wording in the German interview: "Litzmannstädter Transporte" (transports from Litzmannstadt [Polish: Łódź]).

68. The creation of the "Gypsy camp" in Auschwitz-Birkenau followed an order by Himmler dated December 16, 1942. Until July 1944, roughly 23,000 Sinti and Roma had been deported to Birkenau, mostly from Germany and Austria, of whom 85 percent perished or were murdered. Transports from Germany arrived in the BIIe section of Birkenau starting on February 26, 1943; see Michael Zimmermann, *Rassenutopie und Genozid. Die nationalsozialistische "Lösung der Zigeunerfrage"* (Hamburg: Christians, 1996), 295–344.

69. German name used in the interview: Titi (not Gitti)

70. German city name used in the interview: Schurein.

71. Acronym used in the German interview: "FKL" (*Frauen-Konzentrationslager* [(women's concentration camp]).

72. Word used in the German interview: "irritiert" (irritated).

73. On this interview passage, see my essay in this volume.

74. Wording used in the German interview: "Lager Ost" (Camp East).

75. Erich Schoen, later Erich Kulka. This name and the following two are confirmed by Helen Tichauer. Schoen should not be confused with Eric H. Boehm, author of the book *We Survived. Fourteen Histories of the Hidden and Hunted in Nazi Germany* (Boulder, Colo.: Westview Press, 2003).

76. Wording in the German interview: "im Zusammenhang mit einer Bauingenieurin Vera Foltyn, Tschechin" (in connection with a female Czech building engineer [named] Vera Foltyn).

77. Lotte Batscha/Batschowa worked in the Auschwitz prisoner canteen, Vera Foltyn/Foltynowa in the main construction office (SS-Bauleitung); both were members of the communist underground (telephone conversation with HT, January 22, 2008; see also Langbein, *People in Auschwitz*, 496–497; Strzelecka, "Women in the Auschwitz Concentration Camp,"199); and the contribution by Nechama Tec to this volume.

78. Unlike most other names she mentioned in her interview, Zippi did not recall anymore whom she might have been referring to. Perhaps Dr. Alfred Wolff-Eisner, a well-known doctor in Theresienstadt who after the war wrote about camp-related diseases; see H. G. Adler, *Theresienstadt 1941–1945: Antlitz einer Zwangsgemeinschaft* (Tübingen: Mohr, 1955), 508–515.

79. The "I" was typed in between lines. Boder seems to misunderstand this sentence as referring to Zippi as the "draftswoman for Dr. Mengele."

80. Word used in the German interview: "Abschnittslager" (section camps).

81. On DP camp Feldafing and Lieutenant Irving J. Smith, see Atina Grossmann, *Jews, Germans, and Allies: Close Encounters in Occupied Germany* (Princeton, N.J.: Princeton University Press, 2007), 131–147.

82. United Nations Relief and Rehabilitation Agency.

83. Wording used in German interview: "Kennen Sie welche" (Do you know any).

84. Nuremberg is located in the region of Frankonia, not Upper Bavaria.

85. This and the previous sentence not clear in the German interview.

86. Wording used in the German interview: "In diesem Land, wo er alles verloren hat" (In this country where he has lost everything).

87. Additional English sentence in the interview: "The automobile is waiting."

| BIBLIOGRAPHY |

Améry, Jean. *At the Mind's Limits: Contemplations by a Survivor on Auschwitz and Its Realities.* New York: Schocken Books, 1980.

Auerhahn, Nanette, and Dori Laub. "Holocaust Testimony." *Holocaust and Genocide Studies* 5, no. 4 (Winter 1990): 447–462.

Auschwitz 1940–1945: Central Issues in the History of the Camp. 5 vols. Oświęcim: Auschwitz-Birkenau State Museum, 2000.

Bigsby, Christopher. *Remembering and Imagining the Holocaust: The Chain of Memory.* Cambridge: Cambridge University Press, 2006.

Browning, Christopher R. *Collected Memories: Holocaust History and Postwar Testimony.* Madison: University of Wisconsin Press, 2003.

Czech, Danuta. *The Auschwitz Chronicle 1939–1945.* New York: Holt, 1997.

Douglass, Ana, and Thomas A. Vogler, eds. *Witness and Memory: The Discourse of Trauma.* New York: Routledge, 2003.

Felman, Shoshana, and Dori Laub. *Testimony: Crises of Witnessing in Literature, Psychoanalysis, and History.* New York: Routledge, 1991.

Greenspan, Henry. *The Awakening of Memory: Survivor Testimony in the First Years after the Holocaust, and Today.* Occasional Paper. Washington, D.C.: U.S. Holocaust Memorial Museum, 2001.

———. *On Listening to Holocaust Survivors: Recounting and Life History* Westport, Conn.: Praeger, 1998.

Grossmann, Atina. *Jews, Germans, and Allies: Close Encounters in Occupied Germany.* Princeton, N.J.: Princeton University Press, 2007.

Gutman, Yisrael, and Michael Berenbaum, eds. *Anatomy of the Auschwitz Death Camp.* Bloomington: Indiana University Press, 1994.

Hartman, Geoffrey H., ed. *Holocaust Remembrance: The Shapes of Memory*. Oxford: Blackwell, 1995.

———. *The Longest Shadow: In the Aftermath of the Holocaust*. Bloomington: Indiana University Press, 1996.

Hass, Aaron. *The Aftermath: Living with the Holocaust*. Cambridge: Cambridge University Press, 1995.

——— *In the Shadow of the Holocaust*. Ithaca, N.Y.: Cornell University Press, 1990.

Hilberg, Raul. *The Destruction of the European Jews*. New Haven, Conn.: Yale University Press, 2004.

Jacobson, Kenneth. *Embattled Selves: An Investigation into the Nature of Identity through Oral Histories of Holocaust Survivors*. New York: Atlantic Monthly Press, 1994.

Katz, Steven T., and Alan Rosen, eds. *Obliged by Memory: Literature, Religion, Ethics*. Syracuse, N.Y.: Syracuse University Press, 2006.

LaCapra, Dominick. *History and Memory after Auschwitz*. Ithaca, N.Y.: Cornell University Press, 1998.

———. *Representing the Holocaust: History, Theory, Trauma*. Ithaca, N.Y.: Cornell University Press, 1994.

———. *Writing History, Writing Trauma*. Baltimore: Johns Hopkins University Press, 2001.

Langbein, Hermann. *People in Auschwitz*. Chapel Hill: University of North Carolina Press, 2004.

Langer, Lawrence L. *Holocaust Testimonies: The Ruins of Memory*. New Haven, Conn.: Yale University Press, 1991.

Levy, Primo. *The Drowned and the Saved*. New York: Vintage International, 1989.

Niewyk, Donald, ed. *Fresh Wounds: Early Narratives of Holocaust Survival*. Chapel Hill: University of North Carolina Press, 1998.

Perl, Gisella. *I Was a Doctor in Auschwitz*. Tamarac, FL: Yale Garber, 1987.

Roseman, Mark. *A Past in Hiding: Memory and Survival in Nazi Germany*. New York: Metropolitan Books, 2001.

Rosen, Alan. *Sounds of Defiance: The Holocaust, Multilingualism and the Problem of English*. Lincoln: University of Nebraska Press, 2005.

Strzelecka, Irena. "Women in the Auschwitz Concentration Camp." In *Auschwitz 1940–1945: Central Issues in the History of the Camp*. Vol. 2, 171–200. Oświęcim: Auschwitz-Birkenau State Museum, 2000.

Tec, Nechama. *Resilience and Courage: Women, Men, and the Holocaust*. New Haven, Conn.: Yale University Press, 2003.

Wieviorka, Annette. *The Era of Witness*. Ithaca, N.Y.: Cornell University Press, 2006.

Young, James. *Writing and Rewriting the Holocaust: Narrative and the Consequences of Interpretation*. Bloomington: Indiana University Press, 1988.

| ABOUT THE CONTRIBUTORS |

Atina Grossmann is professor of history at the Cooper Union for the Advancement of Science and Art in New York City. Her publications include *Jews, Germans, and Allies: Close Encounters in Occupied Germany* (2007); *Crimes of War: Guilt and Denial in the 20th Century*, ed. with Omer Bartov and Mary Nolan (2002); and *When Biology Became Destiny: Women in Weimar and Nazi Germany*, ed. with Renate Bridenthal and Marion Kaplan (1984).

Konrad Kwiet is professor emeritus of history at Macquarie University, Sydney; he is Adjunct Professor in Jewish Studies and Roth Lecturer in Holocaust Studies at the University of Sydney, Australia. His publications include *Contemporary Responses to the Holocaust*, ed. with Jürgen Matthäus (2005); *Ausbildungsziel Judenmord? "Weltanschauliche Erziehung" von SS, Polizei und Waffen-SS im Rahmen der "Endlösung,"* with Jürgen Matthäus, Jürgen Förster, and Richard Breitman (2003).

Wendy Lower is assistant professor of history at Towson University, Maryland, and the former Director of the Visiting Fellows Program at the Center for Advanced Holocaust Studies of the U.S. Holocaust Memorial Museum, Washington, D.C. Her publications include *The Shoah in Ukraine: History, Testimony, Memory*, ed. with R. Brandon (2008), and *Nazi Empire-Building and the Holocaust in Ukraine* (2005).

Jürgen Matthäus, a historian, is the research director at the Center for Advanced Holocaust Studies of the U.S. Holocaust Memorial Museum, Washington, D.C. His publications include *Atrocities on Trial: Historical Perspectives on the Politics of Prosecuting War Criminals*, ed. with Patricia Heberer (2008); *Contemporary Responses to the Holocaust*, ed. with Konrad Kwiet (2005); *The Origins of the Final Solution: The Evolution* *of Nazi Jewish Policy, September 1939–March 1942,* with Christopher R. Browning (2004).

Mark Roseman is the Pat M. Glazer Chair in Jewish Studies and professor of Jewish studies and history at Indiana University. His recent publications include *Conflict, Catastrophe and Continuity: Essays on Modern German History,* ed. with Frank Biess and Hanna Schissler (2007); *The Wannsee Conference and the "Final Solution"* (2002); and *A Past in Hiding: Memory and Survival in Nazi Germany* (2000).

Nechama Tec is professor emerita of sociology at the University of Connecticut at Stamford. Her publications include *Every Day Lasts a Year: A Jewish Family's Correspondence from Poland,* with Christopher R. Browning and Richard S. Hollander (2007); *Resilience and Courage: Women, Men, and the Holocaust* (2003); *Defiance: The Bielski Partisans* (Oxford University Press, 1993); and *In the Lion's Den: The Life of Oswald Rufeisen* (Oxford University Press, 1990).

| INDEX |

THE OXFORD ORAL HISTORY SERIES

J. Todd Moye (University of North Texas), Kathryn Nasstrom (University of San Francisco),
and Robert Perks (The British Library Sound Archive), *Series Editors*
Donald A. Ritchie, *Senior Advisor*

Doing Oral History, Second Edition
Donald A. Ritchie

Approaching an Auschwitz Survivor: Holocaust Testimony and its Transformations
Edited by Jürgen Matthäus

A Guide to Oral History and the Law
John A. Neuenschwander